"*Ancient Slavery and Its New Testament Contexts* is a crucial rejoinder to persistent trends in modern scholarship and theology of ignoring, excusing, whitewashing, and romanticizing slavery in the New Testament. The volume equips readers with interpretive strategies for centering the wholly human experiences of enslaved people while taking full account of the systemic violence of slavery in the New Testament, its ancient contexts, and some of its ancient and modern interpretations—the harsh realities of coerced labor, racism, physical brutality, sexual exploitation, dehumanization, and commodification. The editors and contributors have translated cutting-edge and ethically reflexive scholarship into an engaging and accessible format for classroom use—a truly remarkable achievement that will make this an indispensable resource for years to come."

—TONY KEDDIE
The University of Texas at Austin

"*Ancient Slavery and Its New Testament Contexts* is an essential resource for anyone seeking to better understand the intersections of enslavement and the New Testament. Cobb and Shaner have assembled a cohort of scholars who stand out for their ability to balance cutting-edge research with clear and accessible prose. This volume includes rich engagement with material and literary evidence alongside New Testament texts, carefully curated images that immerse the reader in the ancient context, and discussion questions designed to facilitate classroom conversations. Teachers in ecclesial, college, and graduate contexts alike will find a wealth of resources for their classrooms in this volume."

—JENNIFER QUIGLEY
Candler School of Theology at Emory University

"*Ancient Slavery and Its New Testament Contexts* represents a must-have resource for any introductory course to the New Testament. Contributors carefully demonstrate that virtually any topic in early Christianity is entangled with the harsh reality of enslavement. The captive, missing in most literary, theological, and historical introductions to the field, occupies the center stage here, urging biblical interpreters to reconsider the ethical foundations of early Christianity."

—LUIS MENÉNDEZ-ANTUÑA
Boston University School of Theology

"*Ancient Slavery and Its New Testament Contexts* is an important and expertly edited collection that will be very useful to students, interested readers, and scholars. The chapters are well-written and clear, with nuggets of insight grounded in nuanced interpretation and analysis. There is a genuine pedagogical care in how each chapter presents the materials, with discussion questions to ponder at the end, and with helpful lists for further reading. This is a great accomplishment, and such a work deserves to be highly recommended."

—RONALD CHARLES
University of Toronto

"This book is an invaluable resource for understanding the complex and brutal realities of ancient slavery, particularly in relation to Jewish, New Testament, and early Christian texts and their diverse audiences. In addition to considering the many metaphors and concepts that deploy slavery motifs in early Christian writings, it examines the everyday realities of the slaves populating their pages. The authors of these essays address common misperceptions while examining how laws, institutions, socioeconomic realities, and societal attitudes regarding slavery influenced Christian teachings and aspirations that continue to this day. I highly recommend this book to students, educators, and anyone interested in exploring this challenging topic."

—HARRY O. MAIER
Vancouver School of Theology

"Confronting the legacy of slavery in the New Testament is challenging. *Ancient Slavery and Its New Testament Contexts* gives readers the background and tools they need to understand the impact of slavery in the world of Jesus and the early Christ followers. Each chapter addresses complex questions in clear and accessible prose, anticipating questions that readers are likely to have. High-quality illustrations bring the text to life. Outstanding scholars, the editors and contributors prove themselves to be excellent teachers—the volume is sure to generate lively conversations in classrooms and congregations."

—JENNIFER A. GLANCY
Le Moyne College, author of *Slavery in Early Christianity* and
Slavery as Moral Problem: In the Early Church and Today

ANCIENT SLAVERY AND ITS NEW TESTAMENT CONTEXTS

Edited by
Christy Cobb
and Katherine A. Shaner

With editorial assistance by
Mallory A. Challis
and Joseph Foltz

WILLIAM B. EERDMANS PUBLISHING COMPANY
GRAND RAPIDS, MICHIGAN

Wm. B. Eerdmans Publishing Co.
2006 44th Street SE, Grand Rapids, MI 49508
www.eerdmans.com

Published 2025

Book design by Lydia Hall

Printed in the United States of America

30 30 29 28 27 26 25   1 2 3 4 5 6 7

ISBN 978-0-8028-8413-8

Library of Congress Cataloging-in-Publication Data

A catalog record for this book is available from the Library of Congress.

Contents

CONTENTS

Figures

Editors' Preface

CHRISTY COBB AND KATHERINE A. SHANER

In all four New Testament gospels, the story of Jesus's arrest is a pivotal moment in the passion narratives that lead up to his crucifixion. Amid Peter's denial, Judas's betrayal, and the interrogation of Jesus by the authorities, a violent moment occurs. One of Jesus's disciples becomes angry and draws his sword. His target? An enslaved man accompanying the high priest. The disciple swings dramatically and cuts off the ear of the enslaved attendant. This moment is brief, and the enslaved character is often overlooked. Yet, this story can tell us quite a bit about ancient slavery and its New Testament contexts.

All four canonical gospels include the enslaved man, making his moment important for Jesus's passion story (Mark 14:43–50; Matt 26:47–56; Luke 22:47–53; John 18:1–11). Like many enslaved people in the New Testament and beyond, in three of the four gospels he has no name and no social connections other than his enslaver. John's Gospel names him Malchus (18:10) and adds another tantalizing detail: his relative is another enslaved person working in the house of the high priest. This relative, John's Gospel explains, questioned Peter about his affiliation with Jesus in the denial scene (John 18:26). Malchus, though enslaved, is not merely the object of the disciple's violence. He has a larger context.

Just like Malchus, this disciple, who reacts so violently, remains unnamed in Mark and Matthew. Luke and John, however, name Peter as the initiator of this violence. Luke alone adds an important detail: after Peter's violent act, Jesus touches the ear of the enslaved man and heals him (22:51). Yet in the three other gospels, the enslaved man's fate dangles unresolved in the narrative. He is hurt, bloody, in pain, missing part of himself. He does not receive medical attention and makes no further appearances in these versions of the story.

Figure o.1. Limestone relief portraying the arrest of Jesus. The figure on the left depicts Peter sheathing his sword after cutting off Malchus's ear, who is seated below. 1264–1288 CE.

Readers are left to wonder about him. Did he return to his household? Would he be able to hear after this altercation? Does his enslaver, the high priest, care about his wounds? Did he recover from them? What kind of a turning point would this have been for his experiences with enslavement?

Both the healing in Luke's narrative and the declaration from Jesus's mouth as he heals Malchus become a point of inquiry for Malchus's enslaved status. Sometimes New Testament scholars assume that the author of Luke's Gospel intentionally added the healing along with this statement to the narrative: "'No more of this!' And he touched his ear and healed him" (Luke 22:51). What is the "this" about which Jesus speaks? The violence generally? The use of swords? Or is Jesus objecting to violence against enslaved people? This healing of an enslaved person has been interpreted as Luke's care for the marginalized and advocacy for the oppressed (and by extension Christian compassion for enslaved people). Yet other literature from the first century CE, in Jewish, Roman, and Greek contexts, demonstrates compassion along these lines as

Figure 0.2. A manuscript leaf that was most likely made for Queen Eleanor of Provence. The bottom illustration depicts Peter with his sword and Jesus reattaching the severed ear of Malchus. Circa 1270 CE.

well. No texts include outright condemnation of slavery. An astute reader must read against the grain of biblical texts for abolitionist ideas. Similarly, other sections of Luke's Gospel (for instance, Luke 17:7–10) include clear disdain for enslaved workers and their "worthlessness." This disdain, along with stereotypes, caricatures, and callus pity, permeates other texts, both scriptural and not, written in this same period. If a New Testament text like Luke holds conflicting views about slavery, the treatment of enslaved persons, and responses to slavery, how can readers—both those reading for religious practice and those reading in religious studies—begin to make sense of the complex world of ancient slavery?

This book, *Ancient Slavery and Its New Testament Contexts*, guides both of these kinds of readers through the complexities of understanding slavery as it is depicted in the New Testament and its historical, literary, and material contexts. The collection of essays within this volume provides pertinent historical context, examines ideologies and attitudes from contemporaneous texts outside the New Testament, and provides strategies for reading and interpreting difficult passages such as the scene with Malchus. Meant as an introduction to the study of slavery in the New Testament, this volume—just as the story of Malchus illustrates—does not provide only one way to view and understand enslavement in antiquity. Instead, it includes a variety of views written by prominent scholars of ancient slavery. Our hope is that it provides a foundation from which students, scholars, and general readers will continue to think, read, and interpret the New Testament with the pervasiveness of slavery in the forefront of their minds.

Why This Volume?

In the early spring of 2021, while still teaching in COVID-19 pandemic mode, we began a conversation about how to teach slavery in our respective classrooms. Both of us taught some version of "Slavery and the New Testament" and drew on our own respective research programs, Cobb working with comparative literature frameworks across early Christian literature and Shaner working with material culture and historiographical frameworks. We realized that we had one thing in common: neither of us were fully satisfied with the accessibility of resources available for our students to understand the complexities and textures of Roman slavery as a context for the New Testament. Certainly, Jennifer Glancy's *Slavery in Early Christianity* (Fortress, 2024), now in an expanded edition, has paradigmatically shaped our scholarly work—and will continue to do so for years. We also agreed that J. Albert Harrill's *Slaves in the New Testament* (Fortress, 2006) is necessary reading for scholars and graduate students working in the field. Sandra Joshel's *Slavery in the Roman World* (Cambridge University Press, 2010) has provided an excellent place to start for many classrooms, but it does not connect specifically with New Testament interpretation needs. We found that beginning students need *both* basic information about slavery *and* reading strategies specific to biblical studies in order to begin to think critically about the ways that slavery is used in the New Testament. Similarly, we knew that ministry professionals and those with Christian faith commitments hungered for the same foundational information and ethical considerations needed in religious studies and seminary classrooms.

Why a Collaboration?

Over the past twenty-five years, a robust scholarly conversation has developed between classicists, historians, archaeologists, scholars of religion, and biblical studies scholars around ancient slavery. Yet, this conversation has not always translated well into the classroom. The technicalities of scholarly writing and analysis sometimes intimidate students. The long-standing arguments among scholars from different schools of intellectual development are not easily traced by early career students and those who are curious but do not have years to devote to discovery.

Early in our planning, we identified a strong desire to have multiple voices in our classrooms, particularly voices of those whose expertise is well recognized across ancient slavery studies. As feminist scholars ourselves, we are committed to drawing from scholarship that does not create a single narrative, but highlights the complexities, ambiguities, and even contradictions of studying ancient slavery. Our commitments to multiplicity in biblical interpretation and attention to the ethics of interpretation have guided our choices. Therefore, this collaboration brought together scholars from around the world, from South Africa to Norway, from the United Kingdom to the United States. It also brought together literary specialists, Roman historians, classicists, archaeologists, ethicists, and religious studies scholars. Emerging scholars and well-established scholars alike agreed to participate in the project. There are still many, many other scholars whose work is fundamental to understanding ancient slavery and the New Testament, and some of their work is represented in the "Further Reading" section at the end of each chapter. The field, however, is emerging—and we are confident that this collaboration was simply the beginning of a larger effort to redesign how ancient slavery is taught in classrooms of many kinds all over the world.

Our Vocational Positions

This collaborative and multifaceted approach also draws together our differences as scholars and teachers. Shaner teaches at a university-based divinity school where pedagogical excellence is highly valued. She is also an ordained

Lutheran (ELCA) pastor who regularly teaches and preaches in churches big and small. She has experienced the hunger among students, pastors, and lay-people for clear-eyed examinations of biblical texts—especially those that have built legacies of oppression. Her teaching frequently focuses on the ethics of specific interpretations for specific contexts. Teaching about slavery in the New Testament is a very different task when speaking to historic mainline white protestant churches in the American South, whose legacy was that of enslaving and its aftermath, than when speaking to African American churchgoers in Northern industrial cities whose legacy was an explicit escape from enslavement and its aftermath during the Great Migration. And there are myriad other kinds of churches in between. As a feminist biblical scholar trained in histories of marginalized peoples, material culture in the Roman Empire, and the politics of biblical studies as a field, Shaner also draws on her pastoral experience accompanying people of faith as they grapple with the ways faith has been both painful and sustaining in their lives.

Cobb began her career teaching undergraduates at a small private liberal arts university in the South that heavily emphasizes teaching; most of her courses were in the common curriculum, and so she taught students from a variety of disciplines. After teaching for a number of years there, Cobb accepted a job in a religious studies department at a larger university, and she now teaches both undergraduate and graduate students (MA and PhD). Both of these experiences have illustrated to her that students are interested in learning more about slavery in the New Testament. Students also ask difficult questions about how the pervasiveness of slavery has affected Christianity today. Further, Cobb's experience in a teaching-focused institution has enhanced her interest in pedagogy, which in turn has fueled her desire to publish an introductory book especially to be used in the classroom. Much of her graduate training was grounded in theory—literary, feminist, and queer—and this foundation has surfaced in her research and teaching. Cobb is also frequently invited to teach in local churches and organizations on the topic of slavery and Christianity. Through these experiences, she has found that the broader public is also interested in understanding how slavery is depicted in the Bible and also how it has impacted our contemporary society.

Both of us are alumnae from the Wabash Center for Teaching and Learning in Theology and Religion and have participated in workshops designed for faculty teaching religion at undergraduate institutions and in theological education. These Wabash Center workshops provided space to ask difficult questions, such as how to address issues of slavery in contemporary classrooms carefully and ethically. Both of us have also published articles about teaching

in our respective classrooms. These publications draw out our individual pedagogical goals. Both of us have been recognized at our respective institutions
for our teaching excellence. All of these experiences and skills have honed our
eyes toward classroom effectiveness and fostered pedagogical skills that have
paved the way for this volume.

Vocabulary Choices

When editing a volume on slavery, one of the first difficult questions to arise
is the language used to represent enslaved persons and systems of slavery in
antiquity. In the ancient world, most of our sources were written by privileged
free persons who were invested in slavery as well as the pervasive ideology that
enslaved persons were enslaved due to "nature" (see chapter 12, "Household
Codes"). Thus, the words used to designate enslaved persons are often dehumanizing and infantilizing. Scholars of slavery must translate these words into
English with care, and there is not yet a scholarly consensus on how we should
approach translation (see chapter 1, "The Language of 'Enslavement' in the
New Testament"). Some scholars prefer to leave the harsh language of slavery
present in their translations and in their own words that discuss slavery. These
scholars note that terms identifying people as "slaves" or "masters" designate a
stark difference in status that is often translated into identity categories—and
the ancient rhetoric bears this out. Other scholars choose to lean into translations and word choices that reveal status connected with personhood. Thus,
"enslaved persons" and "those who enslave" attest to the malleability of status,
even if sometimes only in theory. We have allowed both perspectives to remain
within this book, illustrating the various ways that scholars navigate this complicated question. These choices made by each scholar suggest one opportunity
for a through-going conversation over a semester or series of classes. We believe
that this ongoing conversation would make for a rich learning opportunity.

Additionally, we have chosen to focus our title and this book on the "New
Testament," which needs some explanation. First, we want to acknowledge that
the word "New" has been used historically to elevate the texts within it over
and against the texts in the Hebrew Bible, or the "Old Testament." We do not
share that view. As editors, we recognize the value of the Hebrew scriptures,
both as scriptures in their own right for multiple religious traditions and also
in relation to the study of the Christian (New) Testament. In addition, we
are aware that New Testament texts are not the only valuable resources for
understanding the religious landscape of the earliest Christ followers and the
significant shift in Judaism after the fall of the Jerusalem temple in 70 CE.

While twenty-seven books are included in the canon of the New Testament, the chapters in this book deliver commentary on and integration of many other crucially important texts from Jewish, Roman, Greek, and Egyptian antiquity. Jeremy L. Williams, at the beginning of chapter 8, calls readers to hold this ambiguity in mind as they read by including an asterisk (*) after the term "New." We have chosen to retain the "New" and not thoroughly infuse the asterisk in New* Testament for the sake of reading ease for students for whom such conversations about canon and supersessionist ideologies are unfamiliar. Nonetheless, the term should elicit a point of conversation among students.

Teaching Strategies

We have edited and designed this book as we might teach a twelve- to sixteen-week class on this subject. We highly suggest assigning primary texts alongside each chapter. For upper-level or graduate courses, additional reading could be chosen from the further-reading lists at the end of each chapter. Possible titles for a class where this book could be beneficial are "Slavery in the New Testament," "Enslavement in Early Christianity," "The History of Slavery in Christianity," or "Slavery and Its Repercussions in Christianity." We have arranged the chapters in the order in which we both teach these types of courses. But each of the chapters also can stand alone and be assigned individually to be used for individual modules of a course, for example.

To begin, there are two shorter chapters that address issues of importance when beginning the study of slavery: the language of slavery in the New Testament (chapter 1) and an overview of the challenges to studying slavery through a comparison of ancient slavery to contemporary systems of slavery (chapter 2). Then, we provide a strong historical foundation for understanding the context of the New Testament, specifically Roman and Jewish history. Thus, chapters 3 and 4 both address Roman contexts and chapter 5 addresses slavery in ancient Judaism. After these historical foundations are addressed, we have chosen to move into topically focused chapters that incorporate important facets of enslavement in the ancient world along with a specific focus on New Testament texts that illustrate these facets. These topics include manumission (chapter 6) the slave labor and trade (chapter 7), race and ethnicity (chapter 8), gender and sexuality (chapter 9), metaphors of enslavement (chapter 10), literary constructions and stereotypes of slavery (chapter 11), and household codes (chapter 12). Following these topical chapters, we have added a chapter on slavery in early Christianity in order to show the ways in which slavery continued and also shifted in the following centuries beyond the New Testament (chapter 13). The final two chapters focus on the "so what" of studying slavery in this context. Chapter 14 provides several possible ethical strategies for interpreting these texts, while chapter 15 addresses modern slavery and the ways in which New Testament passages are used to support and challenge slavery in our current context.

Each chapter also has carefully chosen images that enhance the learning experience. All biblical quotations are from the NRSVue unless otherwise noted. Titles of ancient texts use standard English language translations rather than Latin or Greek titles. In order to avoid distraction, we have kept footnotes to a minimum, but have referenced further readings and connections across chapters within the text. At the end of each chapter, teachers will find a set of discussion questions designed for classroom use. The first two questions in each set are meant for undergraduate and general audiences. The third question digs deeper and is meant for graduate students and more advanced audiences. For readers' convenience, we have also included a glossary of uncommon terms before the indices.

Gratitude

Finally, but probably most importantly, we need to recognize Joseph Foltz and Mallory Challis, our editorial assistants, for their enormous contributions to this volume. They have fussed over image permissions, fretted about formats and citations, researched obscure ideas, and made sure that such ideas were understandable. Foltz added a keen acuity with images, a knowledge of the technical aspects of electronic files, and a willingness to doggedly find permissions for the project. Challis lent her sharp editorial eye, incisive organizational skills, and index generation magic to the project. We could not have completed this volume without their passion and dedication. We are also both grateful for the many students we have taught throughout the years at our various institutions, whose curiosity and dialogue inspired this project. We want to thank Trevor Thompson, our editor at Wm. B. Eerdmans, for his encouragement, enthusiasm, and patient shepherding of the project. Gratitude is also due to Jenny Hoffman for her gracious project management and to Michael Helfield for his gentle yet clear editing skill. Of course, we take full responsibility for our infelicities, but cannot take full responsibility for the wealth of knowledge and the clear presentation throughout. What a truly collaborative project this has been!

Abbreviations

AE	*Année Epigraphique*
CIL	*Corpus Inscriptionum Latinorum*
IDR	*Inscripţiile Daciei Romane*
SGDI	*Sammlung der griechischen Dialekt-Inschriften*

1   *The Language of "Enslavement"*
     in the New Testament

EMERSON B. POWERY

In 2012, the state of Pennsylvania passed a resolution to declare that year the Year of the Bible. The resolution gained national attention when American Atheists, an organization committed to the separation of church and state, sponsored a billboard in the heart of Harrisburg that read "Slaves obey your Masters." Crafted as a form of protest against the state-sponsored resolution, the billboard message backfired when it depicted an image of a person of African descent in physical chains to accompany the posted biblical text (Col 3:22). This image created much more controversy within the city of Harrisburg (a city in which 50 percent of the population is African American) than the American Atheists, wanting to mobilize a protest against a violent Bible, had bargained for.[1] Moreover, even if the *intent* of the initiators was to raise awareness about the brutal legacies of slavery perpetuated by sacred texts, the racial dynamics of this reference to enslavement in a demographically mixed city highlight exactly how fraught conversations about slavery and the Bible can be.

With or without reference to this state resolution, readers of the Bible should develop critical awareness about the use of the Bible (and other sacred texts, for that matter) in conversations and media, especially when public figures appropriate the Bible in areas of nationalistic speech and political identity. Rather than assume individuals interpret biblical passages in a historical, polit-

1. Diane Fishlock, "Atheists 'Slaves Obey Your Masters' Billboard Raises Temper in Pennsylvania," *Huffington Post*, March 13, 2012, https://tinyurl.com/SBL6704e3.

ical, and religious vacuum, this conversation needs to be situated in the context of public US history (and/or the public histories of multiple nations).

In the American context, the "Bible" that holds power is an "American Bible." For example, if the year were 1800, because of my skin complexion I would not be able to secure an advanced degree in religion to teach or even to write this piece. If the year were 1830 (or earlier), female students would not be allowed to take classes at colleges, universities, or seminaries. If the year were 1850 (or earlier), a public, collegiate space for gathering a mixed-race and mixed-gender group of students would be very difficult to locate. If the year were 1966 (the year I was born), intimate, interracial relationships could not be sanctioned in marriage—such unions were illegal.[2] If the year were 2014 (or earlier), intimate, same-sex relationships could not be realized in state-recognized marriages, since this legal recognition would be outlawed. For *opponents* of these legal and social changes, it would be common to draw on the Bible to support their claims.[3] In the civil rights era in the 1960s, sacred texts were used in a more generative way to advocate for major accomplishments in social equality. Since that time, however, the Bible has functioned more as a tool for social control than a useful guide for social change. The tension between social reform and social control—and the Bible's role within each—remains an ongoing conversation among religious interpreters. For both Jews and Christians, the Bible has functioned as both a "bridge" and a "boundary marker" in the American context.[4]

As members of the ancient Roman household, the enslaved occupied important, albeit conspicuous, spaces within the family circle. The literature of early Christianity testifies to this experience. The enslaved appear in the parables of Jesus, serve as analogies for discipleship, and even perform as comic relief. Whether used literally, figuratively, or metaphorically, the language of enslavement reveals the earliest Jewish Christian writers as thinkers of their time in a slavocracy that permeated the Roman world. Many early Christ followers utilized the awareness of the human bondage system and the slave discourse that went along with it as one appropriate way to promote the message of this newly

2. See *Loving v. Virginia*, 388 U.S. 1 (1967).

3. None of these resolutions received the national attention of former President Ronald Reagan's declaration of 1983 as the Year or the Bible.

4. Jonathan Sarna, "The Bible and Judaism in America," in *The Oxford Handbook of the Bible in America*, ed. Paul C. Gutjahr (New York: Oxford University Press, 2017), 506, has summed up the understanding of the Bible in Jewish circles using two apt metaphors. He writes: "The Bible served both as a bridge and a boundary marker between Jews and Christians in America."

developing religious movement. Although the metaphorical use of bondage language has attracted much scholarly attention (see chapter 10, "Metaphors of Enslavement"), concentration on the physical presence of the enslaved within early Christ-following communities has received much less attention.[5]

For example, what does it mean to "serve two masters" (Matt 6:24)? Households large enough to host the weekly gatherings of the new Christ-following movement would have used the labor of the enslaved. Among the members of these house churches were the enslaved, persons who served earthly enslavers and persons who prepared for the activities of these house church gatherings. When the Eucharist was administered (1 Cor 11), the enslaved possibly prepared and served the bread and the wine. When common meals were shared, the enslaved likely cooked the fish, baked the bread, and poured the lentil soup. If members traveled from afar for religious gatherings, the enslaved presumably washed their feet and cared for their garments. There was much to do to manage these larger gatherings, and, even if the texts never mention them, it is not hard to imagine who would carry out these responsibilities.

As interpreters, we need to recognize the "gaps" in ancient texts as spaces in which the enslaved were present. In that recognition, we also need to reflect consciously on the enslaved as human actors in their ancient contexts. From another enslaved context—and, from the voices of the formerly enslaved themselves—Harriet Jacobs's deep, reflective words capture the "haunting" of human bondage. She grieves in writing: "There are wrongs which even the grave does not bury."[6] The *presence* of the enslaved lingers in ancient texts and should remain among us still as a type of "haunting."[7]

Translation Matters: The NRSVue (New Revised Standard Version, updated edition)

As we consider ways in which we might acknowledge the presence of the enslaved, we should also attempt to determine how English translations can

---

5. See Emerson B. Powery, "Reading with the Enslaved: Placing Human Bondage at the Center of the Early Christian Story," in *Bitter the Chastening Rod: Africana Biblical Interpretation after Stony the Road We Trod in the Age of BLM, SayHerName, and MeToo,* ed. Mitzi J. Smith, Angela N. Park, and Erica. S. Dunbar Hill (Lanham, MD: Lexington Books, 2022), 71–90.

6. Harriet Jacobs, *Incidents in the Life of a Slave Girl, Written by Herself* (Boston: Published for the author, 1861), 294.

7. Haunting in the spirit of Christina Sharpe, *In the Wake: On Blackness and Being* (Durham, NC: Duke University Press, 2016).

make enslaved people more present or more absent in scripture. In 2022, an updated edition of the NRSV Bible was released. This revision claims to have made over twenty thousand substantial revisions and ten thousand minor revisions.[8] There have been "public" acknowledgments that the updated edition intended to revise its translation of *douloi* (a Greek word for "slaves") to acknowledge—at least in English—the institutional system in which *douloi* found themselves. That is, the NRSVue would provide a more nuanced, contemporary translation in an effort to distance the human subject from any notion that the label indicated the person's "innate" status. One prime example is the change from calling Hagar a "slave woman" in Galatians 4:22–31 to calling her an "enslaved woman." This new contemporary "updated edition" was supposed to provide more suitable language so readers would not confuse the imposed condition *with* the person. But, depending on your perspective, the NRSVue failed in this regard. Instead, the translation's use of the term "slave" rather than "enslaved person" still occurs frequently within the New Testament (164 times).[9] The term "slave" is utilized in various ways, such as when ancient writers make use of characters to speak or narrators to narrate within their stories, or ancient writers write (or dictate) letters in the cultural context of the first century:

Here are several examples:

- "A disciple is not above the teacher nor a *slave* above the master; it is enough for the disciple to be like the teacher and the *slave* like the master" (Matt 10:24–25a).
- "Who, then, is the faithful and wise *slave* whom his master has put in charge of his household, to give the other *slaves* their allowance of food at the proper time? Blessed is that *slave* whom his master will find at work when he arrives" (Matt 24:45–46).[10]
- "You were bought with a price; do not become *slaves* of humans" (1 Cor 7:23).

To expand upon this final example, what meaning would we lose if the latter half of 1 Corinthians 7:23—"do not become slaves of humans"—were rendered as "do not become enslaved to others"? As Laura Nasrallah convinc-

8. "New Testament Studies: NRSVue," Yale Library, https://guides.library.yale.edu/newtestament/nrsvue.

9. The 164 New Testament references to "slave" in the NRSVue account for English translations of several different Greek words in the NT collection: *douloi* (124 times), *diakonoi*, *oiketes*, and *pais*.

10. The NRSVue includes an additional plural, "slaves," in the mouth of the Matthean "Jesus" in Matthew 24 (in a statement in which the Greek did not include *douloi*).

ingly suggests with respect to 1 Corinthians 7, early Christ followers (enslaved, freed, or free) were rhetorically tasked to imagine themselves as "things or commodities."[11] To add to that observation, would not *some* of them also have imagined this enslavement as determined by *forces outside of their control*?

On the other hand, within the NRSVue there are only a few instances in which the term "enslaved" occurs in a nominal sense—only seven by my count. Five of these cases fall within the letter to the Galatians, three within the Hagar and Sarah allegory mentioned above. For example:

- Galatians 4:1: "Heirs, as long as they are minors, are no better than those who are enslaved (*doulos*), though they are the owners of all the property."
- Galatians 4:22–23: "Abraham had two sons, one by an enslaved woman and the other by a free woman. One [was] the child of the enslaved woman (*paidiskē*)."
- Galatians 4:30–31: "But what does the scripture say? 'Drive out the enslaved woman and her child, for the child of the enslaved woman will not share the inheritance with the child of the free woman. So then, brothers and sisters, we are children, not of an enslaved woman (*paidiskē*) but of the free woman.'"[12]

To expand on Galatians 4:30–31, of the Greek terms associated with human bondage, *pais* is perhaps the most ambiguous since it may refer to a "child" (Matt 17:18) or to one who is enslaved (cf. Matt 8:5–13; Luke 7:1–10). Which meaning applies depends on its literary, historical, and ideological contexts, which determine its translation. For example, does the *pais* of one of Jesus's healing stories refer to the Roman centurion's "son," that is, a biological relationship? Does it refer to one enslaved by the centurion? Or does it refer to both? The term *pais* may expose the origins of some enslaved persons who were born into the family but whose birth mother would determine the status of the "child."[13] The Roman centurion could be both a "father" and "enslaver."

For us, language serves a rhetorical function *primarily*. We do not know the people in the New Testament except through its language. In the ancient world, many persons (especially in less populated communities) would likely know the

---

11. See Laura Nasrallah, "'You Were Bought with a Price': Freedpersons and Things in 1 Corinthians," in *Corinth in Contrast*, ed. Steven J. Friesen, Sarah James, and Daniel Schowalter (Leiden: Brill, 2014), 59.

12. The other two passages are the following: Eph 6:9 ("Whether we are enslaved [*doulos*] or free") and Col 3:1 ("There is no longer Greek and Jew, circumcised and uncircumcised, barbarian, Scythian, enslaved [*doulos*] and free, but Christ is all and in all!").

13. Jennifer A. Glancy, *Slavery in Early Christianity*, 2nd ed. (Minneapolis: Fortress, 2024), 4–5; Catherine Hezser, *Jewish Slavery in Antiquity* (Oxford: Oxford University Press, 2005), 442.

Figure 1.1. A funerary monument for Helena, who was an *alumna*, which likely indicates that Helena was a foster daughter or possibly an enslaved girl. 150–200 CE.

origins of many *douloi*, whether they sold themselves, were bought in the market, or were born into the human bondage system—that is, whether they landed in these precarious situations by choice or by chance. Our modern terminology says more about how *we reflect* on these historical periods and how *we think* about these persons.

This difference between the rhetorical and the historical came to the fore when Clarice Martin, in a paradigmatic article from 1990, discouraged the use of "servant" for *doulos* in English translations of the Bible.[14] Martin observed that the softening of the language opened the possibility for a contemporary audience to misconstrue the violent contexts of which we speak. Martin's forceful recommendation to translate *doulos* as "slave" and not "servant" (in the King James Version and elsewhere) was a rhetorical and historical argument. A contemporary group of (religious) readers may feel less comfortable with the rhetorical effect of a phrase like "my good and faithful *slaves*" rather than "my good and faithful *servants*" (Matt 25:23) because of their own collective history. While contemporary church settings might more comfortably and readily repeat Jesus's words with "servant" language, the violent and forceful connotations of Jesus speaking to his followers as "slaves" would literally be lost in translation.

14. Clarice J. Martin, "Womanist Interpretations of the New Testament: The Quest for Holistic and Inclusive Translation and Interpretation," *Journal of Feminist Studies in Religion* 6 (1990): 41–61.

We are left with a number of questions, two of which are, Does the language of the "enslaved" unwittingly mislead in ways the term "slave" does not, *or* is the former translation an appropriate redirection that differentiates between a human subject and the institution in which people (born into or violently forced into) find themselves? Should our language attempt to capture this nuance? One solution may be to distinguish, in our translations, between using "enslaved" to refer to *individual* people and using "slave" for systems. Thus, an individual would be an "enslaved person," but "slave markets," "slave trade," and "slave system" would still be marked with the dehumanizing adjective because these systems and institutions, by definition, attempt to objectify individual people.[15]

Perhaps more challenging than the translation of *doulos*, or even the appropriate recognition of an "enslaved person," is the equal necessity to retranslate the language of the *kyrios* (the Greek word for "Lord") and more closely associate the discourse of "Lord" in first-century religious discourse with "enslaver." At a minimum, we should consider the linguistic connection between Lord and enslaver as an appropriate analogy within the minds of first-century Christ followers. Such an analogy was likely useful for describing and thinking through the relationships between their own newly developing religious practices and their God. The NRSVue has, at least, added in footnotes in several places with the following phrase: "In Greek the same word is used for *master* and *Lord*" (see, for example, Eph 6:9 and Col 3:22). If the double-meaning intends this ambiguity, then Paul's use of *kyrios* (within 1 Cor 7:21–22, for example) as "Lord" and "enslaver" exposes (once again) the apostle's utilization of the human bondage system as a readily available schema for the Christ-following community. The depictions of the *kyrioi* "punishing" their *douloi*—an idea some early Christ followers shared—helps us acknowledge that there are direct efforts that move beyond the metaphor in less than admirable ways.

Nevertheless, the question remains: When we categorize historical people with our contemporary organizing language—whether from the Greco-Roman period or the nineteenth century or the many periods in-between—is our contemporary language sufficient to capture the humanity of these ancient bodies?

Intertwined in this discussion of language is also a recognition that enslaved people can never simply be objects. Walter Johnson attempts to unravel the complexity of this reality when he challenges us to acknowledge and name the many instances in which the enslaved *act out their humanity*.

---

15. Clarice Martin, email exchange with the author, May 14, 2023.

Figure 1.2. A funerary monument for an enslaved boy named Antoninus, who died when he was twelve. This monument was commissioned in the third century CE by his enslaver, Satria Epicharis.

Despite the conditions in which they find themselves (or due to those very conditions), these actions should classify these persons as "agents" of sorts, which is Johnson's attempt to challenge the idea that "agency" should *only* be understood in relationship to radical resistance (or escape).[16] Thus, everyday forms of "resistance"—daily acts that may not be part of an attempt of a formal escape plan—still speak to human actors in an institution that is meant to dehumanize them. As Johnson would put it, these routine practices point to the way some enslaved people "flourished" (Johnson's word) in slavery, "not in the sense of loving their slavery but in the sense of loving themselves and one another."[17] This too, in Johnson's argument, should define what is possible to discern about enslaved people and their agency.

16. Walter Johnson, "On Agency," *Journal of Social History* 37 (2003): 115; this is part of Johnson's critique of James Scott's *Domination and the Art of Resistance* (New Haven: Yale University Press, 1990).
17. Johnson, "On Agency," 115.

Conclusion

Along with colleagues in ancient history, classics, and other historical fields, New Testament scholars are moving in the direction generally of using the language of "enslaved person(s)" as opposed to "slave(s)" in an attempt to recognize, as much as possible, the human dignity of past individuals caught in institutional systems outside of their control. The collection we know as the Bible does not have agency, except through its inheritors and interpreters, nor is the language of enslavement fully revealing of ancient characters, however one publicly uses it in churches, classrooms, or communities—that is, whatever term one uses in a public setting does not tell us all we need to know. Additional explanation always seems necessary. What questions can we raise about those enslaved in these early centuries? What realities did they experience that we can explore or imagine—even if they are *only* minor characters within the central accounts? Are they ancient actors in a story that frequently hides their human activity? We should be attentive to Walter Johnson's critique: granting rhetorical agency to ancient literary characters long ago may not easily transfer into embodied practices of goodwill and recognition of the human dignity of all in our contemporary surroundings.

Discussion Questions

1. What difference does translation make in understanding enslaved people's presence and the legacies of enslavement in the New Testament? What are the ethical decisions that translators make for us?
2. How do our terms describe the literary characters and historical people about whom we speak and write? How are these terms understood in the ears/minds of the most attentive readers and hearers?
3. What "embodied practices of goodwill" can you identify in your own setting that will help you and others recognize the human dignity of all?

Further Reading

Johnson, Walter. "On Agency." *Journal of Social History* 37 (2003): 113–24.

Martin, Clarice J. "Womanist Interpretations of the New Testament: The Quest for Holistic and Inclusive Translation and Interpretation." *Journal of Feminist Studies in Religion* 6 (1990): 41–61.

Nasrallah, Laura S. "'You Were Bought with a Price': Freedpersons and Things in 1 Corinthians." Pages 54–73 in *Corinth in Contrast*. Edited by Steven J. Friesen, Sarah James, and Daniel Schowalter. Leiden: Brill, 2014.

Powery, Emerson B. "Reading with the Enslaved: Placing Human Bondage at the Center of the Early Christian Story." Pages 71–90 in *Bitter the Chastening Rod: Africana Biblical Interpretation after* Stony the Road We Trod *in the Age of BLM, SayHerName, and MeToo*. Edited by Mitzi J. Smith, Angela N. Park, and Erica. S. Dunbar Hill. Lanham, MD: Lexington Books, 2022.

Sarna, Jonathan. "The Bible and Judaism in America." Pages 505–16 in *The Oxford Handbook of the Bible in America*. Edited by Paul C. Gutjahr. New York: Oxford University Press, 2017.

2   *Studying Slavery*

MIDORI E. HARTMAN

As interpreters of biblical texts, we face several challenges when reading difficult passages in which enslavement is woven into the human social fabric of historical time. This chapter explores these challenges and offers strategies for addressing them. First, the intertwining of ethnicity and slavery as a human institution and the question of who was enslaveable in antiquity both have important ethical implications concerning issues of slavery. Second, what are the connections between ancient and contemporary practices of slavery? To explore this question, I turn to a discussion of biblical tradition itself to see how the relationship between enslavement and racialized ethnicity is a post-biblical development that impacted modern New World slavery. My hope is that this background and contextualization will provide a foundation for the study of slavery in the New Testament.

One Challenge in Interpreting the Bible: Enslavement as a Human Institution

A core challenge we face as biblical interpreters is a widespread assumption that the Bible as God's word is inerrant (without mistakes) and infallible (trustworthy). Both of these ideas about scripture were formed within American Protestantism and do not represent a historical view about the Bible, nor do all Christians believe in these ideas. Although the Bible may be understood by many faith communities to be a product of divine inspiration, the texts that constitute the Bible were written and edited by humans over a long period of time. This is important for biblical interpretation because it helps us understand why the Bible contains many diverse and even troubling ideas, including the implicit presumption that enslavement is a "normal" human institution. Because of this, some Christians feel that they cannot criticize limitations of the text and later interpretations. In other words, this default assumption of biblical authority—that the Bible cannot be questioned—limits the ability to see how the Bible is used by people to justify systemic violence and oppression, including enslavement. As Angela N. Parker states, "the doctrines of biblical inerrancy and biblical infallibility are inherently steeped in White supremacist authoritarianism" that impacts modern societies to this day.[1]

One way in which Christians can approach biblical texts is with the understanding that they reflect flawed human institutions, views, and practices. For some people, the Bible also includes inspired and prophetic responses detailing how to address these flaws. If a reader approaches biblical texts in this light, they are invited to critique biblical authority. For example, in the biblical tradition a prophet of the Lord was a person who shared hard messages about society being unjust. Prophets were often not welcomed by their societies for such messages (e.g., Ezekiel, Joel, Jesus). Contemporary biblical interpreters who choose to stand in the biblical prophetic tradition point out the ways in which biblical texts represent social realities that were not just. We should be willing to speak out when the Bible is used to oppress others. The prevalence of enslavement in biblical texts and the justification and support for slavery by Christians using such texts requires a prophetic stance regarding ethical readings of the Bible. The question that arises is how we, as modern readers, should understand ancient enslavement, particularly its differences from and similarities to more modern forms of slavery, especially with respect to ethnicity.

Who Was Enslaveable in Antiquity?

Before we can explore ways to negotiate difficult passages concerning enslavement in the Bible, we must ask a key question: Who, ethnically, were the enslaved in antiquity? This is a natural question to ask because our modern understanding of enslavement comes from a post–New World slavery perspective, in which people were deemed enslaveable in Western colonial institutions because their ethnic and regional origins were tied to the African continent and the Caribbean islands (i.e., West Indies). This perspective shapes our own ideas about enslavement in the Bible, but New World slavery is not a one-to-

---

1. Angela N. Parker, *If God Still Breathes, Why Can't I? Black Lives Matter and Biblical Authority* (Grand Rapids: Eerdmans, 2021), 7.

Figure 2.1. *The Slave Market.* Oil painting by Gustave Boulanger. 1886.

one match with ancient enslavement. At the same time, this point of connection is very important for people who were enslaved in the modern period, many of whom saw their own stories echoed in those of the people of Israel. The Bible became a tool used by colonial enslavers to justify enslavement (e.g., Doctrine of Discovery, Thomas Jefferson's *Notes on the State of Virginia*). Simultaneously, the enslaved *also* used the Bible to counterargue for their own freedom.[2] Ethically, and as inheritors of a long line of liberative interpretations of the Bible, we must acknowledge the power of such readings even as we complicate how ancient people defined who was or was not "enslaveable."

In theory, *anyone* could become enslaved in antiquity due to circumstance. Unlike in New World slavery, physiognomy (facial features) and skin color were not used to justify ancient enslavement. An ancient person's appearance and identity markers such as gender, ethnicity, and class would not automatically protect them from circumstances in which they might be enslaved,

2. See Emerson B. Powery and Rodney S. Sadler Jr., *The Genesis of Liberation: Biblical Interpretation in the Antebellum Narratives of the Enslaved* (Louisville: Westminster John Knox, 2016).

namely through military conquest or human trafficking. Most ancient societies obtained wealth through acts of violence such as war and theft—even theft of human beings. However, each civilization defined the criteria for its own justification of enslavement. Capture by war or by adversarial forces was one reality. Domestic reproduction by existing slaves was another (see chapter 7, "Slave Labor and Trade").

Under these criteria, anyone could be enslaveable in antiquity. There were, however, certain realities that brought ethnicity to the forefront. The fact that a person recently enslaved through war may be a different ethnicity from their enslavers meant that they may not have spoken the same language(s), and their inability to communicate would have played a role in their dehumanization as a war captive. This dehumanization made the enslavement process "easier." Concerning ethnic tensions, ancient Mediterranean societies would often compare themselves with other civilizations based on a free–slave binary logic. One's own people were considered strong and free, while those people from other regions were servile and weak. This ancient binary logic is situated within a larger conversation in antiquity about how enslavement categorized difference. For example, Gaius's *Institutes*, a second-century CE Roman legal text, spells out the free/slave binary clearly: "The main classification in the law of persons is this: all men are either free or slaves" (*Institutes* 1.1.9; see chapter 12, "Household Codes"). This kind of logic shows that enslavement defined freedom. A free person was a citizen with rights unafforded to an enslaved person within a society's population. This is one way enslavement was used to support imperialism at the material level: people went to war with other nations with the understanding that they could enslave their enemies.

Some societies sanctioned the enslavement of one's own people because of an inability to pay debts (see chapter 5, "Jews and Slavery"). Often this indentured servitude would have defined limits. Once debts were paid, freedom would be granted. The presence of debt slavery meant that anyone could hypothetically become enslaved. While people who were enslaved because of debt in the Roman world could be freed once the debt was paid, they were marked with the same "stain of slavery" (*macula servitutis*) because of their former status. While debt slavery and capture in war suggest that ethnic-based enslavement logic was enacted differently in the Roman world than it was in the New World, the impact of this logic was not absent. An ancient person's enslavement was most often based upon the status of the birthing parent—the mother—as the confirmed producer of the child. Since enslaved parents produced enslaved children, both were counted as living property akin to livestock. This legal transfer of enslaved status from parent to child was the same in antiquity as in more modern societies. So, how do ancient social and legal concerns regarding enslavement in the biblical text compare with the postbiblical context (e.g., New World slavery)?

The Biblical and Postbiblical Development of Enslavement Discourses

Ethnic justification for New World slavery draws strongly from interpretations of the Hebrew Bible, namely the so-called Curse of Ham in Genesis 9:25–27. Of the three sons of Noah, Ham was the youngest brother, the grandfather of Canaan, and the one who broke a sexual taboo by seeing and leaving his drunken father naked (cf. Lev 18:7). As a result, Noah cursed Canaan's line—the Canaanites—to be enslaved to the two other brothers, who were blessed for showing piety by respectfully covering Noah up. This story may be understood as an origin story for the "differences in the destinies or fortunes of certain groups or persons."[3] In this reading of the story, the human institution of enslavement was "created" as punishment for a crime. This is a key theme in the narrative passages of Genesis 1–11. However, this connection between racialized ethnicity and enslavement as we know it developed fully in the modern era.

David M. Goldenberg charts the long historical development of how the Curse of Ham was used to justify the enslavement of black Africans. Interpreters misunderstood the origins of the word "Ham" to mean "dark, black, or hot." This association between black Africans and enslavement was an interpretive adaptation to explain why Canaan's line was punished when it was considered "black" Ham's sin.[4] Within later postbiblical and late antique rabbinic contexts, to be described as *kushit* (i.e., descended from Ham) was simply to be considered to have "dark skin" as a result of sun exposure due to manual labor. Thus, it was a descriptor of class and not necessarily a descriptor of ethnicity.[5] Moreover, although there were some associations between black Africans and enslavement, black Africans were a minority ethnicity in the overall slave population in the Greco-Roman world. Their visible foreignness in comparison with other nonindigenous peoples who were enslaved contributed to their association with enslavement.[6]

3. See Cain Hope Felder, *Race, Racism, and the Biblical Narratives: On Use and Abuse of Sacred Scripture* (Minneapolis: Fortress, 2019), 4–5.
4. David M. Goldenberg, *Race and Slavery in Early Judaism, Christianity, and Islam* (Princeton: Princeton University Press, 2003), 167.
5. Goldenberg, *Race and Slavery*, 125.
6. Goldenberg, *Race and Slavery*, 134.

Figure 2.2. Hellenistic bust depicting the head of an "Ethiopian" man found in Egypt. 332–30 BCE.

Black Africans were called "Kushites" (Kush/Cush) in the Hebrew Bible and "Ethiopians" (Nubians) in the Greco-Roman context, and Kush/Ethiopia was imagined as the geographic limit of the known world. In the New Testament, this belief contextualizes Philip's conversion of the Ethiopian eunuch in Acts 8:26–40, which represents an example of the so-called mission to all nations (the gentiles) that Acts depicts (see chapter 8, "Race and Ethnicity"). Thus, this missionary focus means ethnicity was not a limiting factor for the early Jesus movement. Despite this room for more ethnic inclusion in the New Testament, a Eurocentric focus in the text and its interpretation remains. This focus marginalizes Afro-Asian locations in its presumption of Rome as being the center of the world.[7]

This Eurocentric focus became a cultural default to reading and using the Bible. As a result, modern interpreters downplay the impact of non-European Christians in the history and development of the early church (for example, the Ethiopian Orthodox church in Ethiopia, or the Mar Thoma church in India). Eurocentric biblical interpretations have also justified the marginalization of non-European peoples in colonial ideologies. The Bible was employed as justification for the European conquest of Africa and the Americas as an act of "saving" indigenous peoples through conversion to Christianity. For example, the fifteenth-century papal bull *Romanus Pontifex* granted the Portuguese a monopoly of trade over sub-Saharan Africa and included an endorsement of the enslavement of all non-Christians as a determent in practicing their indigenous traditions. Thus, ethical contemporary interpreters must acknowledge a challenging reality. The missionary perspective and drive found in the

7. See Felder, *Race, Racism, and the Biblical Narratives.*

New Testament was used to justify enslavement in modern colonial practices. Moreover, it is important to recognize that the Eurocentric focus of the Bible as it has been constructed and interpreted historically has played a foundational role in the development of the academic field of biblical studies, which continues to marginalize non-European perspectives and interpretations of the Bible as part of a historically embedded colonialist bias to the present day.[8]

In summary, enslavement was an ancient social reality that is represented in the Bible. The evidence of slavery in the Bible can challenge us, as readers, in productive ways to move beyond the comfort zone of doctrine (e.g., biblical inerrancy and infallibility). If we understand that ancient enslavement was viewed broadly as a legal human institution sourced by conflict, trafficking, and domestic production, we can see that ancient enslaveability was tied both to ethnicity and to circumstance. The Bible played a large role in the connection between certain ethnicities and enslavement, eventually tying the Curse of Ham to blackness beginning in late antiquity.[9] How we wrestle with and interpret difficult biblical passages about enslavement remains a challenge. What do we do with passages that have been used to marginalize others? What does it mean that the Bible has been used to these ends throughout the history of Christianity? How do we wrestle with the ways the Bible continues to be used to marginalize others today?

Discussion Questions

1. How has your religious tradition taught you to approach the Bible? How do you handle passages that trouble you personally? Share your insights with several friends by asking them these questions in return.
2. Consider the reality that there are multiple ways to interpret the same text (biblical or otherwise) and that people will see different things depending upon their own context(s). How might your own personhood (age, gender, ethnicity, nationality, etc.) impact how and what you see in scripture?
3. How do you think the fact that enslaveability in antiquity was not solely based in ethnicity will impact how you understand enslaved characters and populations in the Bible moving forward?

8. Andrew M. Mbuvi, *African Biblical Studies: Unmasking Embedded Racism and Colonialism in Biblical Studies* (London: T&T Clark, 2022).

9. See Gay Byron, *Symbolic Blackness and Ethnic Difference in Early Christian Literature* (New York: Routledge, 2002).

Further Reading

Byron, Gay. *Symbolic Blackness and Ethnic Difference in Early Christian Literature.* New York: Routledge, 2002.

Felder, Cain Hope. *Race, Racism, and the Biblical Narratives: On Use and Abuse of Sacred Scripture.* Minneapolis: Fortress, 2019.

Goldenberg, David M. *Race and Slavery in Early Judaism, Christianity, and Islam.* Princeton: Princeton University Press, 2003.

Hicks-Keeton, Jill. *The Good Book: How White Evangelicals Save the Bible to Save Themselves.* Minneapolis: Fortress, 2023.

Mbuvi, Andrew M. *African Biblical Studies: Unmasking Embedded Racism and Colonialism in Biblical Studies.* London: T&T Clark, 2022.

Parker, Angela N. *If God Still Breathes, Why Can't I? Black Lives Matter and Biblical Authority.* Grand Rapids: Eerdmans, 2021.

Powery, Emerson B., and Rodney S. Sadler, Jr., eds. *The Genesis of Liberation: Biblical Interpretation in the Antebellum Narratives of the Enslaved.* Louisville: Westminster John Knox, 2016.

3   *Enslavement in the Roman World*

JAVAL A. COLEMAN

On the back of a gravestone from the second century CE on the Via Flaminia in Rome is inscribed a shocking curse:

> Here are written the eternal marks of disgrace of the freedwoman Acte, sorceress, faithless, deceitful, hard-hearted. A nail and a hemp rope to hang her neck and boiling pitch to burn up her evil heart. Manumitted for free, following an adulterer, she cheated her patron and she abducted his attendants—an enslaved girl and boy—from her patron while he lay in bed, so that he, alone, despaired, an old man abandoned and despoiled. And the same curse for Hymnus and those who followed Zosimus. (*CIL* 6.20905, back)

Acte, a formerly enslaved woman, is accused of infidelity, kidnapping, and slave stealing in this curse, along with co-conspirators who were likely also formerly enslaved, Hymnus and Zosimus. Acte is accused of taking advantage of her patron's age and vulnerability. She is villainized as a sorceress. Whoever wrote it must be quite angry with Acte—or harbor a grudge against her—since it was no small thing to inscribe a curse like this in stone.[1]

---

1. See Katharine P. D. Huemoeller, "Freedom in Marriage? Manumission for Marriage in the Roman World," *Journal of Roman Studies* 110 (2020): 123–39; and Javal Coleman and Dan-El Padilla Peralta, "Rhetorics," in *Writing, Enslavement, and Power in the Roman Mediterranean, 100 BCE–300 CE*, ed. Jeremiah Coogan, Joseph Howley, and Candida Moss (Oxford: Oxford University Press, forthcoming).

Surprisingly, the front side of this gravestone names Marcus Junius Euphrosynus and the girl's mother, presumably Acte, as the owners (dedicators) of the monument to their daughter Junia Procula, who died just weeks short of her ninth birthday. This clarifies that Acte and Euphrosynus were married and even had a daughter together who was named Junia. However, the curse on the back of the monument, which is likely written in Euphrosynus's voice, reveals that Acte was also once his slave.

While the curse speaks to Acte's alleged crimes and wishes unspeakable violence for her demise, the fact that she is both Euphrosynus's wife and former slave adds to the intrigue of the family situation. This curse provides information about the agency of formerly enslaved people in the Roman Empire and the measures they sometimes took to build a life for themselves. Acte was freed from enslavement (manumitted) by Euphrosynus, perhaps so he could legally marry her. This would explain Junia's freeborn status on the front of the monument. After her manumission, Acte left her husband and former enslaver. She even stole enslaved children from Euphrosynus, perhaps her own, born while she was enslaved. She made off with some guys named Hymnus and Zosimus.

Figure 3.1. This inscription is found on the back of a funerary monument memorializing Junia Procula. The text curses Acte, a freedwoman, who is accused of infidelity, kidnapping, and stealing enslaved persons. 69–96 CE.

The complexity and seeming contradictions of this monument raise interesting questions for the study of slavery in the Roman Republic and Empire. What happened between Acte and Euphrosynus? Was this a conspiracy for Acte to create a life and a family of her choosing? How should we understand the entanglement of enslavement, marriage, kidnapping, and liberation in this story? How do this inscription and its curse help us understand Roman slavery more deeply?

Roman slavery is messy, ambiguous, shape-shifting, and difficult to understand clearly because of the scholarly, religious, and ideological pressures placed on its study. Let us look at the historical landscape of Roman slavery, the complex agency of enslaved people within the Roman system, the violence inherent in this system, and the use of ethnically marked war captives for slave trading.

Rome and the Roman Empire

Readers of the New Testament often ask why Roman slavery is even important for a set of texts that are elevated as scripture for Christian practitioners. The texts within the New Testament were written between approximately 50 CE and 150 CE (mid-first to mid-second century CE). The events these texts

Figure 3.2. Another example of a curse against enslaved persons is found on this lead tablet from 100 BCE. On it, these six enslaved workers—Philocomus, Antiochus, Parnaces, Sosus, Erato, Epidia—are cursed after escaping their enslaver. The Latin curse reads: "(May) they dissolve; may they not find satisfaction with (their) masters, these same whose names are here (written). May they disappear/perish for the reason that they also might find satisfaction with (their) property. (May) the things said and done by these (be consigned) to the underworld!"

remember or analyze mostly happened between 30 CE and 100 CE. Some texts tell stories about events in ancient Judea and Samaria but are written decades after the historical memories they hold.

This discrepancy between historical events and writings is extremely important for understanding how the earliest Christ followers made sense of their memories and experience over the first decades after Jesus. Many of these Christ-following communities lived in Greece (Corinth, Philippi, Thessaloniki), Asia Minor (Ephesus, Pergamon, Thyatira, Laodicea), and Syrian Antioch. For all these geographic locations, the era between 30 CE and 100 CE was a time of political and social change, some of it through war and violence, and some of it through an influx of wealth from those most closely connected with the Roman Empire.

In other words, every book of the New Testament was written within a historical era and social context characterized by the Roman Empire, its governing structures, and its social mores. Jewish and Hellenistic political, cultural, and social norms were also embedded in contexts where New Testament texts emerged, as well as the system of slavery within Jewish and Hellenistic societies (see chapter 5, "Jews and Slavery"). And still, the Roman Empire shaped even these sensibilities. So, how did the Roman Empire and its system of slavery emerge in the first century CE?

Rome is a city in modern-day Italy that began as an independent city-state sometime in the fifth century BCE. The city gathered military, economic, and political power throughout the Italian peninsula and formed a senate-led republican government. Eventually, this Roman republic expanded its power to include most areas around the Mediterranean rim and even into Western Europe. By the late first century BCE, the city had incorporated so much territory that it became an *imperium* ("empire") with Rome as its capital.

Multiple military campaigns that consolidated Roman rule on the Italian peninsula and around the western Mediterranean helped facilitate this shift and brought an influx of war captives as slaves to the Italian peninsula. The Punic Wars (264–146 BCE), for example, ended with Rome having control over Carthage on the North African coast. These wars likely kept a steady influx of enslaved war captives flowing into Rome and its environs. During the Republic, several other conquests resulted in mass enslavements, too. In 177 BCE, during a campaign to the island of Sardinia, Tiberius Sempronius Gracchus killed or enslaved 80,000 of the island's locals. Ten years later, in 167 BCE, Aemilius Paullus sacked seventy cities and enslaved 150,000 people from Greece. Ancient historians such as Polybius and Livy wrote about these conflicts extensively and estimated that the Romans enslaved a few hundred thousand people annually.

After the death of Julius Caesar (44 BCE), a power vacuum led to a civil war fought mainly outside of Rome and Italy. Ultimately Marc Antony, having created alliances in Egypt and Asia Minor, fell in battle to Octavian in 31 BCE at Actium off the west coast of Greece. Octavian, known as Caesar Augustus, then became the sole ruler. Having sided with Antony, the cities in Asia Minor spent enormous sums to prove their loyalty to Augustus, competing for the rights to build temples dedicated to the emperor. This influence of the Empire also brought prosperity for some, an influx of people from other parts of the world, and a robust market for slaves.

At the beginning of the Empire, the campaigns that resulted in mass enslavement were not well documented. One exception is a campaign in Galilee, Samaria, and Judea from 66–70 CE called the First Jewish War. Josephus, a Jewish general captured by the Romans early in the campaign, wrote a multivolume history of the Roman takeover of these territories. Especially important for New Testament studies is the long, slow, three-year siege of Jerusalem that ended with the destruction of the Jewish temple in 70 CE. To celebrate this victory, the Romans sent the most "beautiful" war captives and temple plunder back to the city of Rome to be paraded through the streets. Other war captives were sold in slave markets around the Empire (see chapter 7, "Slave Labor and Trade"). Josephus writes that the Romans enslaved 97,000 people (mostly Jews). As a result of this war, the centers of Jewish and early Christ-following religious communities shifted. To be sure, some settlements of both communities remained in the Judean territory taken over by the Romans. But other cosmopolitan centers, such as Antioch, Ephesus, Thessaloniki, Corinth, and Rome, became more important for the development of both religious groups and their relationships to slavery.

Some scholars suggest that the lack of documentation of mass enslavement during the imperial period is evidence for a decrease in the economic dependence of Rome on enslaved labor. Others suggest that once Rome conquered much of the Mediterranean rim, they could no longer rely on warfare to maintain a steady supply of slaves. Instead, enslavers turned to other means of acquiring enslaved labor, such as breeding. And indeed, scholars believe that in the imperial period the breeding of the enslaved became increasingly more common (see chapter 7, "Slave Labor and Trade").

Although it is tempting to oversimplify this difference between the Republic and the Empire and assert a critique of slavery in the later period, the historical reality does not bear this out. We simply do not have texts or other evidence from this period that foreground enslaved experiences from enslaved perspectives. Ancient Roman historians reduced their stories of conquests to numbers. This has had the unfortunate effect of excluding from our histories the experiences of those caught in the violence, enslavement, and aftermath of such conquests.

It is indeed rare that we find information about this experience of enslavement. Ancient historians took as a given that enslavement through warfare was a natural way of doing things. For example, the *Digest* (a collection of Roman laws ranging from the first century BCE to the fourth century CE) notes this about enslavement:

> Slaves come into our ownership either by civil law or the common law of peoples, by the civil law, if anyone over twenty allows himself to be sold in order to benefit by retaining a share of the purchase price; and by the common law of peoples, those who have been captured in war and those who are the children of our slave women are our slaves. (*Digest* 1.5.5.1)

The second part of this quotation is important to notice: it was understood at some level (although how universally is debatable) as a common law among peoples that slaves could be acquired as a result of warfare.

Yet when we discuss warfare captives, we should retain caution in interpreting these numbers as those of newly enslaved people. For example, Polybius states in his *Histories* that "Aemilius Paullus after the fall of Perseus . . . destroyed seventy cities in Macedonia, most of them belonging to the Molotti, and that he sold into slavery 150,000 persons" (*Histories* 30.15). It is difficult to confirm these numbers, though it is not unlikely that a few hundred thousand people would be sold into slavery because of conquest. Nevertheless, it is difficult to know how "correct" these numbers are for this episode. Polybius, in other parts of his *Histories*, is more precise about the fate of captives. In a passage talking about how ten thousand captives were taken after a military victory, Polybius specifies which of the ten thousand captives were sold off into slavery. Selling war captives into slavery was not an automatic process. In another example of imprecision among ancient historians, Livy states that the Romans took thirty thousand enslaved people in the sack of Tarentum in 209 BCE. However, Livy does not specify exactly what this means. Perhaps the Romans enslaved the people of Tarentum, or perhaps the Romans took the slaves who were already in Tarentum, or perhaps it was a mix of both.

Some ancient historians told stories about slaves in their biographies of high-profile figures, but these were mostly illustrations of enslaved workers as tools for powerful people. Philosophers, playwrights, and novelists likewise used stereotypes and stock characters when enslaved people appeared in their writings (see chapter 11, "Literary Constructions and Stereotypes of Slavery"). Nonetheless, some evidence of the lives of those who were enslaved does come from early Christian texts, sale receipts, work contracts, and private letters, as well as inscriptions like the one about Euphrosynus and Acte at the beginning of this chapter. The inclusion of enslaved people in these kinds of ancient sources show us that elite literary texts cannot and do not tell the whole story.

Enslaved Status and Its Imprecisions

Yet ancient historians are not the only ones who struggle with how to write about enslavement and slavery systems. Modern scholars also write about Roman slavery in ways that diminish our view of enslaved people. Two issues are worth our attention in this chapter. The first issue is about the way that slavery is defined in relationship to its inherent brutality. The second issue concerns the perspective through which historians attempt to understand slavery. Let us examine this first issue more closely.

In 1982, Orlando Patterson published a groundbreaking comparative study of slavery across both cultures and time periods. Called *Slavery and Social Death*, this work noted that most slavery systems included three common violations of human rights: slavery enacted a permanent alienation from one's birth family; slavery perpetrated violence against enslaved people's bodies and minds; and slavery was a kind of "social death" that included the inability to form permanent social bonds.[2] Patterson intended this as a description of the kind of experiences enslaved people encountered within slavery systems. Yet a description of the conditions of slavery is by no means a definition of the experience or identity of a person experiencing enslavement.

When historians of slavery use Patterson's definition, however, as a shorthand for slavery and the experience of a slavery system, enslaved persons are not viewed as full humans. The ancient Roman system of slavery was a brutal institution that actively tried to and did dehumanize its victims. In this view, enslaved persons were not viewed as full humans. However, this is simply not true. In fact, the opposite is the case. Slavery was and is a brutal institution that profits on the *humanity* of its victims. Take the example of Acte and Euphrosynus from the beginning of the chapter. Euphrosynus likely had children with Acte, perhaps even the daughter who died. Those children born before Acte's manumission

---

2. Orlando Patterson, *Slavery and Social Death: A Comparative Study* (Cambridge, MA: Harvard University Press, 1982).

would have legally been his slaves, who were bound to his directives in terms of their work. Yet Acte, when she leaves Euphrosynus with several of his slaves, may have left with their common children, who were the same people.

The second issue with modern interpretations of ancient Roman slavery, both in classics and in biblical studies, is that the relationship between enslaver and enslaved is nearly always characterized as a one-way street—previous scholars assumed that the master/owner/enslaver always affected all outcomes of said relationship. The enslaver, however, did not hold all the cards. Enslavers depended on enslaved people not just to *make* their lives easier, but quite literally *for* their lives. Enslaved laborers made large-scale industries with significant profit margins possible. Enslaved people often tended to their ill or infirmed enslavers. Enslaved people cooked meals and transported goods. They built houses and cleaned sewer systems. Enslaved people were not merely tools, automatons of their masters; their work made their masters' lives possible. Acte, again, becomes a good example of this reality. Euphrosynus literally curses her on the back of their daughter's epitaph, but he curses her for her agency apart from him. She determined her own pathway rather than rely on her (former) master to make decisions about the shape of her life. While enslaved people were often met with violence for such acts of "rebellion," their sense of self and purpose need not be determined through their enslavers' views of the world.

At the same time, it is worth exploring how writings from the Roman Empire adopt the perspective of enslavers. This exploration shows us both the idealized perceptions of enslavers and their reliance on the human qualities of enslaved people. Many scholars see a strong influence from Aristotle's *Politics* in the ideologies of slavery in the first century CE. Aristotle suggested that there were people "naturally" suited to enslavement. These people had the capacity for speech, thinking, and task completion, but had only enough rational ability to follow their enslavers' direction (*Politics* 1.1260a30). This claim is echoed in Arius Didymus's epitome of the Roman Empire (Stobaeus, *Eclogues* 2.149.10; see chapter 12, "Household Codes"). Picking up on this lack of rationality, Varro, in his manual for best practices in agricultural estates, suggests that an enslaved workforce provides a set of "thinking tools" for the owner (*On Agriculture* 1.17). Enslaved people, however, could not possibly have been merely tools, either in the master's practical thought or in actual practice. Their value for the enslaver came in their ability to act independently in their work—and sometimes to work for their own benefit beyond the enslaver's prescriptions. Examples of enslaved people saving enough from their extra, freelance work to buy their own or their relatives' freedom are frequent in the historical record (see chapter 6, "Manumission"). These examples show not only that enslaved people were not permanently alienated from freedom, but also that their ties to others defied ideologies of isolation and social death.

Moreover, enslaved status was not always clearly identified in everyday interactions. Roman imperial laws and ideologies attempted to make the lines between slave and free very clear, but often failed (see chapter 4, "Roman Law and Material Culture"). Hence, one of the most famous passages of Gaius is: "The principal division of the law of persons is the following, namely, that all men are either free or slaves" (*Institutes* 1.9). Even with such legal pronouncements, in practice, enslaved status was only clear in the ideological conversation. Some enslaved people, like those enslaved to the emperor, were trusted with governance responsibilities, had access to resources, wielded political influence, and even had a measure of freedom of movement. At the same time, even those enslaved people who lived a relatively privileged existence were also answerable with their bodies and lives for disobedience or mistakes.

These privileged slaves as well as literary texts from elite authors have frequently been the focus of studies of Roman slavery. Yet the ambiguities of enslaved status were much more common than previously thought. Recall the inscriptions about Acte and Euphrosynus from the beginning of the chapter. Although both the curse and the funerary inscription are written from the perspective of the enslaver class (i.e., Euphrosynus's perspective), it is clear that Euphrosynus was not of a particularly high status. Acte, likewise, must have functioned as both enslaved worker and then freed wife at multiple points in the couple's life together. Even the fact of Acte's disappearance suggests an ambiguity about her status—she was able to have enough independence to plot her leaving while also minimally meeting Euphrosynus's expectations. Texts such as these inscriptions provide a different focus for scholars seeking to piece together how Roman enslavement operated in the empire.

As the Acte inscriptions make clear, the difference between free and enslaved is far more complex an issue when one looks beyond legal status. For this reason, scholars more recently have focused heavy attention on examining enslaved people alongside manumitted individuals (people who were set free from slavery). Manumitted people were called freed people—a legal status that signaled they were no longer enslaved but had once been. People who had never been enslaved had the status of a free-born person. Examining these two statuses (slave and freed) alongside one another demonstrates the social elasticity of status in the Roman Empire. For instance, just as enslaved individuals had to answer to their enslavers, most manumitted individuals were legally responsible for maintaining relationships with their former enslavers. This was often worked out through the process known as *operae* or "work days." Here I quote Ulpian's explanation of the practice in full:

> Operae are not things that exist in the nature of things. But personal services cannot be owed to anyone other than the patron, since the ownership of them is established in the person of the one doing them and the one for whom they are done; operae relating to a trade, however, or others of that sort, can be fulfilled by whomever for whomever. For, if they relate to some craft, they can be fulfilled for others by order of the patron. (*Digest* 38.1.9)

Freed people accordingly owed their work service to their former master, who become their patron. *Operae* were typically a set number of workdays that was agreed upon at the time of manumission. Since *operae* were established not by the fact of manumission, but by a legal agreement between two free parties, disputes were seen as breaches of obligation. Although the individuals engaging in *operae* were both free parties, the formerly enslaved individual would carry the stigma of enslavement for the rest of their lives. This stigma marked them as "slave-like" in Roman thought, since they were required to work for the person that previously enslaved them. It is important to note some obvious but nevertheless important aspects of this process. Even though manumitted individuals had to engage in the same kind of labor they would have done as slaves, legally speaking, they were free individuals. They could no longer be beaten, sold, or treated as if they were enslaved people (at least physically; see chapter 6, "Manumission").

Later developments in Roman law suggest a kind of humanitarian turn in Rome's treatment of enslaved people. While we cannot explore these developments systematically, we can look at one example. A rescript from the emperor Antoninus Pius (138–161 CE) is quoted in the sixth-century CE Justinian *Institutes*. It reads:

> The powers of masters over their slaves ought to continue undiminished, nor ought any man to be deprived of his lawful rights; but it is the master's own interest that relief justly sought against cruelty, insufficient sustenance, or intolerable wrong, should not be denied. I enjoin you then to look into the complaints of the slaves of Iulius Sabinus, who have fled for protection to the statue of the Emperor, and if you find them treated with undue harshness or other ignominious wrong, order them to be sold, so that they may not again fall under the power of their master; and the latter will find that if he attempts to evade this, my enactment, I shall visit his offence with severe punishment. (*Institutes* 1.8.1)

While this quotation seems to advocate for the better treatment of the enslaved, Alan Watson (a Roman legal historian) reminds us that we ought to question the ideology behind such texts.[3] The rescript itself does not actually say much of anything about the treatment of slaves. It is more or less about Roman enslavers' practices and how they should behave toward their enslaved property. Even in raising concerns for the condition of enslaved people, Roman law respects the authority of the enslaver as a fairly absolute right. Thus, Pius can reiterate that "the power of masters over their slaves ought not to be diminished."

Violence and the Humanness of the Enslaved

This threat of violence at the hands of enslavers can hardly be understated. If one examines the spectacular level of violence that was inflicted on the enslaved, it is clear that violence and the threat of violence depended on the enslaved individual's capacity to suffer bodily harm. In Rome, this came in the form of anything from insults and whipping to the sexual exploitation of the enslaved. It was accepted that the Roman enslaver class could and did inflict physical, emotional, psychological, and spiritual violence on their enslaved. However, there are instances where excessive violence toward enslaved workers is clearly described as wrong. For example, in his treatise *On Clemency,* Seneca the Younger says the following concerning the treatment of the enslaved:

> Slaves have the right to take refuge at your statue and although one has the right do anything to a slave, in the case of a human being, there are limits to what one can do laid down by the universal law of all living creatures. (*On Clemency* 1.18.1–2)

Seneca notes that unrestrained violence, even against a slave, violates the moral limits of respect for living things. Later in this document, Seneca highlights the excessive violence of a first-century senator, Vedius Pollio, who apparently had the habit of feeding his enslaved to his lampreys (flesh-eating fish) for minor mistakes. After meeting Vedius Pollio, the emperor Augustus had his men break all of Pollio's glassware, something he had threatened a slave's life for. The enslaved person in question apparently fell at Augustus's feet and begged him not to let him die in this particular manner. Thus, it can be surmised that the fear of the enslaved was particularly useful to the enslaver class but was also used to channel pity.

3. Alan Watson, *Roman Slave Law* (Baltimore: Johns Hopkins University Press, 1987).

Several New Testament parables show evidence of this type of excessive violence. For example, in Luke 12:41–48 Jesus tells the parable of the unfaithful slave, which describes the beatings that enslaved people might receive from the enslaved manager of the estate when the enslaver is away (v. 45). When the enslaver returns home, the text says he will "cut him in pieces" for the disobedience (v. 46). It seems that all slaves in this parable will receive some sort of beating, whether it is light (v. 48) or severe (v. 47). While these stories are presented as allegories to represent the believers' respect for God, reading the parables through the lens of Roman slavery suggests that enslaved persons in antiquity would have been fearful of the excessive violence that Seneca and Luke describe.

But all this violence is only useful in slavery systems because enslaved people are actually *not* understood as objects or tools to be used. The very fact of their humanity is precisely why violence perpetuates the system, since slavery profits on the humanity of its victims. In the case of Acte and Euphrosynus, this reality needs to be understood not only in the marriage relationship between the two, but more importantly in the child that they bury and the enslaved children that Acte takes with her. It is clear that, in the relationship between Acte and Euphrosynus, the latter did not see the former as nonhuman, nor does his curse seek to dehumanize her. In fact, it highlights and capitalizes on the humanness of their relationship with one another. From this, we see that Euphrosynus clearly manumitted Acte to meet his own needs (marriage), and Acte decided to reject this relationship at some point. The rejection of Acte clearly upset and angered Euphrosynus very deeply, which led to the curse. Through this, we can see that Euphrosynus did see Acte as a human, even as his treatment of her (and the other enslaved workers in the household) attempted to dehumanize them.

It is also important to mention the fact that intimate relationships between enslaver and enslaved have often been romanticized within the literature of antiquity. The practice of Roman men marrying their formerly enslaved is not an unusual one. In fact, there are over three hundred funerary monuments alone that attest to Roman male enslavers freeing their female enslaved workers for the purpose of marriage. These relationships have often been used as evidence that the Roman enslaver class were benevolent owners since they freed many of their enslaved. However, in the case of Acte we see an outright rejection of this relationship even though she was "manumitted for free." Furthermore, the Acte inscription is unique in that it details some of the sense of agency that formerly enslaved women such as Acte might have had. It is rare that a woman who was previously enslaved, or a freedwoman, would be

Figure 3.3. Funerary monument of Regina, a freedwoman and wife of Barates of Palmyra. Second century CE.

able to leave her circumstances in this way. Even more rare would be if Acte took the two enslaved children with her—perhaps her own two children—so they would be free.

Race, Ethnicity, and Roman Enslavement

Just as the Roman slavery system was complex in its marking of enslaved people's status, the system was also complicated in terms of the race and ethnicity of enslaved people. Roman slavery was not a skin-color-based system as in the Americas, but skin color did factor into perceptions of enslaved people. Roman slavery was not an ethnically driven system either. But the ethnicity of enslaved people did influence their roles within the system.

Although warfare played a significant role in the obtainment of Rome's enslaved, the evidence we have tends to focus on the numbers of those enslaved and rarely if ever provides an account of what this experience would have been like. Take, for example, the passage of Polybius mentioned above. In discussing the Aemilius Paullus episode, Polybius makes note that seventy cities were destroyed and over 150,000 people enslaved. It is important to understand that this meant loss of lives, culture, and knowledge. The annihilation of a knowledge system, or epistemicide, has been recently traced as a salient feature of the mass enslavements of the Roman Middle Republican period. For example, in 150 BCE the praetor Sulpicius Galba ordered that several Lusitanian tribes be murdered and enslaved. Although a capital charge was brought against him at Rome, he defended himself through alleging that the Lusitanians were plotting against him, or that they were into sacrificing human beings. What is key in this episode is that certain Lusitanian religious practices and ways of life should be heavily monitored, and furthermore that even some should be erased. Mass enslavement was a method by which this could be accomplished.[4]

Through this understanding of the ways in which Romans enslaved people, we can point out that Rome enslaved all kinds of people from different races and regions. If they fought with Gauls, they enslaved Gauls. If they fought with Greeks, they enslaved Greeks. Although there was not a single race the Romans desired to enslave above all others, there were certainly races which they found to be more worthy of enslavement, thus more agreeable for slaving. This can be seen in texts describing the process of sale at the slave markets:

---

4. See Coleman and Padilla Peralta, "Rhetorics"; and Dan-El Padilla Peralta, *Divine Institutions: Religions and Community in Middle Republican Rome* (Princeton: Princeton University Press, 2020).

Those who sell slaves must state the race of each at the sale; for the race of a slave frequently encourages or deters a prospective buyer; hence it is advantageous to know his race since it is reasonable to suppose that some slaves are good because they come from a tribe that has a good reputation, and others bad because they come from a tribe that is rather disreputable. (*Digest* 21.1.31.21)

It is clear from this passage that the Romans *did* consider race and ethnicity important factors in determining how good or not good a potential slave might be (see chapter 8, "Race and Ethnicity," for more information on these connections). Nevertheless, it is important to keep in mind that, generally speaking, Romans were "equal opportunity" enslavers; hence, they did not focus on enslaving a specific people. That does not mean, however, that the Romans did not have a racializing discourse concerning slavery, since the above passage makes it clear that they did. Romans tended to acknowledge the ethnicity of certain enslaved while at the same time rejecting their origin. They made every effort to reduce their enslaved into what made them useful. There are vast references in Plautus's plays to racial stereotypes that made certain types of slaves desirable (see chapter 11, "Literary Constructions and Stereotypes of Slavery").

Two examples illustrate this point. The first is the idea that Greek slaves were more educated, sophisticated, and able to perform higher-level tasks. Slaves of Greek origin were often seen as status symbols to their owners, teaching their children, writing their letters, and attending to accounting matters. In another example, an Egyptian woman's brown skin was seen as beautiful and enchanting—she looked "exotic" to the Roman eye. Nonetheless, this exoticism was valued for the price she would command as an enslaved sex laborer. At the end of the day, whether the enslaved person was from Egypt or from Corinth, what mattered to Roman slaveholders were the uses to which the former could be put.

Conclusion

As we have seen, understanding Roman slavery is vital to understanding the historical context of the New Testament. As described above, the texts within the New Testament were written within the context of ancient Judaism as well as the ancient Greek and Roman worlds. Each of these contexts play a part in the texts of the New Testament. Considering the facets of Roman slavery described in this chapter, for example, can help the reader to understand Paul's letter to Philemon. In this letter, Paul writes to Philemon about the fate of

Onesimus, a person enslaved to Philemon, whom Paul meets while in prison. Depending on the way one reads this letter, Paul could be advocating that Philemon treat Onesimus better or even that Philemon free Onesimus through manumission. In this case, the reader of Philemon might question the possible repercussions of manumission for Onesimus. Even if Philemon did choose to manumit Onesimus, there could have been *operae* outlined in the manumission agreement so that Onesimus might have still had to regularly work for Philemon. Similarly, while we cannot know the race of Onesimus, after recognizing Rome's tendency to enslave people of many races, we can imagine Onesimus perhaps being a different race than his enslaver, Philemon.

Furthermore, the parables of Jesus in the Synoptic Gospels include a number of allusions to the violence done to enslaved persons by their enslavers. This overview of Roman slavery can assist us as we try to make sense of these parables. While the parables do not clearly recount a historical story, they incorporate the extreme violence inflicted upon enslaved persons, which was supported and sustained by the Roman Empire. The parables reveal to us just how "normal" these views about slavery were, even to Jesus's followers.

Returning to Euphrosynus's curse of Acte presented at the opening of this chapter, let me reiterate my main point: enslaved persons in the Roman Empire were human beings. While much ancient literature and scholarship on slavery has emphasized the dehumanization of enslaved persons, we need to complexify our view of slavery systems to recognize how much they rely upon the humanness of enslaved persons, especially in terms of violence. While enslavers did not often recognize it, we can identify moments of agency,[5] like the actions that Acte took, within an enslaved person's (or a manumitted person's) life while still understanding the exploitative components of the slavery system.

5. The matter of enslaved agency is widely debated; however, some scholars have made great strides in this area, particularly scholars who have adopted Saidya Hartman's lens of "critical fabulation," which is defined as a mode of storytelling rooted in archival material and approached through a critical lens: "listening for the unsaid, translating misconstrued words, and refashioning disfigured lives . . . respecting the limits of what cannot be known" ("Venus in Two Acts," *Small Axe* 12 [2008]: 1–14, here 1–4). Scholars who have fruitfully applied this approach include Candida Moss, *God's Ghostwriters* (New York: Little, Brown, 2024); Deborah Kamen and Sarah Levin-Richardson, "Approaching Emotions and Agency in Greek and Roman Slavery," in *Les lectures contemporaines de l'esclavage: Problématiques, méthodologies et analyses depuis les années 1990* (Besançon: Presses universitaires de Franche-Comté, 2022); and Kamen and Levin-Richardson, "Epigraphy and Critical Fabulation: Imagining Narratives of Greco-Roman Sexual Slavery," in *Dynamic Epigraphy: New Approaches to Inscriptions*, ed. Eleri H.Cousins (Havertown, UK: Oxbow, 2022), 201–22.

Discussion Questions

1. What is the most surprising aspect of Roman slavery addressed in this chapter? What aspect of Roman slavery would you like to know more about?

2. In addition to Philemon and Jesus's parables, is there another text or section of the New Testament that can be more clearly understood after reading this chapter on Roman slavery?

3. Return to the curse tablet focused on Acte from the beginning of the chapter. How do situations like the one described here complicate our understanding of enslavement in the Roman world? What other situations can you imagine occurring in the context of Roman slavery that might be similarly complicated?

Further Reading

Callahan, Allen Dwight, ed. *Slavery in Text and Interpretation*. Atlanta: Society of Biblical Literature, 1998.

Coleman, Javal, and Dan-El Padilla Peralta. "Rhetorics." In *Writing, Enslavement, and Power in the Roman Mediterranean, 100 BCE–300 CE*. Edited by Jeremiah Coogan, Joseph Howley, and Candida Moss. Oxford: Oxford University Press, forthcoming.

Huemoeller, Katharine P. D. "Freedom in Marriage? Manumission for Marriage in the Roman World." *Journal of Roman Studies* 110 (2020): 123–39.

Joshel, Sandra R. *Slavery in the Roman World*. Cambridge: Cambridge University Press, 2010.

Patterson, Orlando. *Slavery and Social Death: A Comparative Study*. Cambridge, MA: Harvard University Press, 1982.

Roth, Ulrike. *Thinking Tools: Agricultural Slavery between Evidence and Models*. London: Institute of Classical Studies, School of Advanced Study, University of London, 2007.

4   *Roman Law and Material Culture*

F. MIRA GREEN

According to Acts 16, when Paul and his companions arrive in Philippi in Macedonia to begin their proselytizing efforts, a slave girl who was also a diviner—that is she performed divination and fortune-telling—followed Paul and his friends around Philippi for a few days yelling that they were "slaves of the Most High God" and brought a new salvation to the city. Paul, however, did not appreciate her endorsement. After a while, he became annoyed and ordered the fortune-telling spirit in her to leave. The spirit subsequently withdrew from her, which resulted in her inability to perform divinations. This situation created even more problems for Paul and his companions. The enslaved girl's gift of divination had made money for her enslavers. Angered by this loss of income, the enslavers grabbed ahold of the proselytizing men and brought them to the center of town in front of some local magistrates. As a crowd started to gather, it began attacking Paul and his friends. Meanwhile, the magistrates stripped the men of their clothing, flogged them publicly, and then brought them to prison. These humiliations were all extreme violations of the protections that Paul's Roman citizenship should have provided (Acts 16:16–40).

This story in Acts not only shows us an interaction between an enslaved person and a Roman citizen, but also indicates that Roman citizens did not simply live in Rome. Citizenship was a force of cohesion within the Empire: It connected different individuals across a wide space. This was the result of imperial policies of extending Roman citizenship to those outside of Italy who met certain qualifications. The first emperor, Augustus (27 BCE–14 CE), reimagined Roman citizenship to include more people living in the provinces.

Eventually, the emperor Caracalla in 212 CE would grant Roman citizenship to all free persons living in the Empire. The effect of the extension of Roman citizenship created multiple identities for people like Paul. He identified as a Jew, a Tarsian (from the city of Tarsus), and a Roman citizen. Yet, when historians shift focus to the daily realities of marginalized people living in the Roman Empire, this story from Acts also reveals and obscures many things about the life of the enslaved girl whose gift of divination was stolen from her by an annoyed Paul. She had a spiritual gift that was exploited by her enslavers and taken from her by a strange man. Throughout the story, she remains unnamed and the harm she suffers from Paul is immediately interpreted through the lens of what her enslavers lose, not her own loss. We know nothing of how she dealt with the loss of her gift or what it might have meant for the rest of her life as an enslaved person.[1] What we know and do not know of her is consistent with what we see in many literary sources that survive from the Roman world—that is, her life is used as a means to advance the story of the free people living in the Roman world, but all the other details of her life are either afterthoughts or not mentioned at all in Acts. What is more, other passages found in the New Testament indicate that some authors acknowledged and upheld the power dynamics that defined relationships between free and enslaved persons in the Roman Empire (Titus 2:9; 1 Tim 6:1; 1 Pet 2:18; Eph 6:5).

In this chapter, I propose that understanding the legal landscape of Roman slavery and the material conditions of enslaved persons offers a richer understanding of the world in which the texts of the New Testament were composed. Unfortunately, there are almost no documents from the Roman world that allow modern scholars or students to know how a slave experienced or thought about her life.[2] Rather, the sources we have about their lives were written from the perspective of enslavers, and ancient authors make it clear that free persons viewed the lives of slaves in instrumental terms. Thus, it requires a bit of imaginative thinking to get at the material lives and experiences of enslaved people living in the Roman world.[3] In the pages that follow, I will begin with what we can learn from Roman law about the lives of slaves in the Roman

1. See Christy Cobb, *Slavery, Gender, Truth, and Power in Luke-Acts* (London: Palgrave MacMillan, 2019).
2. On female authorship of graffiti from Pompeii offering us a possibility of thinking about how to recover some lost voices from the Roman world, see Sarah Levin-Richardson, "*Fututa Sum Hic*: Female Subjectivity and Agency in Pompeian Sexual Graffiti," *The Classical Journal* 108 (2013): 319–45.
3. See Sandra Joshel and Lauren Hackworth Petersen, *The Material Life of Roman Slaves* (Cambridge: Cambridge University Press, 2014).

world. Then I will consider what some artifacts and art might communicate about the daily, physical experiences of slaves in Roman homes.

Slavery in Roman Law

Conquest and ecological good luck allowed the Roman state to become the first to unite the entire Mediterranean under one political domain.[4] The proceeds of its empire were immense as Rome harnessed resources from local communities and put them into circulation. Prospering often to the detriment of its neighbors and subjects, Rome opened some communities to the broader Mediterranean world and made their resources available to the Romans. Roman imperialism unlocked the economic potential of the Mediterranean world, which helped launch new markets that responded to Romans' exploitation of the wealth of empire.[5] The redistribution of wealth and economic resources was the single most dynamic aspect of the growth of Rome's economy.[6] Land and human property were some of the resources that were redistributed. Particularly, Rome's conquest of its neighbors and wider regions often resulted in colonization and enslavement. Colonization meant that thousands of people were resettled and granted land allotments, taking land away from those who were colonized. Simultaneously, thousands of people were forcibly removed from their homelands and enslaved, often in Italy, the heart of Rome's empire.

A major consequence of Rome's conquest of the Mediterranean world was the founding of one of the largest slave societies in history.[7] Unlike slavery in the American South, Roman slavery was not race-based (see chapter 2, "Studying Slavery"; and chapter 3, "Enslavement in the Roman World"). Thus, Roman slavery encompassed many races, nationalities, and/or ethnic groups (see chapter 8, "Race and Ethnicity"). Romans recognized the origins of slaves, but a person's origin became a sort of personal characteristic that often was deeply discrediting. For example, in Roman legal documents we see that a slave's place of origin could hinder a sale:

> Those who sell slaves must state the *natio* [place of origin] of each at the
> sale; for the *natio* of a slave frequently encourages or deters a prospective

4. See Walter Scheidel, "Slavery," in *The Cambridge Companion to the Roman Economy*, ed. Walter Scheidel (Cambridge: Cambridge University Press, 2012), 89–113.

5. Peter Fibiger Bang, "Predation," in *The Cambridge Companion to the Roman Economy*, ed. Walter Scheidel (Cambridge: Cambridge University Press, 2012), 201.

6. Bang, "Predation," 200–203.

7. See Scheidel, "Slavery," 89.

buyer; hence it is advantageous to know his *natio*, since it is reasonable to suppose that some slaves are good because they originate from a tribe that has a good reputation, and others bad because they come from a tribe that is rather disreputable. (*Digest* 21.1.31.21)

In effect, the origin of a slave was a measure of their usefulness and potential.

Rome's slave system was relatively well developed. Seneca the Younger notes the market behind the Temple of Castor and the Saepta Julia in the Campus Martius as the most well-known locations in Rome to buy slaves (*On Firmness* 9.59; 13.4). An integrated system of enslavement, slave trading, and recapturing runaway slaves supported Roman slaveholding.[8] The *Digest* (a collection of Roman laws and discussions about Roman laws) reveals that every level of state authority, from the emperor to local magistrates, was involved in coordinated efforts to pursue and recover runaway slaves (*Digest* 11.4).[9]

Rome's institution of slavery was upheld by both elite and ordinary Romans' reliance on slave labor. Slaves engaged in a wide variety of activities, and their labor supported various modes of production in the Roman world. They worked in agriculture as estate managers, field-hands, shepherds, and dung-pile movers. Slaves were also domestic servants on country and urban estates, such as wait staff, doorkeepers, cooks, hairdressers, wet nurses, and tutors. Slaves labored as craftspeople, construction workers, retailers, miners, clerks, textile workers, and potters. Some slaves were doctors and midwives, while others were entertainers and gladiators. They also worked in public administration and served in military supply functions. Their labor catered to almost every aspect of free Romans' lives and thereby supported the economy.

Romans practiced chattel slavery, treating people as property or commodities. Not only were enslaved persons seen as property, but they were also referred to explicitly as tools. The Roman scholar Varro (who lived during the second and first centuries BCE) called the slave an *instrumentum vocale*, a "talking tool" (*On Agriculture* 1.17). Unlike inanimate property, slaves spoke, thought, and had will. As tools of their owners, the actions of slaves were understood by their owners almost as extensions of themselves. In this way, they were often most useful as tools because they were able to think and speak.[10]

8. See Sandra Joshel, *Slavery in the Roman World* (Cambridge: Cambridge University Press, 2010), 78–110.

9. Christopher J. Furhmann, *Policing the Roman Empire: Soldiers, Administration, and Public Order* (Oxford: Oxford University Press, 2012), 31–43.

10. For a counter-argument for interpreting *instrumentum vocale* as a talking tool, see Juan P. Lewis, "Did Varro Think That Slaves Were Talking Tools?," *Mnemosyne* 66 (2013): 634–48.

No matter their level of integration within a family or society, they were always considered outsiders. Although the slave was conceived of as the property of another, Roman law acknowledged slaves as people and distinguished human property from other kinds of property. Yet, these distinctions are difficult to see. Slaves, like land, could be sold, lent, mortgaged, given away, or bequeathed in a will. One jurist cited in the *Digest* claims that "if a slave woman or a mare has a miscarriage because of a blow struck by you, Brutus says . . . that you are liable to an Aquilian action [suit for damage to property] just as in the case of a breaking" (*Digest* 9.21). Just as the loss of the enslaved girl's divination in the story above is interpreted as a loss of wealth for her enslavers, the enslaved woman's loss of a child in this legal text is considered in terms of a loss the enslavers suffer. In other words, if a slave was hurt or killed, the master (*dominus*), not the slave, was hurt. The enslaver could sue for damage to property or for insult to his person if another person was implicated in the harm done.

One of the other characteristics of Roman enslavement was the inability of the enslaved to control what happened to their own bodies. This lack of physical integrity that enslaved people endured is also reflected in Roman laws surrounding *iniuria* ("injury"):

> A slave was not considered personally to suffer *iniuria* ("outrage," "injury"), but an injury is held to be committed through him on his owner, though not in all the ways in which it was held to be committed on us through our children and wives, but only if the act is specially shocking and obviously intended as an insult to his owner, as where one flogs another's slave. (Gaius, *Institutes* 3.222)

Again, we see how Roman law undermines the physical integrity of the slave. Any injury a slave suffered was seen as an injury inflicted on the enslaver. The physical vulnerability of a slave was also underscored by the fact that in a criminal trial the testimony of a slave had to be obtained through torture to discover the truth of it (*Digest* 48.18.1–22).

In addition to facing physical vulnerability, enslaved persons also could not own property or have legal kin relationships. While slaves could not legally marry or have a family, they nevertheless had parents and siblings. If they could marry and have kids, that privilege depended on the circumstances of their enslavement. Yet, if they did have a family in enslavement, the acknowledgment of those familial relationships was granted by the enslaver and could be withdrawn. In effect, family relationships among slaves were always threatened by sale and by the death of the owner. In the latter case, the enslaved family might be broken up by arrangements of the owner's will (see chapter 9, "Gender and Sexuality").

Not only did they control the familial connections of the enslaved members of their homes, but enslavers also capitalized on enslaved women's sexuality for profit inside a brothel or as instruments to control their enslaved men. Roman prostitution made use of the bodies of enslaved people in a variety of ways, such as fulfilling the sexual needs of lower-class men, earning money for their enslavers, and fulfilling the fantasies of elite men.[11] The use of enslaved people's sexuality in brothels was a lucrative enterprise for many elite slave owners. The jurist Ulpian claims that brothels were operated on the property of "many honorable men" (*Digest* 5.3.27.1). Members of Rome's elite would most likely have also profited from the business of prostitution, especially as landlords of brothels. There were, however, consequences to running a brothel. In the *Tabula Heraclensis* (108–124), we learn that anyone who has run (or will run) a brothel could not serve in the Senate. Therefore, upper-class men would use an intermediary, or middleman, to distance themselves from the business of running a brothel.[12]

Roman slave owners also benefited from the exploitation of the sexual lives and reproductive abilities of female slaves. When discussing the labor herdsmen performed, Varro claims that enslaved men's relationships with enslaved women made them more diligent in their work because the latter kept the former sexually satisfied. Enslaved women could also work alongside herdsmen when they followed the herd (Varro, *On Agriculture* 2.10.6). Like Varro, Columella, another Roman writer who lived in the first century CE, claimed that male slaves, who were valued for their labor potential, would be more diligent in their work and more controllable if they were tied sexually to a female slave (Varro, *On Agriculture* 1.17.5; Columella, *On Agriculture* 1.8.5). By creating sexual relationships between male and female slaves, the enslaver also benefited economically from their female slaves' reproductive abilities. Roman authors viewed enslaved women's sexual reproduction as being the primary means of the slave population's growth in Rome. Columella asserts that he would reward an enslaved woman who gave birth to three children and manumit one who bore four children (Columella, *On Agriculture* 1.8.19). An enslaved woman could expect to be sold during her childbearing years because

11. F. Mira Green, "Witnesses and Participants: The Sexual Lives of Enslaved Women and Boys in Ancient Rome," *Helios* 42 (2015): 143–62.

12. T. A. J. McGinn, *The Economy of Prostitution in the Roman World: A Study of Social History and the Brothel* (Ann Arbor: University of Michigan Press, 2004), 32–34.

that was the time when she was economically most valuable. In fact, most sales records for enslaved women include the expectation that she would bear children and be available as a wet nurse. This evidence suggests that enslaved women were valued more for their breeding potential than their labor potential.[13] Yet, the exploitation of both enslaved women's labor and reproductive abilities significantly contributed to their slave owners' wealth. Female slaves usually performed manual labor (specifically textile work), which also allowed them to care for children.[14] Through this type of forced labor, enslaved women produced a material product for sale while simultaneously including their children from an early age in the process of production. Thus, their children were socialized into enslavement, their enslavers benefited from enslaved children's labor, and the enslavers added valuable, well-trained slaves to their wealth.

The sexuality of enslaved women was also treated as a tool to control enslaved men. Slave owners' instrumental vision of their sexuality precludes any notions of the personal choice in the sexual partners of female slaves. Although slave owners valued female slaves for their physical ability to have sex and profited from their reproductive capacities, enslaved women enjoyed no protection against sexual or physical violation. A cross-cultural comparison provides insight into the enslavement of women in ancient Rome. Discussing the legal implications of slavery and rape in the American South, Saidiya Hartman claims that notions of enslaved individuals as both property and persons complicated issues of sexual consent and agency. She states: "As the enslaved is legally unable to give consent or offer resistance, she is presumed to be always willing."[15] Because enslaved women in Rome had no legal protection and they were valued for their sexual and reproductive capacities, they were open to sexual violation not only by free men, but by enslaved men as well. Simply put, enslaved women were treated as though their sexual lives did not belong to them.

Two of Ovid's poems about his relationship with his lover's maid, Cypassis, give us an example of the lack of physical integrity and control over her own sexual life that a female slave might face. In the first poem, Ovid addresses his

13. Keith Bradley, *Slavery and Society at Rome* (Cambridge: Cambridge University Press, 1994), 53–56.

14. Ulrike Roth, *Thinking Tools: Agricultural Slavery between Evidence and Models* (London: Institute of Classical Studies, School of Advanced Study, University of London, 2007), 1–24.

15. Saidiya V. Hartman, *Scenes of Subjection: Terror, Slavery, and Self-making in Nineteenth-Century America* (New York: Oxford University Press, 1997), 81.

lover, Corinna, and in the following poem he turns his attention to Cypassis. Declaring his fidelity to Corinna, he cruelly dismisses her slave girl:

> Behold this new crime! Cypassis who fixes your hair
> is accused that she defiled her mistress's couch.
> Gods grant me better than if my libido is such that I sin
> with a dirty girl of a contemptible type!
> What free man would willingly have sex with a house-slave
> and grab a back scarred by the whip? (*Amores* 2.7)

Attempting to hide behind the notion that no Roman man of taste or manners would have sex with his lover's slave, Ovid verbally attacks the telltale signs of Cypassis's enslavement. We might imagine that the enslaved girl who followed Paul had similar marks on her body as a result of the violence she experienced in bondage. It is only in Ovid's next poem that it is revealed that Cypassis is present during his defense of his sexual loyalty to Corinna, and thus she hears Ovid demean her:[16]

> But if you say no, stupid girl, I will become the informer of
>   our deeds
> and I will come forward as the betrayer of my own guilt,
> in what places, how many times, Cypassis, how many ways
> and what ways, I will tell your mistress that I met with you.
>   (*Amores* 2.8)

The alliance between the free is so focused in the first poem that neither Ovid nor Corinna makes a remark about Cypassis.[17] Cypassis becomes a shadow—present, and even discussed, but not directly addressed. In the next poem, addressed to Cypassis, Ovid blackmails and threatens her. Because he has diverted Corinna's suspicion, he bullies Cypassis into more sexual favors. If she refuses, he promises to inform Corinna of their previous escapades. Cypassis's situation speaks to the everyday conditions of enslaved women like the one who followed Paul. Like Cypassis, enslaved women were placed in

---

16. William Fitzgerald, *Slavery and the Roman Literary Imagination* (Cambridge: Cambridge University Press, 2000), 65.

17. Fitzgerald, *Slavery*, 63–65.

F. MIRA GREEN

difficult situations that demanded all of their tactical abilities to divert power and anger that could be directed toward them at any moment.[18]

Material Evidence for the Daily Lives of Slaves

Another way to get at the daily experiences of people living in slavery in the Roman world is through material evidence, such as daily tools, domestic fixtures, art, and funerary reliefs. I will consider only a few examples of these.

Since the 1990s, scholarly research on Roman homes and slavery has experienced some important shifts. During the course of the nineteenth century, aristocratic bias pervaded the initial work done on Roman domestic architecture focusing on spectacular finds made in Pompeii and Herculaneum. Yet in the 1990s, a shift toward studying domestic architecture in combination with Roman social history acted as a starting point for other scholars interested in the daily lives of non-elite people living in the Roman world.[19] Indeed, this scholarly trend has stimulated important work on the lives of enslaved household members, who had been previously overlooked. It also has brought some aspects of their daily lives to the foreground.[20] For example, building on the work of scholars interested in the archaeology of Greek, Roman, and American slavery, Sandra Joshel and Lauren Hackworth Petersen's work offered a new method of making the archaeological record readable for the material lives of Roman slaves.[21] Using Roman literature and law to recover where the movement and actions of slaves were represented, this work explored some of the enslaver strategies, enslaved tactics, and rival geographies that could be recovered in the structures and settings of Roman homes, city streets, workshops, and villas.

This new method for seeing the everyday lives of enslaved people extends to physical exchanges that occurred between the human body and household tools.[22] Enslaved people interacted with kitchen hearths, braziers, pots, and ceramic jugs through nonverbal codes of status. These codes were inherent

18. This paragraph comes from Green, "Witnesses and Participants," 156–57.
19. See Penelope Allison, "Using the Material and Written Sources: Turn of the Millennium Approaches to Roman Domestic Space," *American Journal of Archaeology* 105 (2001): 181–208; Andrew Wallace-Hadrill, *Houses and Society in Pompeii and Herculaneum* (Princeton: Princeton University Press, 1994).
20. Michele George, *Roman Slavery and Roman Material Culture* (Toronto: University of Toronto Press, 2013).
21. See Joshel and Petersen, *Material Life of Roman Slaves*.
22. See Mira Green, "Cooking Class," in *Public and Private in the Roman House and*

44

Figure 4.1. A Roman cooking bench from an excavated villa in Oplontis, Italy.

in the design of household fixtures and tools. They also played a fundamental role in routine activities involving food preparation. Roman homes and daily objects manifest design decisions that encouraged users' physical responses to objects—specifically bending, stooping, or crouching—and these responses framed Roman interpretations of domestic hierarchies. Not only does the built environment set the stage for repeated nonverbal codes signaling class and gender to outside observers, but it also shapes an individual's experience with her own body through quotidian household routines. For example, the evidence of kitchen benches' dimensions, in combination with the average height of Roman men and women, makes transparent the physical demands made upon peoples' bodies as they prepared and cooked food.

To explore this human–object interaction, I studied the archaeological remains of domestic structures from four well-known sites in central Italy that were destroyed when Mount Vesuvius erupted in 67 CE: Pompeii, Herculaneum, Oplontis, and Stabiae. I measured a sample of the average dimensions and construction in their kitchens. Since my height (167.64 cm or about 66

Society, ed. Kaius Tuori and Laura Nissin (Portsmouth, RI: Journal of Roman Archaeology, 2015), 133–47.

inches) falls within the range of the average height of people who lived and died in the Bay of Naples when Mount Vesuvius erupted, my body was at points useful in the attempt to evaluate encounters between humans and tools. Out of the forty-six domestic structures I studied, I found twenty-two intact, or nearly intact, kitchen benches in atrium homes in Pompeii and Herculaneum. Considering the additional 30–35 cm (about 12–14 inches) that would be added to the benches' height because of braziers or ceramic cooking devices holding a pot, the combined height of each bench and the accompanying tools would still require a man or woman of average height to bend forward to use it. Only two houses out of the twenty-two have more comfortable working heights that fall between 80 and 89 cm (31.5 and 35 inches), and four houses have kitchen benches with heights between 90 and 99 cm (35.5 and 39 inches) that allow for an erect posture during use. Thus, the material evidence suggests that kitchen benches generally required either a deeply bowed or a slightly concave posture while preparing food. Indeed, an upright pose seems to signal deviation from common practices inside atrium homes.[23]

Moreover, visual representations of food preparation and cultivation indicate that bowed or crouching poses inscribed status on the enslaved bodies engaged in domestic cooking practices (see figure 4.2). Notice how the image of an enslaved worker on this silver cup from the House of Menander suggests this posture. The confluence between body, tool, and movement during food preparation collapses the distinction between the person, object, and task. Intimately connected to this person's hunched body is an internal and external audience. The external audience is anyone who viewed the image, such as the patron of the home, guests, family members, and slaves. The internal audience is often, but not always, found within the image itself (i.e., the other characters in the cup). Notably, neither the internal nor external audience makes eye contact with the laborer. The mutual lack of interest between laborer and internal audience suggests the mundaneness and routine work of food preparation. The external audience for this representation varied along class lines: homeowner and guest/visitor, free and enslaved, slave owner and slaves. For these different audiences, this image reinforced nonverbal codes and interpretations of daily activities involving food preparation and subtly instructed what the proper performance and reception of these labors should involve.[24] Domestic spaces, fixtures, and visual imagery came together to help manage and main-

23. All the information in this paragraph comes from Green, "Witnesses and Participants," 135–38.
24. All the information in this paragraph comes from Green, "Cooking Class," 133–47.

Figure 4.2. Silver cup from Casa del Menandro depicting enslaved workers in a bowed or crouched position while preparing food.

tain domestic hierarchies. In essence, the physical encounters between human and household objects comprise a set of actions that bring together different elements that at once create, communicate, and sustain Roman social norms and domestic hierarchies. And these daily, repetitive exchanges helped inscribe status and gender on people's bodies through encoded messages sent both to workers/performers and observers of domestic labor.

Not only did Roman household tools and spaces encourage repeated daily actions that inscribed class and gender on bodies, but wall paintings also communicated the power dynamics that enslaved people experienced in these households. Wall paintings expressed a male gaze that is inflected by slaving values, according to Beth Severy-Hoven. She observes that status and gender often mingle in wall paintings found in Roman houses—especially in the scenes of corporal punishment and sexual violence found in the House of the Vettii at Pompeii. Representations of sexual and physical violence in domestic settings encode messages about the homeowner's status as a *dominus* ("slave owner") by displaying his wealth alongside his "mastery over the rest of the household in terms of religion, sexuality, and corporal punishment."[25] Indeed, she asserts that such scenes portray the enslaver as someone able to penetrate both male and female bodies as he wills. They also remind enslaved household members of the various servile duties they must perform and the vulnerability they endure in that labor.

Like images of cooking, sexually charged scenes found in domestic settings frequently had internal and external audiences. For example, a mosaic from

25. Beth Severy-Hoven, "Master Narratives and the Wall Painting of the House of the Vettii, Pompeii," *Gender and History* 24 (2012): 540–80, here 551, 566.

Figure 4.3. A mosaic depicting a male-female couple on a bed with two enslaved attendants nearby. First century CE.

the Villa Centocelle portrays a scene of male–female eroticism (see figure 4.3). Although the couple is not having sex, there is obviously some sort of flirtation or foreplay in the scene. The focus of the mosaic is on the body of the woman and her receptive eye contact with the male figure. Her fixed look and seductive, slightly reclined pose suggest that she is willing and open to the man's advances. The male figure leans in toward her, which makes his gaze more assertive and intrusive into her space and foreshadows the physical intimacy that will likely follow. Notably, the couple is oblivious to the two enslaved women flanking them. These women are not positioned as sexual objects, but rather observe or attend the sexual activities of the central figures. Even though the couple is unaware, or at least does not care about their presence, the two women act as an indifferent and intent audience, respectively. For instance, the enslaved woman on the left appears uninterested in the couple's love-play as she pours wine or water into a vessel. Yet, the enslaved woman on the right actively observes the couple's interaction as she pitches her body forward and directs her eyes on their performance. In essence, these enslaved women see the central woman's desire for the man and this man's powerful, dominating posture and intentions. These images suggest that slaves were commonly imagined to be present during the sexual activity of others, implying their sexual lives were indirectly co-opted by the free.

Conclusion

From Roman texts and material culture, we can fill in some of the silences about the slave girl in the apostle Paul's story. Roman law and literature reveal that slaves were viewed as property and lacked the physical integrity Roman citizens enjoyed, and enslaved women's reproductive and sexual lives were exploited for others. Material culture from Roman homes indicates that daily tools and fixtures helped to manage and maintain domestic hierarchies through daily human–object interactions that demanded stooped or concave poses. Wall paintings also projected the power dynamics enslaved household members navigated. Female slaves were valued for their reproductive capacities, and their sexual lives could be used for profit and control over male slaves. Wall paintings and mosaics also suggest that slaves were expected to be present during the sexual interactions of others as attendants to their needs. While we cannot know who the slave girl in Paul's proselytizing mission to Philippi was and what the exact details of her life were, we can assume she too faced a lack of physical integrity, that her kin relationships were governed or unacknowledged by her enslaver, and that her sexual life was exploited, much like her gift of divination was.

Discussion Questions

1. After finishing this chapter, return to the story of the enslaved prophet in Philippi (Acts 16:16–40). How does knowledge of Roman law and material culture enhance her story? How can you reimagine her daily life using this information?

2. How did the Roman laws discussed in this chapter impact the lives of enslaved workers? How might an enslaved woman (or child) be treated differently than an enslaved man as a result of these laws?

3. Go to the website of the Metropolitan Museum of Art. Search for other examples from the first or second century CE of objects that include examples of enslaved persons doing daily work. Share your object with the class or in a group. What information does this example of material culture provide about the daily lives of enslaved persons during the time in which the New Testament was written?

Further Reading

Cobb, Christy. *Slavery, Gender, Truth, and Power in Luke-Acts*. London: Palgrave MacMillan, 2019.

Gardner, Jane. "Slavery and Roman Law." Pages 414–37 in *The Cambridge World History of Slavery*. Vol. 1. Edited by Keith Bradley and Paul Cartledge. Cambridge: Cambridge University Press, 2011.

Green, F. Mira. "Cooking Class." Pages 133–47 in *Public and Private in the Roman House and Society*. Edited by Kaius Tuori and Laura Nissin. Portsmouth, RI: Journal of Roman Archaeology, 2015.

Joshel, Sandra. *Slavery in the Roman World*. Cambridge: Cambridge University Press. 2010.

Joshel, Sandra, and Lauren Hackworth Petersen. *The Material Life of Roman Slaves*. Cambridge: Cambridge University Press, 2014.

Roth, Ulrike, ed. *By the Sweat of Your Brow: Roman Slavery in Its Socio-Economic Setting*. London: Institute of Classical Studies, School of Advanced Study, University of London, 2010.

Scheidel, Walter. "Slavery." Pages 89–113 in *The Cambridge Companion to the Roman Economy*. Edited by Walter Scheidel. Cambridge: Cambridge University Press, 2012.

5   *Jews and Slavery*

CATHERINE HEZSER

Just as in other ancient societies, slavery was taken for granted as an established socioeconomic institution in ancient Israelite culture and in postbiblical Jewish societies of Hellenic and Roman times. In ancient Jewish literary sources, Jews feature as both slave owners and slaves. While there are many similarities between post-70 CE rabbinic and Roman slave law and practices, mass slavery was a Roman imperial phenomenon that was distinctive to Roman society. In Jewish Palestine of the first four centuries CE, enslaved workers would have been present on a much smaller scale alongside free laborers and tenant farmers. Rabbinic sources mostly mention household slaves who included wet nurses and pedagogues.

Slaves were not a homogeneous social group but differed widely among themselves regarding their education and skills, occupations, and lifestyles. Some slaves were their masters' secretaries or business partners, whereas others were simple farm hands. Slaves could also become wealthy and own slaves themselves. Some slaves were able to purchase their freedom, while others remained enslaved until their masters had no use for them anymore. In this chapter, we shall look at the various aspects of ancient Jewish slavery in more detail. What do the Jewish literary sources tell us about slaves, and how does this representation compare with what we know about slavery in Greco-Roman society? The following topics will be discussed in this chapter: ancient Jewish sources on slaves and slavery; how one became enslaved; the occupations of slaves; the treatment of slaves; and the possibility of manumission.

Ancient Jewish Sources on Slaves and Slavery

Slaves are mentioned in ancient Jewish texts from the Hebrew Bible, probably edited in the early postexilic period, to rabbinic literature from late antique and early Byzantine times. The compilations and authored works span a period of at least one thousand years. They are written in Hebrew, Palestinian and Babylonian Aramaic, and Greek, and include traditions from various geographical regions of the Near East. When using this material for information on Jewish slavery practices, several methodological considerations need to be addressed. First, these are literary sources that, with the exception of Flavius Josephus's writings, are not historiographical and should not be considered to provide historically reliable information on slaves. This means that the texts need to be examined within their literary contexts and questioned regarding the underlying ideology and perspective of those who formulated them. Only if several traditions in different literary forms and contexts point in the same direction can a certain amount of sociohistorical reliability be assumed. This reliability is higher if there are other sources outside of the text itself that support a phenomenon (e.g., documentary evidence and/or Roman sources).

Second, all the available literary sources are formulated from the perspective of the literate elites. Not all were slave owners themselves, but they may have represented the perspective of those who were. Unfortunately, we lack firsthand evidence from Jewish slaves or slaves owned by Jews and are therefore unable to reconstruct their real-life experiences, and only one slave biography still exists of any slave from classical antiquity.[1] Third, the literary sources tend to present slaves as a single collective at the very bottom of the social hierarchy (see chapter 12, "Household Codes"). The authors categorically distinguish between slaves and free people and do not properly account for the different backgrounds, skills, and lifestyles among slaves.

Unfortunately, hardly any nonliterary documentary evidence is available for the study of ancient Jewish slaves and slavery. Two inscriptions about synagogue donors from Hammat Tiberias (in the Galilee, Israel) mention a certain Severus, who is called a *threptos* of the Jewish patriarchs. This term is commonly used for abandoned children, who were mostly used as slaves and in some cases reared as adopted children. The fact that Severus is mentioned by name and donated a significant amount of money to the synagogue indicates that he was wealthy. The inscription notes that with his donation he

---

1. See Keith Hopkins, "Evidence for Roman Slavery," in *Studies in Ancient Greek and Roman Society*, ed. Robin Osborne (Cambridge: Cambridge University Press, 2004), 206–25.

Figure 5.1. Mosaic floor from a synagogue in Hamat Tiberias, Israel, that includes the name of Severus, who was most likely a freedman. 337–286 BCE.

"completed" the mosaic floor. Since non-Jewish slaves were unlikely to have been members of a synagogue community, and even less likely to have been commemorated as wealthy sponsors, Severus was probably raised as a child by the patriarchal family. When the inscription was set up, he would have grown into a wealthy member of the patriarchal household. He may have been a wealthy freedman who converted to Judaism.

That the term *threptos* was used for manumitted slaves is evident from Jewish manumission inscriptions from the Bosporan Kingdom dated to the late first to early second century CE.[2] Additionally, a significant proportion of the Jewish inhabitants of Rome would have descended from Jews who were brought to Rome as enslaved war captives as a consequence of Pompey's capture of Jerusalem in 63 BCE and a century later after the first Jewish revolt against Rome (66–73 CE), as reported by Flavius Josephus. However, this phenomenon is not reflected in the Jewish grave inscriptions from Roman cata-

2. See E. Leigh Gibson, *The Jewish Manumission Inscriptions of the Bosporus Kingdom* (Tübingen: Mohr Siebeck, 1999).

combs. As one scholar has noted: "Of more than 500 Jewish grave inscriptions from Rome, not one attests that the deceased was either a slave or a freedman."[3] As a possible reason, this scholar suggests the descendants of freeborn Jewish slaves may have deliberately avoided any reference to their deceased relatives' servile origins. As is known from both rabbinic and Roman literature, a stigma was attached to a servile and manumitted status, which persisted for several generations (see chapter 3, "Enslavement in the Roman World").

How Did One Become a Slave?

According to both rabbinic and Roman law, the child of a female slave had the status of a slave, irrespective of who the father was.[4] This rule enabled masters to engage in sexual relations with their female slaves without having to acknowledge the offspring of such unions as potential heirs. Children born to enslaved women, whether fathered by other enslaved or freeborn men, were slaves within their master's household. Although slave owners would have had an interest in increasing their number of slaves through breeding,[5] they would have had to bear the costs of rearing the child until it could profitably work for them. This consideration indicates that enslaved persons were counted among the householder's possessions, which he could use as he saw fit. Thus, many of his considerations about them would have been economic rather than humanitarian or social. Some rabbis were opposed to the forced procreation of slaves, which they considered a form of prostitution. They also considered sexual unions between free male Jews and female slaves illegitimate and urged men to avoid them, in contrast to Roman cultural practices that perceived sex with one's own slaves as acceptable common practice as far as male owners were concerned. Marriage between slaves and free persons was generally outlawed under Jewish law, although rabbis agreed that if someone had sex with a slave woman who later became free and he married her, "they do not take her away from him" (Mishnah Yevamot 2:8).

Freeborn individuals of Jewish ancestry could become enslaved in several ways, all of them based on unfortunate circumstances (see chapter 7, "Slave Labor and Trade"). The reason most often mentioned by Flavius Josephus is the Roman capture and enslavement of Jews in the context of Roman imperialism.

3. Gideon Fuks, "Where Have All the Freedmen Gone? On an Anomaly in the Jewish Grave-Inscriptions from Rome," *Journal of Jewish Studies* 36 (1985): 30.

4. See Catherine Hezser, *Jewish Slavery in Antiquity* (Oxford: Oxford University Press, 2005), 194–201.

5. See the story in Midrash Leviticus Rabbah 8:1 par. Pesiqta de Rav Kahana 2:4.

Mass slavery developed in Rome as a result of Roman military conquests in more or less distant regions. Political subjugation and enslavement were closely linked, both in reality and in the ancient imagination. They involved the loss of freedom and independence and were associated with weakness and humiliation. In his account of the Masada episode, Josephus raises the question of which is preferable: dying as a free person, who has only God as his or her master, or survival and enslavement to the Romans (*Jewish War* 7.324–382).[6] Even though suicide is prohibited in biblical law, the Jewish rebels and their families who hid themselves at the fortress toward the end of the first Jewish revolt against Rome decided to kill themselves rather than become the slaves of their enemies. Jews who were captured by Romans would have been sold as slaves at local and regional slave markets. Some were brought to Rome to be paraded as war trophies in military parades. In times of military campaigns, such as the Hasmonean and Herodian wars, Jews took war captives themselves.[7] Since these campaigns were much more limited than those of the Romans, however, they did not result in mass slavery. Sometimes the conquered populations were Judaized (this included circumcision if they were male) rather than enslaved.

Another reason for enslavement was poverty. Families who became indebted risked being seized by their debtors and forced to work for them until their debts were paid off. A parable in Midrash Sifre Deuteronomy 26 presents the situation of a man who borrowed wheat from a king and failed to pay back his debts in time. Consequently, "the king entered his house and seized his sons and daughters and put them on the auction block" to sell them as slaves. A similar situation is mentioned in a parable in Matthew 18:24–34, where a man is said to have owed his debtor one thousand talents: "His master commanded him to be sold, and his wife and his children and all that he had and payment to be made" (Matt 18:25). In the Near East, impoverished families might also decide to abandon newborn babies or to sell their children into slavery, hoping for their survival if they could not feed and maintain them themselves. Whereas Roman law prohibited self-sale and the sale of freeborn citizens, rabbis permitted such actions to poor people (see Lev 25:39). The rabbis were especially concerned about the sale of girls and women beyond the age of puberty, because of the danger of sexual exploitation.[8]

6. See Jodi Magness, *Masada: From Jewish Revolt to Modern Myth* (Princeton: Princeton University Press, 2021).

7. See Hezser, *Jewish Slavery in Antiquity*, 227–28.

8. See Hezser, *Jewish Slavery in Antiquity*, 190; and the so-called Concubine Law of Exod 21:7–11 (cf. Mishnah Ketubbot 3:8; and Mishnah Qiddushin 1:2).

Another way to become enslaved was ill fortune while traveling on the road or staying at an inn. Ancient land travel was dangerous because of bandits who might kidnap travelers in unsettled areas or lure them out of inns and hostels at night. Ships sailing along the coasts of the Mediterranean could be intercepted by pirates who captured people and sold them as slaves (see chapter 7, "Slave Labor and Trade"). Rabbis condemned human trafficking, irrespective of the kidnapped person's gender and social status.[9] Anyone venturing out too far from his or her hometown was endangered; therefore, travel was avoided unless it was necessary.

What Do We Know about the Occupations of Male and Female Slaves?

Although slaves were also used in agriculture, Jewish literary sources from the Roman and early Byzantine periods mostly mention occupations in households. As New Testament parables suggest, it may have been more cost-efficient for landowners to employ free day laborers during the harvest seasons (cf. Matt 20:1–16) and tenants for more permanent agricultural tasks (Mark 12:1–12; Matt 21:33–46; Luke 20:9–19; Gospel of Thomas 65). Day laborers could be exploited more since the landlord did not have to care about their physical well-being. They also did not need to be fed, clothed, and housed year-round, so the overall costs would be less. With tenant farmers, the only task left would be to collect the proportion of the harvest agreed with them. In the parable of the wicked tenants (Mark 12:1–12), enslaved farm workers are sent to collect fruit, but they are not involved in the agricultural work themselves. They rather have the function of intermediaries who deal with the tenants on behalf of the landlord. Yet there are also parables that address issues of agricultural slavery (e.g., Matt 24:45–51; Luke 12:42–46).[10] In the parable of the wise slave, a servile steward "whom his master has made ruler over his household" is mentioned, that is, a slave in charge of overseeing and managing other slaves who work on his master's estate. This slave is presented as particularly reliable here. Such enslaved overseers would have had a much higher status and better life than the simple farmhands. Wealthy landowners tended to live in the cities, enjoying an urban lifestyle, while having their farms managed by servile stewards. This phenomenon is indicated here and in other parables that thematize the slave owner's absence and return (cf. Matt 25:14–30; Luke 19:11–27).

9. Tosefta Bava Qamma 8:1.
10. See Llewellyn Howes, "Agricultural Slavery and the Parable of the Loyal and Wise Slave in Q 12:42–46," *Acta Classica* 58 (2015): 70–110.

Figure 5.2. Second-century CE marble relief showing a porter, who was most likely enslaved, delivering amphoras to a merchant.

Rabbinic texts mention slaves involved in a variety of household tasks. Women who were enslaved domestic workers, often called handmaids, whom wives brought into the marriage, could take over tasks wives were expected to do, such as food preparation (e.g., grinding flour), cooking and baking, doing the laundry, wet nursing (i.e., suckling a child), and tidying the householder's bed. According to Mishnah Ketubbot, female slaves may be used as substitutes for all these tasks, but the wife should not be left idle. According to Rabbi Eliezer, "Even if she brought in for him a hundred slave girls, one forces her to work in wool, since leisure leads her to unchastity" (Mishnah Ketubbot 5:5). In the Jerusalem Talmud's discussion of this part of the Mishnah, Rabbi Bun explains that "it is because these sorts of work are menial that they assigned them to the slave girl," and R. Huna insists that the more intimate tasks should be done by the wife herself: "She anoints his body with oil, washes his feet, and mixes his cup" (Jerusalem Talmud Ketubbot 5:5, 30a). The discussion suggests that, to some extent, enslaved women's and free wives' roles and functions within the household overlapped.

This was also the case regarding the upbringing and education of children. In wealthy families, wet nurses would feed babies, offering their breastmilk to drink. While Jewish families would employ non-Jewish midwives and wet nurses in their households, rabbis were opposed to the opposite scenario: Jewish women were not supposed to serve as midwives and wet nurses for gentile women.[11] The reason probably was that these tasks were considered too demeaning and intimate to carry out for members of another ethnic group. It is also possible that the rabbis did not want Jewish women to be involved in the birth and nurturing of the children of their Roman enemies.

Male slaves are mentioned in parables about kings as pedagogues for the householders' sons.[12] Enslaved pedagogues would deal with all aspects of the sons' upbringing, making sure they ate regularly and accompanying them to school. Educated Greek and bilingual slaves could also teach and tutor the children themselves. They would be involved in elementary education, that is, the teaching of the alphabet and the reading and memorizing of short texts. Children, or rather sons, since girls may not have received the same type of education, could develop such a close relationship with their pedagogues that their relationships to their own parents could seem under threat. Rabbinic king parables often express the ambiguities involved in son–pedagogue relationships, which shifted between beneficial and malevolent.[13]

Specially educated and proficient slaves could serve as their master's secretaries or business managers, sometimes becoming their confidants. Such slaves could hold slaves themselves and oversee their master's finance and business undertakings (cf. the Roman institution of the *peculium*). Both rabbinic and Roman law point to certain advantages when using enslaved people as one's representatives. While the proceeds of slaves' business undertakings would belong to the master, he would not be held responsible if certain problems occurred, such as if the buyer did not receive the purchased goods in time or if they were damaged.[14] While slaves could sell or acquire goods on behalf of their master, the slave was not his own agent but acted under the authority of his master. Yet the master could not be held responsible if his enslaved intermediary caused the damage of the borrowed or purchased object.[15] Slaves could even purchase other slaves "on condition that his master will not have authority over them," in which case the slaves are the servile buyer's possession (Jerusalem Talmud Yevamot 7:1, 8a). These texts show that slaves could not only have a significant amount of authority and leeway in conducting

11. Mishnah Avodah Zarah 2:1, cited in the story about Rabbi Gamliel and Roman "spies" in Jerusalem Talmud Bava Qamma 4:3, 4b.

12. See, for example, Midrash Leviticus Rabbah 2:5.

13. See Hezser, *Jewish Slavery in Antiquity*, 147–48, 359–62.

14. See Tosefta Bava Qamma 11:2.

15. See Mishnah Bava Metzi'a 8:3.

their master's business but could also be quite wealthy themselves, exerting authority over other slaves whom they controlled or even owned. Such slaves could eventually purchase their freedom and become wealthy freedmen. Their relationship to their master, who depended on them, and their elevated lifestyle would have been very different from the sit-

Figure 5.3. Mosaic featuring grain measurers from Ostia, Italy.

uation of the many lower-rank slaves in the same household. Such great differences among enslaved people in a household are believed to have impeded joint action against householders, for example planning slave revolts.

Jewish writers such as Philo, Josephus, and Paul would have used enslaved secretaries, copyeditors, and translators to create their literary works. In antiquity, authors dictated their compositions to literate slaves, who were the actual, physical writers of the texts. Household slaves functioned as scribes since writing was a technical skill rather than a symbol of higher education. Jews whose mother tongue was Aramaic, such as Josephus, would have needed assistants whose mother tongue was Greek to write down, copyedit, correct, and improve their formulations. Josephus admits that his active knowledge of Greek was rather rudimentary (*Jewish Antiquities* 20.11.2). In the same text, he associates expertise in the Greek language with scribes, probably alluding to his secretaries. It is likely that he used a slave who was literate in Greek to translate an earlier Aramaic composition of the *Jewish War* into Greek (*Jewish War* 1.1.1). Paul, who was a native Greek speaker, probably dictated his letters to scribes, whose identity he does not always reveal. Paul mentions his own clumsy handwriting in Galatians 6:11, and in Philemon 19 he verifies a promise by writing with his own hand. In Romans 16:22, Paul's scribe and the writer of the letter identifies himself as Tertius and sends greetings of his own. Ultimately, we do not know the extent of slaves' involvement in ancient literary compositions but can assume that such involvement would have been larger if the authors were not native speakers in the languages in which they composed their works.[16]

16. See Candida Moss, *God's Ghostwriters* (New York: Little, Brown, 2024).

Were Slaves Mistreated by Their Masters?

The ways in which slaves were treated in Jewish contexts would have depended on their number and roles within the household and farm and on their owners' attitudes and values. Simple farmhands whose jobs could easily be completed by other slaves or day laborers could be exploited more readily than servile managers and business executives on whose good work and trust the master depended. A master who owned only one slave and used him or her for various tasks would have been more careful about this slave's physical and mental well-being than those who owned large numbers of slaves who fulfilled similar tasks. Besides these economic considerations, the master's predisposition played an important role. Like Stoic philosophers and some early Christians, rabbis admonished their fellow Jews to treat their slaves mildly (see chapter 12, "Household Codes"). Whereas Roman masters had the right to kill their slaves, biblical and rabbinic law prohibit such behavior, since slaves were seen as human beings rather than as mere possessions. Some rabbinic narratives present rabbis as role models for ideal master–slave relationships.

Hellenistic Jewish writings already urge Jewish masters to behave properly toward their slaves. Thus, Sirach writes: "Do not ill-treat a slave who works honestly, or a hired servant whose heart is in his work. Love a good slave from the bottom of your heart and do not grudge him his freedom" (Sir 7:20–21). This recommendation does not exclude the possibility of physical punishment of slaves altogether. It merely warns masters against punishing good slaves unjustly. Philo goes further and suggests that the master's treatment of his slave has consequences for the slave's own behavior. If slaves are provided with proper clothes, food, care, and time for unwinding, they will carry out their tasks much more efficiently than those who are overloaded with work and neglected as far as their living conditions are concerned (*On the Special Laws* 2.83). Similarly, Pseudo-Phocylides writes: "Provide the slave with the tribute he owes his stomach. Apportion to a slave what is appointed so that he will be as you wish." And he goes on to also consider the slave's mental state: "Do not brand [your] slave, thus insulting him. Do not hurt a slave by slandering [him] to [his] master. Accept advice also from a judicious slave" (Pseudo-Phocylides 223–227). Although these writers were members of the upper strata of society who likely owned slaves themselves and were concerned about their economic efficiency, they were also guided by Jewish religious values and the biblical notion of justice in the treatment of members of their households. The Hebrew Bible already warns owners not to treat (Hebrew debt) slaves harshly (Lev 25:43) and reminds them of the slave's humanity and creation in the image of God (Job 31:15).

Rabbis were particularly concerned about their impoverished fellow Jews who might become the debt slaves of wealthy Jewish masters. According to a tannaitic Midrash, such individuals should not even be treated as servants: "He is not to go behind you carrying you in a sedan chair; and he is not to go before you in the bathhouse carrying your utensils"; rather, he should "be with you in food, in drink, and in clean clothes" (Midrash Sifra Behar 7:2, 80a), that is, he should eat the same food and wear the same kind of clothes as his master. In the context of ancient society, where slaves had a status at the very bottom of the social hierarchy, the suggestion of such egalitarian treatment in defiance of status differences is striking. A tradition in the Jerusalem Talmud presents Rabbi Yohanan as a role model in this regard: "Now did not Rabbi Yohanan from whatever he would eat give to his slave and recite the following verse in this connection: 'Did not he who made me in the womb make him?' [Job 31:15]" (Jerusalem Talmud Ketubbot 5:5, 30a; Bava Qamma 8:5, 6c). The religious motivation for such behavior is evident from the quotation of scripture here.

At the same time, slave owners' rights to physically punish their slaves were taken for granted in antiquity. According to Proverbs 29:19, "a slave cannot be disciplined by words. Though he may comprehend, he does not respond." Such procedures were part of the power relationship between master and slave and indicated the latter's basic vulnerability. What ancient Jewish sources prohibit is the execution of undue punishment and the use of overt cruelty in the treatment of one's slaves. Exodus 21:20–21 considers the corporal punishment of slaves legitimate, since they are their masters' property. However, if a slave dies immediately after having been struck with a rod, that is, if the action leads to the slave's imminent death, the master should be held responsible for the killing. Such restrictions to corporal punishment were expanded by rabbis, who distinguished between the master's own and others' slaves and Jewish versus non-Jewish slaves. According to Mishnah Bava Qamma 8:3, someone who wounded his own Jewish slave or someone else's non-Jewish slave is liable to a penalty. The rule excludes an enslaver who wounded his own non-Jewish slave. A subsequent portion even states explicitly: "He who wounded his Canaanite slave is exempt on all counts" (Mishnah Bava Qamma 8:5). The Tosefta disagrees here. Literally an "addition" to the Mishnah, the Tosefta is an important rabbinic document that contains tannaitic traditions beyond the scope of the Mishnah. It prohibits violence against such slaves as well: "He who wounds . . . his male or female Canaanite slave, is liable on all [counts]" (Tosefta Bava Qamma 9:10). The master is supposed to pay a fine imposed by the court. The Tosefta also expands the biblical ruling of Exodus 21:20 by stating that a master who kills his slave in his domain is liable to punishment, irrespective of whether the slave dies immediately or only later (Tosefta Bava Qamma 9:21–22). As long as a slave is his possession, the master is held responsible for his death. This limitation of physical punishment stands in contrast to Roman slave owners' right of life and death over their slaves. It is based on the biblical notion that slaves were human beings and the killing of human beings was prohibited by divine law.

Some rabbinic narratives paint an ideal picture of friendly and harmonious relations between rabbinic masters and their slaves. In contrast to similar Roman stories, which emphasize the slaves' courage when rescuing their masters in dangerous situations, the rabbinic narratives express rabbinic religious values.[17] For example, Tabi, the slave of Rabbi Gamliel, is presented like a disciple of sages eager to follow rabbinic halakhic rules. Allegedly, Rabbi Gamliel's relationship to his slave was so close that he even accepted condolences on his account: "Tabi, my slave, is not like the rest of the slaves. He was worthy" (Mishnah Berakhot 2:7). This explanation already indicates that such behavior was considered appropriate in exceptional circumstances only, when slaves stood out and were particularly dear to their masters. In other stories, Tabi is said to have put on *tefillin*, a practice that women, slaves, and minors were exempted from. He is also said to have slept under his master's bed in the *sukkah* during the Sukkot festival, although slaves are exempt from dwelling in the *sukkah* during that period (Jerusalem Talmud Sukkah 2:1, 52d). These stories give the impression of a slave who went far beyond what was necessary to practice Jewish religious obligations that were binding for free male Jews only. For that reason, his rabbinic master is said to have treated him differently from other slaves.

Altogether, only a few particularly prominent and wealthy rabbis are presented as slave owners in rabbinic texts. Since the majority of rabbis did not belong to the upper strata of society but were part of what is sometimes called the "middling class" of artisans and merchants, they may not have needed them and/or could not afford to own them. Since slaves also served as status symbols, the possession of a slave was seen as a necessary "accessory" for a person who stemmed from an aristocratic family (Tosefta Pe'ah 4:10). For

17. For Roman examples, see Valerius Maximus, *Nine Books of Memorable Deeds and Sayings* 6.8 ("On the Loyalty of Slaves").

other rabbis, their students seem to have fulfilled functions often associated with slaves: they constituted their entourage when walking in public, carried their utensils to the bathhouse, prepared their food, served their drinks, helped them to get dressed, and fanned them when the weather was hot. All of this was part of the "service of sages" (*shimush hakhamim*). The Babylonian Talmud even states explicitly: "All manner of service which a slave must render to his master, the disciple must render to his teacher, except for taking off his shoe" (Babylonian Talmud Ketubbot 96b). The practice mentioned at the end of this statement would humiliate the student too much, whereas other services were part of the hierarchical master–disciple relationship.

How Could Slaves Become Free?

The biblical rules concerning the release of Jewish-born slaves in the seventh year of their service (Exod 21:2–3) or in the Jubilee year (Lev 25:40–41) do not seem to have been practiced in the first centuries CE. They were perhaps not practiced in earlier times either as the admonitions in Jeremiah 34:8–16 and Nehemiah 5:1–13 suggest. Nonetheless, various possibilities existed for slaves to be manumitted (see chapter 6, "Manumission"). In the case of debt slaves, that is, indebted free people and/or their family members who were seized by the creditor if they were unable to repay their debts, we may assume some or perhaps even most of these creditors would have released such individuals once the debt was paid off by their work. The assumption of the literary sources is that debt slaves were enslaved only temporarily. Female slaves could be manumitted if the householder intended to marry them. In Mishnah Yevamot 2:8, rabbis do not advocate such unions but nevertheless legitimize them if they had already happened. Since, at least in theory, polygamy was legal, some wealthy Jewish householders may have married the enslaved women with whom they had romantic and/or sexual relationships. For example, Josephus accuses Pheroras, the brother of King Herod, of "mad love" when he prefers his formerly enslaved wife to Herod's daughter (*Jewish Antiquities* 16.194–195). Such cases would have been exceptional, however, as were the ones in which masters rewarded their most valued slaves by granting them freedom.

Manumission could serve as a forceful motivator to elicit the best behavior and outstanding work from enslaved workers. Slaves who gained some income through business undertakings or received gifts from third parties could purchase their freedom. Others could be redeemed by relatives or communities, as the rabbinic discussion about the redemption of Jewish war captives enslaved by Romans indicates. The redemption of freeborn Jews who had become the war captives of Romans was a religious duty. At the same time, rabbis urged their fellow Jews to "not redeem captives for more than their actual value" on the slave market (Mishnah Gittin 4:4–6) to prevent Romans from profiting from the practice of taking Jews captive. Nevertheless, Rabbi Yehoshua is said to have paid a large amount of money to redeem a Jewish boy who was about to be sold in the slave market in Rome. In general, women and girls were supposed to be redeemed before men to prevent their sexual exploitation and dishonor (Tosefta Horayot 2:5–7).

In general, manumission under Jewish law involved the payment of money and a manumission document (Mishnah Qiddushin 1:2–3). How much money had to be paid was complicated, however, since the slave's purchase price, current value, and remaining years of service were considered (Mishnah Qiddushin 1:5). Another form of manumission was the oral declaration of a dying person who said on his deathbed: "I make so-and-so, my slave, a free person" (Tosefta Bava Batra 9:14). Whereas the patriarch Rabbi Yehudah ha-Nasi was willing to grant such a slave immediate freedom, other rabbis suggested one should "force the heirs to fulfil the words of the deceased" (Tosefta Bava Batra 9:14). Some rabbis even required a written manumission document to supplement an oral declaration that might be ambiguous or lack sufficient witnesses (Jerusalem Talmud Gittin 1:6, 43d). In Roman society, masters would also release slaves when they were no longer useful to them economically, that is, when they were old and/or sick. The continued support of aging and sickly slaves could be seen as a *mitzvah* (religious duty) when manumission would lead to decrepitude. Manumission did not erase the formerly servile status entirely. The stigma of slave ancestry haunted the descendants for many generations and involved legal restrictions in both rabbinic and Roman law.

Discussion Questions

1. Three methodological considerations about the material within ancient Judaism that addresses slaves open this chapter. What are those three considerations? How do they affect the way we understand slavery within these texts?

2. Having read chapter 3 on Roman slavery and now chapter 4 on Jews and slavery, what differences are noted between the two systems? How is slavery similar within Roman and Jewish contexts?

3. Consider the treatment of slaves in Jewish contexts. What violence was legally allowed and what was prohibited? How does this affect our understanding of New Testament texts about violence toward enslaved persons?

Further Reading

Fuks, Gideon. "Where Have All the Freedmen Gone? On an Anomaly in the Jewish Grave-Inscriptions from Rome." *Journal of Jewish Studies* 36 (1985): 25–32.

Gibson, E. Leigh. *The Jewish Manumission Inscriptions of the Bosporus Kingdom.* Tübingen: Mohr Siebeck, 1999.

Hezser, Catherine. *Jewish Slavery in Antiquity.* Oxford: Oxford University Press, 2005.

Hopkins, Keith. "Novel Evidence for Roman Slavery." Pages 206–25 in *Studies in Ancient Greek and Roman Society.* Edited by Robin Osborne. Cambridge: Cambridge University Press, 2004.

Howes, Llewellyn. "Agricultural Slavery and the Parable of the Loyal and Wise Slave in Q 12:42–46." *Acta Classica* 58 (2015): 70–110.

Magness, Jodi. *Masada: From Jewish Revolt to Modern Myth.* Princeton: Princeton University Press, 2021.

6   *Manumission*

CHANCE EVERETT BONAR

Manumission is a complex topic that is plagued with popular misconceptions. The process of freeing enslaved people, as well as the social and legal construction of a category of persons called *freedpeople* or *formerly enslaved people* (in Latin, *liberti*), had profound effects on the world within which early Christians lived. Consequently, slavery and manumission shaped the ideologies, cosmologies, ethics, and community-building strategies of early Christians.

This chapter provides a background on practices of manumission in the Roman Mediterranean and dispels common myths about it. Additionally, we will explore some examples of how the practices and ideologies that ancient Mediterranean people held about manumission impacted New Testament literature and early Christian history. Three sections organize the chapter: (1) an overview of manumission and its complexity; (2) a discussion of manumission in the New Testament; and (3) a look at manumission in some other early Christian literature and church practices.

Practices and Ideologies of Manumission in the Ancient Mediterranean

Manumission comes from the Latin verb *manumitto*, referring to freeing or emancipating an individual by "sending them from the hand" (*manū* + *mittō*). Within Roman law, there are various procedures by which manumission could take place. Formal options included manumission by a juridical official's rod (*vindicta*), through having an enslaved person's name added to the Roman citizen census list (*censu*), or through the enslaver's will (*testamento*). The Roman emperor Constantine later added a fourth type of formal manumission before a church congregation (*manumissio in ecclesia*). Informally, enslaved people could be manumitted through an enslaver declaring it in front of friends (*inter amicos*) or through a letter (*per epistulam*)—although informal manumission did not give an enslaved person legal freedom in the Roman Republic or Empire. In some circumstances, male enslavers would manumit enslaved women in order to marry them (see chapter 3, "Enslavement in the Roman World").[1] Roman enslavers expressed an ideal (that they did not always follow) that enslaved people who expressed loyalty (*fides*) were those who ought to be manumitted. In reality, qualifications or rationales for manumission varied widely.

Enslaved people sought out freedom from slavery through armed rebellion, escape from their enslaver's household or villa, accumulating funds for the cost of manumission, and other means. Notably, writers in the Roman imperial era recognized that freedom was a concern that impacted the bodies and psyches of the enslaved. For example, Artemidorus's second-century CE *Interpretation of Dreams* (*Oneirocritica*) contains dozens of dream interpretations in which enslaved persons' dreams signified manumission in the near future; some dreams also signified that an enslaved person would not be manumitted. In describing how to interpret a dream about flying depending on the dreamer's social context, Artemidorus claims that "enslaved persons, following this dream, will be freed, since in fact all birds that fly are also without an enslaver and have no leader" (*Interpretation of Dreams* 2.68).[2] While we are rarely able to investigate or gain firsthand accounts of the inner lives of enslaved persons in the Roman Mediterranean, sources like the *Interpretation of Dreams* give us a better idea of how the hope of freedom could manifest for an enslaved person, as well as how enslaved persons sought out dream interpreters to help them understand, navigate, and change the social conditions in which they lived.

Perhaps one of the best-known characteristics of manumission in the Roman Mediterranean is its frequency: Roman enslavers freed their enslaved people at a rate far beyond neighboring societies. This has led to a common misconception that Roman slavery was more "temporary" or "gentle" than other forms of chattel slavery, since freedom and citizenship were possible for some

1. Katharine P. D. Huemoeller, "Freedom in Marriage? Manumission for Marriage in the Roman World," *Journal of Roman Studies* 110 (2020): 123–39.

2. Translation from Daniel E. Harris-McCoy, *Artemidorus' Oneirocritica: Text, Translation, and Commentary* (Oxford: Oxford University Press, 2012), 247, modified slightly. On slavery and dream interpretation, see Edith Hall, "Playing Ball with Zeus: Strategies in Reading Ancient Slavery through Dreams," in *Reading Ancient Slavery*, ed. Richard Alston, Edith Hall, and Laura Proffitt (London: Bristol Classical, 2011), 204–27.

Figure 6.1. A marble funerary altar for Q. Fabius Diogenes and Fabia Primigenia, placed by his freedmen, freedwomen, and enslaved household workers. Diogenes himself was possibly a freedman. 14–68 CE.

enslaved people. However, this does not seem to be the case for a majority of people enslaved in the Roman Mediterranean. Large numbers of informally manumitted people during the Roman Republican era, for example, experienced no change in their legal status. Depending on the whims of the enslaver, if they believed an enslaved person had not exhibited adequate loyalty (*fides*), they had the capacity to prohibit their manumission (*Codex Justinianus* 3.36.5; 7.12.2). Additionally, the enormous number of funerary portraits and epitaphs we have of freedpeople likely represent only a fraction of (formerly) enslaved populations in and around Rome. Only those who were wealthy enough—or whose former enslavers were wealthy enough—were memorialized. Often this form of commemoration was done either to

Figure 6.2. Funerary relief with busts of Gaius Popillius Salvius, freedman of a woman, and Calpurnia Nice, freedwoman of a woman and Octavius.

make the enslaver look benevolent or to highlight the achievements of the freedperson.[3] Manumission may have been a relatively more common process in Roman society, but it was still selective and a majority of enslaved people never experienced manumission.

Those who were manumitted acquired a complex legal and social status. For example, Gaius's *Institutes*, a second-century CE textbook on Roman private law, notes that manumission made some into Roman citizens while others were granted Latin status (that is, the level of citizenship granted to inhabitants of Latin colonies) depending on a variety of factors (*Institutes* 1.16). Those granted only Latin status could not make a legal will, and any property they accrued over their free lifetime would be given to their former enslaver upon their death (*Institutes* 3.56). The Roman emperor Augustus also established legal barriers to prohibit the manumission of many enslaved people before

3. Maureen Carroll, "The Mourning Was Very Good: Liberation and Liberality in Roman Funerary Commemoration," in *Memory and Mourning: Studies on Roman Death*, ed. Valerie M. Hope and Janet Huskinson (Oxford: Oxbow Books, 2011), 126–49.

Figure 6.3. Funeral stele of M. Cocceius Alcimus, a freedman of the Roman emperor, dedicated by his own freedwoman (and possibly his wife) Cocceia Lolia. Second century CE.

the age of 30, and stripped the automatic right to citizenship upon manumission some gained if they were formerly deemed criminals and had been chained, branded, or fought as gladiators.[4] While gaining the ability to conduct business for their own financial gain, legally marry, and birth children as freeborn Roman citizens, many freedpeople still faced legal restrictions, such as being barred from holding public office. Enslaved women who were manumitted for marriage to their former enslavers were unable to legally divorce or to separate their property from that which belonged to their new husband (see chapter 3, "Enslavement in the Roman World").

Greek manumission practices during and after Roman colonial expansion into the eastern Mediterranean (second century BCE–second century CE) are equally complex, involving either a publication of the names of enslavers and their freed enslaved people before the city-state (*polis*) or forms of what is often called "sacral manumission," in which an enslaved person is sold to a deity like Apollo, the Autochthonous Mother of the Gods, or the Jewish God.[5] Unlike with Roman manumission practices, Greek manumission did not allow the possibility of conferring citizenship upon a freedperson, or the ability to vote,

4. On the effects of Augustus's *Lex Aelia Sentia* (4 CE) on criminalized people, see Ulrike Roth, "Men without Hope," *Papers of the British School at Rome* 79 (2011): 71–94.

5. Maria Youni, "Transforming Greek Practice into Roman Law: Manumissions in Roman Macedonia," *Tijdschrift voor rechtsgeschiedenis* 78 (2010): 311–40; E. Leigh, *The Jewish Manumission Inscriptions of the Bosporan Kingdom*, TSAJ 75 (Tübingen: Mohr Siebeck, 1999).

own land, or lend money. Sacral manumission is of particular interest to students of the New Testament and early Christianity, given how figures like God, Jesus, and sin are characterized as (former) enslavers in some literature. Most notably, some sacral manumissions included a *paramonē* clause that essentially delayed the process of manumission, forcing the enslaved person to continue laboring for their former enslaver until the enslaver's death, even while they themselves were enslaved to a deity.[6] Both Greek and Roman practices and ideologies of manumission are important to keep in mind when considering how early Christians encountered and characterized freedom from enslavement.

Along with the frequent rate of manumission, another well-known characteristic of Roman slavery and manumission is the *peculium*. The term refers to the property granted by an enslaver to be administered by an enslaved person, sometimes described as an "allowance" that was wholly controlled by the enslaver (*Digest* 15.1.4). A *peculium* could include money, goods, land, other enslaved people, or livestock. While some scholars in previous decades argued that enslaved people were able to save up their *peculia* in order to pay for their manumission, more recent scholarship has recognized that a *peculium* is primarily intended to sustain enslaved people and ensure they continue functioning effectively as their enslaver's business agents.[7] In other words, a *peculium* shifts the responsibility of feeding oneself and paying for exploited labor onto enslaved people through this "allowance." Additionally, scholars have recognized that only a small number of enslaved people were able to use their *peculium* to purchase their freedom, suggesting that the norm was not manumission but rather subsistence in one's enslaved condition. While it is common to mischaracterize enslaved people in the Roman Mediterranean as being able to easily purchase their freedom, our data shows that this was not the most likely situation for most of those subjected to enslavement.

Just because manumission was relatively more common in the Roman Mediterranean does not mean that Roman enslavers were innately more benevolent. Rather, enslavers had much to gain from the legal and social processes of manumission. Even as early as the fourth century BCE, Aristotle's student Theophrastus wrote in his *Economics* about the importance of setting freedom as a "prize" (*athlon*): if an enslaved person knew manumission was possible

6. Joshua D. Sosin, "Manumission with Paramone: Conditional Freedom?," *Transactions of the American Philological Association* 145, no. 2 (2015): 325–81.

7. This is discussed in depth by Ulrike Roth, "*Peculium*, Freedom, Citizenship: Golden Triangle or Vicious Circle? An Act in Two Parts," in *By the Sweat of Your Brow: Roman Slavery in Its Socio-Economic Setting*, ed. Ulrike Roth, Bulletin of the Institute of Classical Studies Supplement 109 (London: Institute of Classical Studies, 2010), 91–120.

Figure 6.4. An Egyptian mummy portrait of a young, manumitted teenager named Eutyches. 100–150 CE.

after a set amount of time or labor, they would work harder to achieve this goal (*Economics* 1.1344b). Theophrastus places this statement alongside another strategy to encourage enslaved productivity: allowing enslaved people to start families and have children, so they would be less likely to flee or rebel. Roman enslavers and writers who elaborated on the logics of slavery followed suit, arguing that enslavers needed to balance punishment and reward so as to make enslaved people believe manumission was possible and worth striving toward through their labor. Enslavers hoped the belief that manumission was an attainable reward would be deeply ingrained among both fellow enslavers and enslaved people, encouraging compliance in the present in exchange for the hope of experiencing freedom in the future. This ideology still influences popular conceptions of Roman slavery as "gentler" or less permanent than other forms of enslavement.

Enslavers financially and socially gained from the manumission of the enslaved. Part of Augustus's legal reforms to curb excessive manumission practices in the first century CE targeted enslavers who would manumit all of their enslaved people *in testamento* upon their deaths in order to appear benevolent (Dionysius of Halicarnassus, *Roman Antiquities* 4.24). The praise of former enslavers on their tombstones and those of their freedpeople, similarly, reveals how deeply the appearance of beneficence mattered to elites. The lives of enslaved people were commodified to celebrate and glorify their enslavers. Likewise, the cost of manumission paid by some enslaved people through their *peculium* essentially purchased their replacement for the enslaver. An older enslaved person (thirty-plus years) whose use value had decreased in the eyes of the enslaver could be manumitted and their manumission cost recapitalized to purchase a younger, more "valuable" enslaved person. In many cases, enslavers also received a portion of their freedperson's inheritance upon the freedperson's death, meaning that enslavers financially benefited from whatever labor a formerly enslaved person did after their manumission.

Enslavers could also enforce certain legal obligations upon their freed-people, even after manumission. These obligations are usually grouped into two categories: *obsequium* (behavioral deference and obedience) and *operae* (physical or intellectual labors).[8] Formerly enslaved people were prohibited from taking any legal action or from providing incriminating evidence in court against their former enslavers and could be compelled to take actions such as providing financial support or childcare for their former enslavers. *Operae* were a set number of days of labor a freedperson had promised to an enslaver as (partial) compensation for their manumission, often fulfilled through surrendering a portion of their income from business ventures or through personally tending to the needs of their enslaver.

Finally, it is worth noting that freedpeople were also, at times, treated as a concept that elite Romans could "think with." For example, Rose MacLean's scholarship has shown how the Roman aristocracy made sense of their new role as socially superior to most Romans but socially inferior to the new emperor Augustus. They looked at how freedpeople positioned themselves and claimed characteristics like virtue and honor, and they attempted to do the same.[9] The *concept* and *ideals* of formerly enslaved people could be borrowed from and applied to new contexts or could be used as an analogy for another type of experience.

My goal in this brief introduction to manumission in the Roman Mediterranean is to highlight its complexity. Not every enslaved person could expect to be manumitted, and yet Roman elites and their literature often depended on creating the impression that manumission was common and feasible in order to incentivize and control enslaved people. Additionally, manumission did not mean that one was absolutely freed from one's former enslaver. Rather, freed-people were still deeply integrated into their familial and social structures.

Manumission in the New Testament

Now that we have explored some of the complexity of manumission, we can turn to the New Testament. How do New Testament texts talk about formerly enslaved people? How do they use "freedpersonhood" as a concept when mak-

---

8. These stipulations are laid out especially in Justinian, *Digest* 38.1.

9. Rose MacLean, *Freed Slaves and Roman Imperial Culture: Social Integration and the Transformation of Values* (Cambridge: Cambridge University Press, 2018).

ing claims about Jesus, God, ethics, or Christian community? In this section, we will focus on three examples that come from the letters of the New Testament's most prolific author: Paul. In his letters to the Corinthians, Romans, and an individual named Philemon, Paul discusses formerly enslaved people as a social reality in the Roman Mediterranean and as an idea that could be used to explain Jesus-adherents' relationships to Jesus and God.

The first example comes from 1 Corinthians 7. In the midst of a long passage about sexual ethics and properly intervening to stop a community member's illicit behaviors, Paul turns his attention in this chapter to the various social roles that people hold: being married or unmarried, circumcised or uncircumcised, enslaved or free. Because Paul is an apocalyptic thinker who believes Jesus will return soon—likely within his own lifetime—he urged the Corinthian community to remain as they were and not try to change the situation(s) they were living in. As he puts it: "Let each of you lead the life that the Lord has assigned, to which God called you. This is my rule in all the churches" (1 Cor 7:17). One of the more controversial and difficult parts of Paul's argument consists in his claims about slavery and freedom among the Corinthians (1 Cor 7:21–24):

> Were you a slave when called? Do not be concerned about it. Even if you can gain your freedom, make the most of it. For whoever was called in the Lord as a slave is a freed person belonging to the Lord, just as whoever was free when called is a slave belonging to Christ. You were bought with a price; do not become slaves of humans. In whatever condition you were called, brothers and sisters, there remain with God.

Scholars have long debated the first few sentences (1 Cor 7:21) in particular, because the Greek phrase underlying "make the most of it" (*mallon chrēsai*) is famously ambiguous. It could be literally translated as something like "rather, use it" or "rather, do it" but is a shortened phrase that leaves us guessing about what it refers to. Is Paul saying, "Even if you can gain your freedom, rather, use *your enslavement*" or "Even if you can gain your freedom, rather, *take advantage of freedom*"? If Paul is arguing that enslaved believers should take advantage of the opportunity to be manumitted, then this passage seems to be an exception to his rule elsewhere that people should stay in their social conditions until Jesus's return. Conversely, if Paul is arguing that enslaved believers should reject the opportunity to be manumitted in order to stay enslaved until Jesus's return, Paul's argument raises a host of other ethical questions for modern readers of the New Testament.

Equally tricky are the following verses about slavery and freedom under Jesus (1 Cor 7:22–24).[10] Paul argues that the social conditions a person was in when they were called will reverse: the one who was enslaved when called becomes a "freed person belonging to the Lord," and a free person becomes a "slave belonging to Christ" (7:22). Paul then goes on to remind the Corinthians that they were "bought with a price"—a phrase he also uses in 1 Corinthians 6:20 to urge the Corinthians to glorify God with their bodies by avoiding sexually illicit acts. I want to emphasize that Paul's argument that believers are "bought with a price" applies to both enslaved and free people in Corinth. Those who were free are made into Christ's enslaved people through his purchase of them, but enslaved people who are manumitted *also* have their manumission paid for by the Lord. In both situations, Paul depicts Jesus as making a payment to enslave or manumit believers in order to change their social condition. Manumission not only comes at a cost on behalf of enslaved Corinthians, but also implies that they owe some form of *obsequium* (behavioral deference and obedience) and *operae* (physical or intellectual labors) to Jesus as their former enslaver.

Paul again discusses manumission from slavery in Romans 6. In this chapter, Paul spends time explaining to his Roman audience that, just because God has provided grace that covers sin, it does not mean that Jesus-followers should continue to live sinful lives. Rather, Paul urges his readers to consider themselves dead to sin and to avoid succumbing to their bodily desires. To make this point, Paul turns to the analogy of slavery, arguing that people are enslaved to the one they obey, whether to sin and death or to obedience and righteousness. Paul celebrates that believers are "set free from sin, hav[ing] become enslaved to righteousness" instead (Rom 6:18). For Paul, obedience to God is an action that manumits a person from their enslavement to sin and places them under a new enslaver. The believer's obligation thus shifts to obedience and righteousness. Additionally, Paul claims that believers "have been freed from sin and enslaved to God," which leads them to sanctification and eternal life (Rom 6:22).

What is perhaps most important to note here is that Paul does not imagine freedom in Romans 6 as a lack of accountability or responsibility to another. Instead, Paul characterizes humans as having to choose to whom they will be enslaved. There is not an option provided for freedom *beyond* or *without* enslavement to either God or sin. By depicting obedience as enslavement, Paul does not

---

10. Laura S. Nasrallah, "'You Were Bought with a Price': Freedpersons and Things in 1 Corinthians," in *Corinth in Contrast: Studies in Inequality*, ed. Steven J. Friesen, Sarah A. James, and Daniel N. Schowalter (Leiden: Brill, 2014), 54–73.

make use of the concepts of manumission and "freedpersonhood" fully, but only borrows parts of them to claim that believers are manumitted from enslavement to sin and no longer need to live under its grasp. In this passage, manumission is intricately intertwined with enslavement, since leaving behind one enslaver necessitates becoming obedient to and subject to a different enslaver.

Finally, Paul's short letter to Philemon offers a glimpse into how Paul and other early Jesus-adherents may have thought about the manumission of enslaved people beyond analogical or theological changes in one's social condition (see chapter 14, "Ethics of Interpretation"). In this letter, Paul appeals to Philemon on behalf of Onesimus, a man who is likely enslaved to Philemon, and orders that whatever complications their relationship may have had in the past need to be rectified. Paul urges Philemon to welcome back Onesimus "no longer as a slave but more than a slave, a beloved brother" (Phlm 16).

This passage has been controversial among scholars because, like 1 Corinthians 7, Paul's language is ambiguous. Some debate whether Onesimus is an enslaved person at all, since he is described as being treated "as a slave" (*hōs doulon*). Does this phrase mean that Onesimus *is* an enslaved person, or that he is being treated "as if he was an enslaved person" but actually is not one? Additionally, the phrase "more than a slave" (*hyper doulon*) is difficult to interpret. Does Paul's call for Philemon to treat Onesimus as "more than a slave" imply Onesimus should be manumitted? Or is Paul simply telling Philemon to be less harsh to Onesimus, treating him more like a brother than an enslaved person? The letter to Philemon is especially controversial because of its use by antebellum pro-slavery white supremacists to justify the enslavement of Africans and return of fugitives, since these interpreters claimed Paul returned the fugitive enslaved person Onesimus to Philemon and upheld the status quo of slavery (see chapter 2, "Studying Slavery").[11]

Discussions of manumission and "freedpersonhood" are rare in New Testament literature, but when they appear they are often very controversial. What does freedom from sin look like if it involves enslavement to God? Is Paul a theological resource for abolitionism, or does he encourage Onesimus and enslaved people at Corinth to remain enslaved? We are not given straightforward answers by Paul, and we continue to debate how Paul's vision for early church communities and Christian ethics are shaped by the realities and concepts of slavery and freedom.

---

11. Allen Dwight Callahan, "'Brother Saul': An Ambivalent Witness to Freedom," in *Onesimus Our Brother: Reading Religion, Race, and Culture in Philemon*, ed. Matthew V. Johnson et al. (Minneapolis: Fortress, 2012), 143–56.

Manumission in Early Christianity

Beyond New Testament literature, manumission is a significant point of discussion in early Christian literature and practice.[12] We have evidence of early Christians participating in the manumission of enslaved people, as well as pushback against manumitting through the church itself (see chapter 13, "Early Christian Slavery"). Additionally, some early Christian texts tell parables about slavery and freedom that highlight some of the more uncomfortable rationales behind manumission in the Roman Mediterranean.

One of the most revealing pieces of evidence we have for how early Christians interacted with the legal practice of manumission comes from Ignatius, a bishop of Antioch and composer of various letters in the early second century CE. In his letter to Polycarp, a fellow bishop in Smyrna, Ignatius provides a set of commandments that include regulations for enslaved people in the community:

> Do not treat slaves, whether male or female, contemptuously, but neither let them become conceited; instead, let them serve all the more faithfully to the glory of God, so that they may obtain from God a better freedom. They should not have a strong desire to be set free at the church's expense, lest they be found to be slaves of lust. (*To Polycarp* 4.3)[13]

This passage has troubled scholars because it appears that Ignatius argues for the continued enslavement of enslaved Christians, deferring any chance for freedom to a hypothetical future point when God might grant it. Ignatius especially criticizes the desire of some enslaved people to have the cost of their manumission covered *at the church's expense*. Ignatius links moral and legal problems in this passage, believing if enslavers are too harsh or too lenient on their enslaved people, their desire for manumission (and expectation that churches fund their manumission) might overwhelm the social and economic system he and other church leaders are constructing.

Other early Christian texts take a different approach, even explicitly supporting the communal funding of manumission. For example, we might turn

---

12. J. Albert Harrill, *The Manumission of Slaves in Early Christianity* (Tübingen: Mohr Siebeck, 1995).

13. All translations of Ignatius, *To Polycarp*, and the Shepherd of Hermas come from Michael W. Holmes, *The Apostolic Fathers: Greek and English Translations*, 3rd ed. (Grand Rapids: Baker Academic, 2007).

to the *Teachings of the Apostles* (*Didascalia Apostolorum*), a third-century CE text of church orders likely composed in Syria that claims to be written collectively by Jesus's twelve apostles. The *Teachings* mentions manumission in the midst of an exhortation that bishops should only receive financial gifts from people who are faithful and just Christians. If the gifts offered to a bishop is acceptable, he is encouraged to

> distribute from what is given by them for ransoming the faithful, for the redemption of slaves, captives and prisoners, and those treated with violence, and those condemned by the mob, and those condemned to fight with beasts, or to the mines, or to exile, or condemned to the games, and to those in distress. (*Teachings of the Apostles* 18.4.2)[14]

The writer of the *Teachings* refers here to multiple situations enslaved people experienced: exploited labor in mines, condemnation to fighting fellow enslaved gladiators or animals for Roman blood spectacle, and incarceration. They suggest that it is the role of a bishop to financially support the redemption of enslaved people with ethically sourced financial resources and to avoid taking money from those who incarcerate, oppress, or act hypocritically (*Teachings of the Apostles* 18.3.1).

Likewise, the first- or second-century CE text known as the Shepherd of Hermas, likely composed in or around Rome, is often treated as evidence of early Christian practices of manumission.[15] In two of the parables and commandments offered to the text's protagonist, Hermas's angelic interlocutor claims that God expects believers to serve widows, care for orphans and the poor, "deliver God's enslaved people from distress," act hospitably, endure insults, and uphold various other ethical norms (Shepherd of Hermas, Mandate 8.10). Later in the text, Hermas is again encouraged to "buy souls that are in distress" (along with supporting widows and orphans) and is told that they ought to spend all of their wealth and possessions on these activities (Shepherd of Hermas, Similitude 1.8). Some scholars have interpreted these passages as ethical exhortations to manumit enslaved people through either individual or corporate wealth. However, it is less clear in the Shepherd than it is in the *Teachings* that manumission is the topic under discussion, since the act of

---

14. The translation is from Alistair Stewart-Sykes, *The Didascalia Apostolorum: An English Version* (Turnhout: Brepols, 2009), 199.

15. See Chance E. Bonar, *God, Slavery, and Early Christianity: Divine Possession and Ethics in the Shepherd of Hermas* (Cambridge: Cambridge University Press, forthcoming).

"buying" is used metaphorically to refer to materially and financially supporting marginalized people.

Beyond debates over whether church communities should be involved in the manumission of enslaved people, some early Christian literature uses manumission as a concept to "think with." This is to say that early Christians used the idea of "freedpersonhood" to think about their ethics or relationship to God. One of our best examples also comes from the Shepherd of Hermas in a parable told to Hermas about enslaved workers in a vineyard. Parables that represented enslaved people as bodies to think with are common in New Testament gospels, where Jesus tells stories about enslaved people obeying or disobeying their enslavers. In these parables, the positive and negative consequences the enslaved experience range from being given *more* responsibilities for their loyalty to being dismembered for their disloyalty (for example, see Matt 18:23–35; 24:45–51; Luke 19:11–27). Note that Jesus never claims that freedom is an option for loyal enslaved people in his parables. By contrast, a parable about enslaved vineyard workers in the Shepherd imagines that manumission is an incentive for them to work harder for their enslaver, and then applies that logic to how believers ought to relate to God.

The parable of the vineyard (Shepherd of Hermas, Similitude 5) opens with an enslaver leaving his field in the hands of a trustworthy enslaved person, telling him to fence the vineyard in before his return and to do nothing else to it. As a reward for his obedience, the enslaver promises that "you will gain your freedom from me" (Shepherd of Hermas, Similitude 5.2.2). The enslaved person goes on to fence and weed the vineyard, going above and beyond what was asked of him. Upon his return, the enslaver celebrates how the enslaved person both obeyed and exceeded his command and plans to make the enslaved person a joint heir with his son. The enslaver celebrates with a feast, sending food to the enslaved person that he subsequently distributes to his fellow enslaved people, which caused the enslaver even more joy. The interpretation of the parable offered within the Shepherd is incredibly complex, but in short it is used to teach Hermas about the Son of God's obedience to God, as well as about how believers ought to serve the Holy Spirit that dwells inside their bodies in order to receive a reward from God.

Scholars often turn to this parable in the Shepherd as an example of an early Christian using manumission as a conceptual resource to explain how God rewards obedience. This is especially notable, since the writer and protagonist of the Shepherd, Hermas, was likely an enslaved or formerly enslaved person. Some scholars posit that he may have been writing, in part, from his own experience of enslavement and desire for (or achievement of) manumission. Unlike in the case of Jesus's parables, which at best offer the "reward" of more responsibilities for loyal enslaved people, the Shepherd's parable sees manumission as conceptually comparable to God's treatment of believers. It is worth noting the Shepherd does not critique the idea that one needs to be loyal or obedient to an enslaver in order to "deserve" manumission. Rather, the parable reinforces ancient Roman enslavers' ideologies and encourages the text's audience to accept these ideologies in their relationship with God.

Additionally, the *promise* of manumission is more present in the Shepherd's parable than the act of manumission itself. For example, the parabolic enslaver tells his enslaved person "you will gain your freedom" (Shepherd of Hermas, Similitude 5.2.2) and that he "wishes to make him joint heir with" his son (Shepherd of Hermas, Similitude 5.2.7). The enslaved person is still presented as enslaved at the end of the parable and is not even included at the enslaver's feast; rather, he is sent food that he goes on to share with his fellow enslaved people (Shepherd of Hermas, Similitude 5.2.9–10). Even though the parable emphasizes the *ideal* of manumission for enslaved loyalty, the story itself fails to follow through with the process of manumission beyond its promise. This distinction between the rhetoric and reality of manumission in the Roman Mediterranean is worth keeping in mind when examining New Testament and early Christian literature, since such texts and their writers are shaped by the practices and discourses of slavery and freedom in which they participated.

Conclusion

My goal in this chapter was to offer an introduction to practices and ideologies of manumission in the Roman Mediterranean, as well as to how they might manifest in or influence early Christian texts and ideas. Manumission in antiquity—just as in the Atlantic world—is a complex phenomenon, not least because those who gained freedom still dealt with the "stain of slavery" that haunted and limited their lives as freedpeople. Manumission complicates the free–slave binary by introducing freedpeople as inhabitants of a gray zone between the two, often not quite free of some obligations to their former enslavers and not quite accepted as full participants in Roman society like their freeborn counterparts. Early Christianity had practitioners with social statuses among the enslaved, freed, and free. Consequently, early Christian texts and historical actors responded in various ways to the social and legal realities of enslavement and freedom and left behind a complex legacy for scholars, students, and Christian practitioners today to wrestle with.

Discussion Questions

1. Read this portion of an inscription from Delphi in Greece, which records the sale of four enslaved people to Apollo:

   > Philon, son of Straton, sold to Apollo Pythion for the purpose of freedom bodies whose names are Stephanos, Eukleidas, Ktema, Mochion, for the price of three *minai* of silver for each, and he received the full price. [. . .] Stephanos, Eukleidas, Ktema and, Mochion shall remain (*paramenein*) with Philon and Euameris, Philon's wife, throughout the entire lifetime of Philon and Euameris, serving them and doing all they can and are ordered to do by Philon and Euameris. If they do not remain or obey, Philon and Euameris shall have power to punish those who do not obey and to whip, put in fetters, and let out for hire the labor of the one who does not remain with them. (*SGDI* 2156, lines 2–5, 12–19)[16]

   Should we classify this scenario as "manumission" or "freedom" for the four freedpeople listed? Why or why not?

2. The practice of selling enslaved people to deities continued well into the first and second centuries CE in the eastern Mediterranean. What role does the inscription give the god, Apollo, in this scenario? How might this practice have impacted how early Christians imagined their relationship to God, or how they read Paul's or Jude's claims to be an "enslaved person of Jesus Christ" (Rom 1:1; Jude 1)?

3. Take a look at the funerary relief below of Lucius Antistius Sarculo and Antistia Plutia, and the translation of the inscription underneath their portraits. What is the relationship between the freeborn man Sarculo and the freedwoman Plutia? Why do Rufus and Anthus claim they are having these portraits made? How does doing so relate to the obligations that freedpeople were expected to fulfill?

   > Lucius Antistius Sarculo, son of Gnaeus, of the Horatia tribe, Salian priest of the Alban association, as well as Master of the Salian priests. Antistia Plutia, freedwoman of Lucius. Rufus, freedman, and Anthus, freedman, had these portraits made for their patron and patroness, because they deserved it.[17]

16. From Delphi, first century CE. The translation is from Eftychia Bathrellou and Kostas Vlassopoulos, *Greek and Roman Slaveries* (Hoboken, NJ: John Wiley & Sons, 2022), 260–61.
17. Translation from Bathrellou and Vlassopoulos, *Greek and Roman Slaveries*, 273.

Figure 6.5. Marble funerary monument of Lucius Antistius Sarculo and his wife, Antistia Plutia, who was a freedwoman. The monument was dedicated by Rufus and Anthus, who were freedmen of Sarculo and Plutia. 30–10 BCE.

Further Reading

Bonar, Chance E. *God, Slavery, and Early Christianity: Divine Possession and Ethics in the Shepherd of Hermas.* Cambridge: Cambridge University Press, forthcoming.

Harrill, J. Albert. *The Manumission of Slaves in Early Christianity.* Tübingen: Mohr Siebeck, 1995.

Mouritsen, Henrik. *The Freedman in the Roman World.* Cambridge: Cambridge University Press, 2011.

Nasrallah, Laura S. "'You Were Bought with a Price': Freedpersons and Things in 1 Corinthians." Pages 54–73 in *Corinth in Contrast: Studies in Inequality.* Edited by Steven J. Friesen, Sarah A. James, and Daniel N. Schowalter. Leiden: Brill, 2014.

Petersen, Lauren Hackworth. *The Freedman in Roman Art and Art History.* Cambridge: Cambridge University Press, 2006.

Zelnick-Abramovitz, Rachel. *Not Wholly Free: The Concept of Manumission and the Status of Manumitted Slaves in the Ancient Greek World.* Leiden: Brill, 2005.

7   *Slave Labor and Trade*

ULRIKE ROTH

This chapter explores some of the key economic aspects of ancient slaving: slave labor and the trade in slaves, including discussion of the slave supply. While slaving in the ancient Mediterranean happened in diverse settings—for example, Roman, Jewish, and Christian—these settings were not categorically separate from one another—a point that the study of economic aspects of slaving specifically brings to the fore. In fact, exploration of the mechanisms by which ancient societies and communities satisfied their demand for enslaved labor highlights the seemingly boundless collaboration of enslavers across vast distances and diverse cultures. Studying the economics of slaving also demonstrates the enormous scale of slaving in the world in which Christianity began. Indeed, understanding slavery's economic dimensions is essential for interpreting specific references to slavery in the New Testament. Additionally, this chapter highlights the broader structures underpinning missionary efforts and subsequent church-building—another complex issue that students of the New Testament must confront.

Slave Labor

Slavery fulfilled multiple functions, one of which was the creation of a labor supply. The role of enslaved labor in any one slaving culture and setting depended on numerous factors, as did the range and type of occupations in which enslaved people found themselves. Economically modest enslavers, controlling only a few or just one enslaved person, regularly privileged multitasking, rather than the occupational specialization of the enslaved, a fact strikingly encapsulated, for example, in the New Testament parable about a single

83

enslaved man undertaking multiple (and highly diverse) chores (Luke 17:7–8). Paul's description of the enslaved Onesimus (in the letter to Philemon), as of other enslaved individuals in the early Christ groups, is likewise indicative of occupational generalization. Domestic slavery was especially prone to such generalization, while craft and industrial production, as well as clerical work, favored specialization. Some enslaved people—mostly enslaved men—worked in highly skilled occupations for which the Roman Empire's administration offers many examples (see further below).[1] But the distinction breaks down in elite slaving contexts.

Josephus's account of King Herod's eunuchs is instructive in this regard. They were charged individually with minute tasks in the domestic setting, such as the pouring of wine or the serving of dinner (*Jewish Antiquities* 16.230–231). Ancient inscriptions also attest to various specialized occupational roles among those enslaved in the households of the Roman emperors: numerous epitaphs (memorials) from the early first century CE columbarium (a large underground burial space) of Augustus's wife Livia illustrate an extraordinarily wide-ranging occupational spectrum for her enslaved workers, from doorkeepers to wardrobe managers and doctors (e.g., *CIL* 6.8964; 3985). These epitaphs suggest simultaneously a sense of occupational pride on the part of the enslaved.[2] Critiques of such domestic specialization, however, existed in the Roman imperial world. Roman satire mocks this specialization on the example of enslaved people whose task is indicated by their name, such as an enslaved meat carver in Petronius's *Satyricon*, who is named Carpus. In Latin, whenever someone called for Carpus, they would call "Carpe." But the word *carpe* is also the command to pluck or to cut (the imperative of *carpere*). So whenever the man is called, he is simultaneously named *and* ordered to undertake his task (Petronius, *Satyricon* 36.8), and the task thus becomes the man, and vice versa. While this example is supposed to be funny, it strikingly highlights the symbiosis of slavery and labor.

While domestic and more generally urban slavery left profuse evidence, the numbers of those enslaved in rural settings, and specifically those set to agricultural work, far exceeded the numbers of urban enslaved people. Agricultural slavery was widely familiar in the first century CE. This familiarity can be seen in several New Testament parables (e.g., Matt 13.24–30; 21:33–39).

1. See P. R. C. Weaver, *Familia Caesaris: A Social Study of the Emperor's Freedmen and Slaves* (Cambridge: Cambridge University Press, 1972).

2. See Susan Treggiari, "Jobs in the Household of Livia," *Papers of the British School at Rome* 43 (1975): 48–77.

But rural slavery, too, hovered between the specialization and generalization of labor roles, depending on the wealth level of the landowner. The multitasking slave in Luke (17:7–8) stands beside the specialized vine dresser whom the Spanish-born Columella describes in his agricultural manual as fetching up to 8,000 sesterces (perhaps the cost of a fancy modern car) on the market. Such a high value reflected this slave's expert training and skill (*On Agriculture* 3.3.8). As with wealth derived from slave trading, the intrinsic relationship between slavery and the prosperity of landowners raises difficult questions regarding their contribution to and support of Christ groups. This relationship gains even sharper edges concerning the land and related slave owning of the developing church. In the early third century CE, Origen mentions the administration of income derived by the church from its land holdings, potentially opening a window onto land-based slaving by the church.[3]

Enslaved labor was not typically separate from free labor. Therefore, in principle, it was impossible to identify someone's enslaved status through their occupational role, even if some tasks were readily associated with enslavement, such as the heavy labor of grain milling in bakeries, the clerical work of serving as a personal scribe, or the personal service of attending one's enslaver to the baths. Overall, occupational association with slavery depended strongly on context. For example, Josephus reports that two of Herod's sons threatened to make the mothers of their brothers "work at the loom along with the slave-girls" (*tais doulais*; *Jewish War* 1.479), associating weaving with enslavement even though the task was widely performed by free women, especially those of lower social status. Conversely, the above-mentioned occupational specialization in elite households gave some female textile workers specific job titles, such as seamstress (*sarcinatrix*: e.g., *CIL* 6.6350) or spinner (*quasillaria*: e.g., *CIL* 6.6342), removing them from the generic notion of "slave-girls" while simultaneously illustrating the hierarchies that such specialization engendered. These hierarchical structures—themselves embedded in wider societal status distinctions—form a backdrop for appreciating the radicalness of Jesus's contention that service and subservience is leadership (Mark 10:42–45). They also provide a lens through which to scrutinize the occupational hierarchies in the already mentioned emerging institutional church.

Perplexing only at first sight, many ancient slaving cultures preferred enslaved individuals for confidential duties. Notably, enslaved people were often preferred as secretaries, accountants, supervisors, and in other administrative and managerial positions. Moreover, ancient enslavers sometimes transacted business

---

3. In Patrologia Graeca 13:1696–97.

through the enslaved, as the Tosefta illustrates (e.g., Bava Qamma 11:2, 7). Enslaved personnel also coveted important public roles. Indeed, even public law and order regularly fell under the remit of slave labor. For example, Pliny, a Roman governor of the province of Pontus and Bithynia, on the southern Black Sea coast, encountered issues in the staffing of prison wards. He consequently communicated with the emperor Trajan in (probably) 109 CE over his concern with "using the public slaves in the various towns as prison wardens"—a practice Trajan approved because it was "the custom of the province" (*Letters* 10.19–20). In another intriguing example about enslaved people's role in public life, Josephus reports that one of Herod's eunuchs was not only responsible for seeing the king off to bed, but also for state business (*Jewish Antiquities* 16.230–231). The seemingly odd overlap between the most private and public confidentialities in the eunuch's role exemplifies a paradox in many ancient slaving cultures. While ancient thought configured the enslaved often as unreliable and devious, ancient enslavers placed nonetheless enormous trust in enslaved people to perform certain duties deemed unsuitable for free servants to perform. This was because free people could change allegiance, whereas those controlled by slavery were expected to remain loyal to their enslavers for fear of repercussions. This troubling logic is strikingly embedded in New Testament parables that depict trust being invested in enslaved individuals (notably Matt 24:45–50; 25:14–30).

Like Herod, the Roman emperors, too, availed themselves of slave labor for the Empire's administration, with enslaved (as well as freed) staff coveting the most important roles. Musicus Scurranus, for instance, enslaved to Emperor Tiberius, served in the imperial treasury in Gallia Lugdunensis, in the role of *dispensator* (*CIL* 6.5197). Civic entities, too, are documented to have owned their (clerical) staff, such as four men enslaved to the Colonia Iulia Augusta Philippensium (the Roman colony of Philippi) in the second century CE. These four administrators also engaged in independent cult activity through worship of the god Silvanus. They did so together with free cult participants, as was also the case in the Christ groups (*CIL* 3.633; with, e.g., 1 Cor 7.21–22). The financial cost of such cult activity was possibly covered by proceeds from extra work (so-called slave personal production), which augmented the private purses (called a *peculium*) of the enslaved. Scholars are divided on the interpretation of such work. Some say it was imposed as a gracious allowance, while others argue that it enhanced exploitation.[4]

---

4. Such personal funds are discussed in Roman law under the term *peculium*; they also enhanced the basic maintenance of the enslaved. See Ulrike Roth, "Food, Status and the *Peculium* of Agricultural Slaves," *Journal of Roman Archaeology* 18 (2005): 278–92.

This symbiosis of enslavement with elevated positions of trust is highly relevant when studying the impact of slavery on the organization of the Christian mission and early church (see chapter 13, "Early Christian Slavery"). Notably, when (forced) trust becomes the basis for the privileging of slave labor in some circumstances, the use of enslaved individuals in Christ-following communities acquires an additional dimension. Clearly, enslaved workers did not merely provide cheap labor. Furthermore, if only the enslaved could be fully trusted for the thorniest assignments, becoming a "slave of god" emerges as a mandate for Christ devotees (see chapter 10, "Metaphors of Enslavement"). The adoption of this notion in the Christian movement sets up the idea that the Christian God demands obedience, and in turn punishes the delinquent worker for failing to have such obedience. This analogy is adapted from slaving mechanisms and strategies designed to enforce the trust expected of the enslaved. The study of slave labor in relation to its New Testament contexts thus sits at multiple conceptual and practical crossroads.

Slave Supply

Given the extent of slave labor in ancient societies, it is unsurprising that enslavement happened throughout the ancient Mediterranean region. Simultaneously, everyone in this vast region could potentially be subjected to slavery, especially Roman slavery. But while in the centuries in which the Christian faith took root slaving under Roman conventions exceeded other slaving systems significantly in numerical terms, the ways Romans supplied slaves were not unique. Moreover, Roman slavery did not operate in isolation from enslavement under other, non-Roman conventions and juridical systems (such as among Jews in Judea, the Gauls in Western Europe, or the Garamantes in North Africa).

Apart from its numerical dominance, the means by which the Romans satisfied their demand for enslaved labor are well known because relatively rich evidence remains from the time period (see chapter 3, "Enslavement in the Roman World"). From this evidence, scholars document a notable range of supply sources. Nonetheless, which of the various means to enslave people was numerically most important is not certain, and this was even less clear for other slaving systems at the time. In principle, the quantitative assessment of any one supply source is analytical guesswork.[5] This methodological uncer-

---

5. On the demographic study of Roman slavery (in Italy), see Walter Scheidel, "Human Mobility in Roman Italy, II: The Slave Population," *Journal of Roman Studies* 95 (2005): 64–79.

Figure 7.1. The Column of Marcus Aurelius, Rome, Italy. 193 CE.

tainty notwithstanding, it is clear warfare was a key driver for the subjection of individuals to slavery in the ancient world. This was already the case in the Roman Republican period, but also applies to the imperial period.

A striking example is the depiction on the Column of Marcus Aurelius in Rome of women, girls, and even infants being seized by Roman soldiers during the Marcomannic Wars in the late second century CE (e.g., on scene CII). Likewise, when Titus conquered Judea and sacked Jerusalem in 70 CE, several hundred of those captured were paraded in his triumph in Rome—a standard procedure that vividly demonstrated the subjection of those who suffered defeat at the hands of the Romans. Many of these war captives were consequently enslaved, and the event was preserved for future generations on Titus's victory arch in Rome. Josephus, a contemporary of the events, claimed in his historical account of Jerusalem's destruction that in addition to a huge number of killings, nearly 100,000 persons became enslaved (*Jewish War* 6.420). Whether these numbers are overall accurate or inflated, the fighting undoubtedly produced a massive volume of newly captured people who would consequently become enslaved. Such practices of enslavement were paradigmatic of ancient warfare, as Jesus knew well (Luke 21:24).[6] Probably in

Figure 7.2. Scene on the Column of Marcus Aurelius in Rome. This scene depicts women, girls, and infants being seized by Roman soldiers to be enslaved. 193 CE.

the late second century CE, the Roman legal scholar Florentinus went even so far as to suggest ways that the words for enslavement were derived from defeat in battle, such as *servi* from being sold after a battle rather than being killed in it, and hence spared in the sense of being preserved or saved (*servare*), and *mancipia* from being in the hand (*manus*) of the enemy (*Digest* 1.5.4.2–3).

While warfare produced conspicuous evidence of enslavement, capture that took place separately from military engagements must have played an equally important or perhaps even greater role in enslaving people (even if less evidence for this exists). Such capture took place everywhere in the ancient Mediterranean and its diverse hinterland (notably across different parts of Europe, sub-Saharan Africa, the Levant, the Black Sea region, as well as Persia and India). In the early second century CE, the learned writer Suetonius commented that during the Augustan age many individuals of all legal statuses, whether free or (already) enslaved, were subject to violent seizure and subse-

6. See generally Hans Volkmann, *Die Massenversklavung der Einwohner eroberter Städte in der hellenistisch-römischen Zeit*, 2nd ed. (Stuttgart: F. Steiner, 1990).

Figure 7.3. The Arch of Titus, Rome, Italy. 81 CE.

quent exploitation on the rural estates of large landowners (*Augustus* 32). Likewise, in the generation before Jesus's birth, Diodorus Siculus, a native of Sicily, enshrined in his voluminous history the practice of organized plots to capture people for sale into slavery by painting a slanderous portrait of wine-loving Gauls in modern-day southern France who exchanged an amphora of wine for a fellow human with traders headed for Italy (*Library of History* 5.26.3).

Arguably of lesser quantitative relevance for the slave supply overall was enslavement through state punishment and tax or tribute payments. So-called debt slavery probably filled notable labor requirements throughout time and space, albeit primarily at an individual level. Conversely, infant exposure and

Figure 7.4. A detail from the Arch of Titus in Rome, commemorating Rome's victory in Jerusalem. 81 CE.

sale into slavery, including self-sale (potentially in consequence of prior debt slavery) have been regarded as practices that helped satisfy the demand in slaves markedly. Poverty was the chief motivation behind such acts, even if the notion of choosing to become enslaved to improve one's standing is also floated in the sources (e.g., Petronius, *Satyricon* 57). Often discouraged in prescriptive writings, such as in a sapiential text from Qumran (4Q416 2.2.17), self-sale was a widespread response to pressing socioeconomic challenges and may even have occurred in a variant in Christian contexts as a means to resource support for the poor (1 Clem. 55:2).

The real-life backdrop of being sold into slavery provides a canvas for the Acts of Thomas, an early Christian text in which Jesus is depicted as selling Thomas, the carpenter, to an Indian merchant. In practice though, individuals who were sold into slavery were predominantly minors whose families experienced severe economic hardship. Even when desperate parents felt forced to leave a very small child or infant exposed to the elements without care, they presumably knew that others might raise that child in slavery. The widespread nature of this practice can be deduced from correspondence from around 110 CE between the aforementioned Pliny the Younger and the emperor Trajan concerning foundlings called *threptoi* in Pliny's province (*Letters* 10.65–66).

Inscriptions from various gods' sanctuaries in Asia Minor and Macedonia illustrate a related practice of giving children to the gods as enslaved laborers: whatever other purposes this practice served, it functioned to satisfy the sanctuaries' labor requirements. Importantly, handing individuals over to a god's service has chronologically earlier roots in the Greek world, providing a framework for understanding the practice of using enslaved individuals in missionary service, as well as for the broader notion among early Christ devotees of becoming a "slave of god" (*doulos theou*; Jas 1:1; Titus 1:1; also "slave of Christ"; Rom 1:1).

The most striking source of enslaved people, however, was itself a direct product of slavery: birth into slavery, or what scholars call natural slave reproduction. Typically, anyone born into slavery would automatically be enslaved, thus procuring future generations of enslaved persons through birth (see chapter 9, "Gender and Sexuality"). In principle, in many ancient slaving cultures the legal status of the mother determined that of the child, while that of the father was irrelevant. Thus, the offspring of enslaved women held servile status. Roman slavery provides once again detailed documentation; the chief rules (and exceptions) were succinctly summed up by the legal scholar Gaius in the later second century CE (*Institutes* 1.82–89). It is widely assumed that in the first three centuries of Roman imperial rule, natural slave reproduction constituted a numerically significant supply source (even if the extent to which ancient enslavers actively encouraged natural slave reproduction remains unquantifiable).[7] The large number of people born into slavery in the period suggests that a significant proportion of the enslaved had no experience of (legal) freedom. This reality fueled a system designed to reproduce itself in demographic *and* conceptual terms.

Overall, ancient enslavers drew on a diversity of sources, differently configured in each slaving culture, time, and place. Nonetheless, all these systems were successfully geared toward satisfying the demand for enslaved laborers. Notwithstanding the lack of reliable quantitative data, Roman slavery was undoubtedly the single largest consumer of enslaved humans in the first few centuries CE and in the regions in which the early Christ groups met and the earliest Christian churches formed. This was the result of the spread of Roman power across the Mediterranean, and with it of Roman civic status and legal rule, which facilitated and even promoted human enslavement. Thus, while

---

7. See further Ulrike Roth, *Thinking Tools: Agricultural Slavery Between Evidence and Models* (London: Institute of Classical Studies, 2007); Walter Scheidel, "Quantifying the Sources of Slaves in the Early Roman Empire," *Journal of Roman Studies* 87 (1997): 156–69.

slaving was near universal in antiquity, the growth of Rome's influence can be seen as synonymous with the diffusion of large-scale slavery, raising deeper questions about the role of the Roman Empire in the spread of Christianity. Scholarly arguments that implicate Rome's imperial system in explaining the successful expansion of the Christian faith need to grapple with Rome's slaving culture and its impact on the development of Christian theology and the institutional church.

Slave Trade

Whatever the mechanism that led to an individual's enslavement, the majority were likely sold at least once, either between individuals and/or through larger slave-trading networks and systems. The trade in enslaved persons thus created a huge movement of people across diverse cultures. Those engaged in the selling and trading of other humans hailed from all parts of the Mediterranean, too. As such, the trade in humans constitutes a prime example for the fundamental promiscuity of slavery in the ancient Mediterranean. Seen the other way, slave trading benefited from frictionless collaboration across varied cultural, religious, and political settings.

Large-scale, systematic trading of humans existed in various forms. Recognizably similar structures, however, characterized these various forms. For example, the documentation of Roman (Dressel 1) wine amphorae (clay jugs) in Gaul as the medium of exchange for captured Gauls illustrates an extensive trade in people destined for Italy, at least until the Augustan age. This human merchandise has been estimated to have constituted up to one-third of the exchanged goods in the region. Whatever the precise figures, the underlying raiding and slaving processes on Gallic territory must have been considerable. Undoubtedly, these processes created widespread fear of enslavement among local communities.

The same basic structure can be inferred for other regions. Especially notable (for their imprint on our sources) are various peoples inhabiting the Black Sea coast who sold humans captured in their hinterland. As the Arcadian Polybius records in the second century BCE, these captured people were then further sold to maritime traders—together with cattle, honey, and wax (*Histories* 4.38.4–6). The longevity of this practice can be deduced from Procopius of Caesarea's very similar comment in the sixth century CE (*Persian War* 2.15.5).

Seaborne piracy, too, augmented the trade. During Jesus's lifetime, Strabo, a native of Amaseia in Pontus, reports such piracy in and around Colchis. Critically, Strabo adds that the Colchian pirates "readily offer to release their captives

Figure 7.5. An example of a Roman wine amphora. Circa 100 BCE.

for ransom" to the captives' relatives (*Geography* 11.2.12). This comment illustrates another dimension of contemporary people raiding and the interrelatedness of localized, short-term "ransom slavery" with more permanent medium- and long-distance slave trading.

North Africa was another significant trading zone that supplied slaves to the territories in which the early Christ groups met. There, the Garamantes of southern Libya open a window onto the pre-Islamic Saharan and trans-Saharan trade. Archaeological evidence documents sub-Saharan as well as Mediterranean trade connections (again through amphorae, but also pottery, glass, faience, gold, silver, copper, coins, beads, ivory, etc.). These connections suggest trading in multiple directions, including people trading, also within Africa. Perhaps unsurprisingly, the sea-trading handbook known as the *Periplus of the Erythraean Sea*, of unknown authorship, written in Greek, probably in the mid-first century CE, specifies trading ports for slaves even much further east. Especially noteworthy is the entry for the port of Opone (in modern-day Somalia) in the Horn of Africa, renowned for its spices, tortoise shell, and "better-quality slaves, the greater number of which go to Egypt" (*Periplus of the Erythraean Sea* 13). From Egypt, these slaves were likely sold north (e.g., to Greece and Asia Minor) and west (e.g., to Rome and Carthage). Trade links with Persia and India may document additional resources for human merchandise that was trafficked west via Africa. These markets augmented Persian and Indian land traffic moving toward the Mediterranean, sometimes also via Babylon (Rev 18:13). Perhaps this is the route envisaged for the merchant in the above-mentioned Acts of Thomas. Plainly, the multidirectional trading links across numerous regions in and beyond the Mediterranean shine a spotlight firmly on the geographic boundlessness of ancient slave trading.

The clearest description of how people raiding worked in antiquity comes from an African context (see chapter 8, "Race and Ethnicity"). In the early fifth century CE, Augustine, the bishop of Hippo, lamented the violent raiding and widespread social complicity in and around Hippo, a town which fed the trade. Augustine described the volume of captured people as a "never-ending stream" (*Letters* 10*.5). But this sense of massive movement is not unique to the African continent. In an image that foreshadows Augustine's by three centuries, the Roman satirist Juvenal depicts a river of people from Syria as "for a long time now polluting" Roman culture, "bringing with it its language and customs" (*Satires* 3.58). Notwithstanding Juvenal's problematic critique of specific ethnicities, the result of these diverse yet interlinked raiding and trading zones was an enslaved population that lacked a singular physical characteristic (such as skin color) or cultural attribute (such as language). The enslaved could thus not be identified in a generic fashion, even if such identifications occurred in localized contexts. This Mediterranean-wide diversity provided the platform from which to apply the concept of enslavement irrespective of ethnicity and race (see chapter 8, "Race and Ethnicity"). Paul and other Christ devotees used this lack of a single ethnicity or race-based identity metaphorically when conceptualizing themselves as "slaves of God."

Professional traders, too, hailed from all corners and quarters. Two examples illustrate this point. First, the Roman freedman Aulus Kapreilius Timotheus, likely a contemporary of Paul, and identified as a "body merchant" (*somatenporos*) on his tombstone, proudly displayed a coffle of individuals chained at their necks (*AE* 1946, 229) and traded out of Amphipolis in Macedonia (which Paul visited on his second missionary journey, reported in Acts 17:1). Second, and roughly in the same period, the freeborn Roman Gaius Aiacius, of Italian origin, operated as a slaver in the province of Germania (in the area of Cologne in modern-day Germany) (*CIL* 13.8348).

Ancient texts also provide insights into the functioning of the trade in humans. Moreover, these texts demonstrate the involvement of persons of elevated social status in this trade. Notably, an 81 BCE court defense speech by Cicero reveals that a company in which the defendant was involved traded, among other things, boys from Gaul (*For Quinctius* 6.2). Apart from illustrating the combined trading of humans with other merchandise, this text speaks unambiguously to the involvement of the upper strata in human trafficking, despite the public disdain that elite discourse loaded onto slave trading and traders. Such disdain for the slave trade appears in multiple ancient texts, in-

Figure 7.6. Fragment of the tombstone of Aulus Kapreilius Timotheus, a slave-trader. The lower scene depicts enslaved individuals chained by their necks. First century CE.

cluding the vice list in 1 Timothy 1:10. Although the proportion of people traders among the general trader population is unknown, it cannot be doubted that several of Cicero's imperial peers who made money from trade were profiting also from human merchandise. In Augustine's above-mentioned letter, the involvement of fellow citizens in people raiding, capturing, and trading is spelled out explicitly (*Letters* 10*.6). But the recognition that members of the elites, including local elites, engaged in slave trading and associated practices carries wide-reaching consequences for the modern appreciation of the involvement of those from the middle and upper social strata in the Christ groups and the early church. Thus, students of the New Testament must reckon with slave trading as a possible source of the wealth that helped to build the early church.[8]

The debate on where and how exactly people were traded and sold is ongoing. Besides organized vending after warfare or other large-scale capture,

8. On Roman slave traders, see John Bodel, "*Caveat Emptor*: Towards a Study of Roman Slave-Traders," *Journal of Roman Archaeology* 18 (2005): 181–95.

structured marketing might have taken place just about everywhere, notably in port cities (like the above-mentioned Opone), but also at inland auctions, fairs, and in busy town centers. For first-century CE Rome, the Stoic Seneca singled out "the men who traffic in wretched human chattels, buying and selling near the temple of Castor, whose shops are packed with a throng of the meanest slaves" (*On the Firmness of the Wise* 13.4). The use of raised platforms or blocks to display the human ware is the source of the phrase *de lapide* (*emptus*), or "(bought) from the block." This slur was associated with lesser, or devalued purchases by Seneca's contemporary and fellow-Spaniard Columella (*On Agriculture* 3.3.8). A generation later, another Spaniard, the poet Martial, referenced "tender boys" who were not displayed "in the booths in front" but "kept in reserve on the boards of a privy platform" (*Epigrams* 9.59). This comment opens moreover a window onto the sex work imposed on the enslaved as well as the significant sexual exploitation widely experienced in enslavement (see chapter 4, "Roman Law and Material Culture"). Overall, the selling and purchasing of people became so normalized that the Roman legal scholar Papinian, himself from Syrian Emesa, spoke around 200 CE of "the regular, daily traffic in slaves" (*Digest* 41.3.44 pr.).

In Roman society, the legal requirement to declare bodily defects underpinned the commodification of those offered for purchase. This commodification increased further when potential buyers pulled off "the garments from slaves that are advertised for sale" to check for physical imperfections (Seneca, *Letters* 80.9). Roman law also required merchants to state the enslaved person's ethnicity (*natio*; *Digest* 21.1.31.21), whether they be Jews (e.g., Philo, *On the Special Laws* 2.123), Moesians (e.g., Juvenal, *Satires* 9.142–144), or Africans (e.g., Petronius, *Satyricon* 34.4). This requirement reflected the profound interconnectedness of the ancient Mediterranean that enabled people trading across myriad cultures and enormous distances. But whatever the peculiarities of the Roman settings and rules, there is no reason to think Rome was unique in its approach to the trading and selling of people. Notably, apart from specific restrictions in Jewish contexts,[9] the proximity of the venues where people were sold in ancient towns to important civic spaces strongly suggests urban Christians—whether the well-off in Carian Laodicea (Rev 3:17) or the hungry in Roman colonial Corinth (1 Cor 11:21–22)—were confronted with the practice on a regular basis. Regardless of their own legal status—free or enslaved—early Christ followers were likely either actively involved in purchasing "from the

9. Discussed in Catherine Hezser, *Jewish Slavery in Antiquity* (Oxford: Oxford University Press, 2005), 254–58.

block" or witnessed the practice regularly just passing by (see chapter 13, "Early Christian Slavery").

A person's commodification and uprooting through sale was not limited to professional and structured trade settings but extended also to individually organized sales. Such sales not only illustrate the complexities of slavery, but also document the influence of Rome on slaving across the Mediterranean at the granular level. A good example is the contract recording the sale of the approximately six-year-old girl Passia, possibly a former foundling. A man called Dasius, from the tribe of the Pirustanians, in the Roman province of Dacia, offered her for sale in 139 CE to a man called Maximus (*IDR* 1.360). While neither the seller nor the purchaser is likely to have held Roman citizenship, the contract, which was in Latin, followed closely the expectations of Roman law, illustrating Rome's influence on slaving practices even outside its own jurisdiction.

The geographical and cultural implications of such sales are embodied in another contract from the mid-second century CE, which was found in the Fayum in Egypt. This contract was brokered between a freeborn man from Miletus (where Paul received the church leaders from Ephesus, reported in Acts 20:17) and a Roman sailor based in Ravenna in Italy (another trading center for slaves) concerning a mature woman of likely Greek origin (*AE* 1922, 135). The underlying interconnectedness here between Egypt, Asia Minor, Greece, and Italy enabled slavery's pervasive reach. Clearly, Roman customs and imperial structures facilitated and constituted a kind of global framework for slavers of diverse cultural, religious, and civic pedigrees. This reality has direct consequences for interpreting how enslaved Christ devotees would have understood discourses referencing the trade in humans, notably the idea that they were "bought for a price" (e.g., 1 Cor 6:20; 2 Pet 2:1).

Conclusion

The combined study of the dimensions explored in this chapter—the exploitation of the labor capacity of the enslaved, the different supply sources for slaves, and the trade that arose from the enslavement of other human beings—emphasize the vast economic role that slavery played in antiquity. While quantitative documentation is lacking, slaving may well have been the single largest continuous driver of the ancient economy. Moreover, although slavery was of different economic importance in different slaving cultures, it is clear Rome consumed slave labor at a scale that rendered the income of its elites dependent on it.[10]

10. The classic exposition (wrapped into a discussion of the rise and decline of ancient

It is in this world of massive slaving that Christianity took hold and through which the references to slavery in the New Testament must be interpreted—many of which, as this chapter has illustrated, make sense only when one takes into account the commodification of human life through capturing, trading, and selling. Enslaved labor, too, is part of this economic equation, constituting another deeply troublesome dimension for New Testament interpretation. Such labor was as familiar to Jesus as it was drawn on by Paul, and even more so in generations to come when the Christian faith became institutionalized.

Given slavery's huge role in wealth creation, the procurement of financial assets for the early missionary work as well as subsequent church-building must be scrutinized critically from this angle. Confrontation with slavery in New Testament interpretation has traditionally focused on specific issues concerned with matters of status—notably, the question of whether Paul recommended or discouraged manumission when stating that there was neither slave nor free (e.g., Gal 3:27–28; 1 Cor 12:13), or the discussion about how enslavers and enslaved should relate to one another in the Christian community (e.g., Col 3:22; Eph 6:5–9; 1 Pet 2:18–21). By contrast, engaging with the wider economic setting of ancient slavery foregrounds the broader structures that underpinned the Christian movement, irrespective of the handling of status anxieties and dissonances within specific communities. It is with this troublesome underpinning that students of the New Testament must wrestle. In particular, how does the income generation and wealth creation that derive from slavery impact our understanding of the early missionary work and the subsequent growth of the institutional church? And more broadly: what role must this entanglement with slaving play in coming to terms with Christian legacies of slavery?

Discussion Questions

1.   Would the specific labor exploitation of enslaved individuals (accountant versus vine dresser, seamstress versus sex worker, etc.) have an impact on their ability to participate in the Christian community?

2.   How might an enslaved person's specific route into slavery (through warfare, capture, sale, birth, or otherwise) affect how they experienced the conceptual leanings on slavery in the early Christ groups and the emerging

---

slavery) is Moses Finley, *Ancient Slavery and Modern Ideology* (New York: Viking, 1980), 67–92, 123–49.

institutional church? What might the challenges be when slave traders and enslaved persons met in the Christian community?

3. How might the ubiquity of slave trading in and beyond the ancient Mediterranean have impacted the spread of Christianity?

Further Reading

Bradley, Keith. "'The Regular, Daily Traffic in Slaves': Roman History and Contemporary History." *The Classical Journal* 87 (1993): 125–38.

———. "The Roman Slave Supply." Pages 31–56 in *Slavery and Society at Rome*. Edited by Keith Bradley. Cambridge: Cambridge University Press, 1994.

Roth, Ulrike, ed. *By the Sweat of Your Brow: Roman Slavery in Its Socio-Economic Setting*. London: Institute of Classical Studies, School of Advanced Study, University of London, 2010.

Scheidel, Walter. "Real Slave Prices and the Relative Cost of Slave Labour in the Greco-Roman World." *Ancient Society* 35 (2005): 1–17.

Silver, Morris. "The Role of Slave Markets in Migration from the Near East to Rome." *Klio* 98 (2016): 184–202.

Trümper, Monika. *Graeco-Roman Slave Markets: Fact or Fiction?* Oxford: Oxbow Books, 2009.

8   Race and Ethnicity

JEREMY L. WILLIAMS

Several features of contemporary thought concerning race and ethnicity provide helpful tools for exploring ancient enslavement in and around the New* Testament.[1] Many scholars claim that race functioned differently in antiquity than it does in contemporary times—if it even existed in antiquity at all. In Roman antiquity, enslaved people were those who had been prisoners of war, conquered, or unable to pay a debt. Although some enslaved people were born into enslavement, there was not an industry built around breeding enslaved people like animals. Ancient Roman and antebellum enslavement were indeed distinct iterations of enslavement, but there are similarities between the two practices. The similarities are significant for our discussion on race and ethnicity in ancient enslavement.

Race or racialization is a sociopolitical process that hierarchizes some humans as full humans, others as not quite human, and others still as nonhuman. Although race and ethnicity operated differently in ancient times than in current times, especially around enslaved people, both contexts involved groups of human beings racializing other human beings to legitimize the sociopolitical processes and the power networks that made and make enslavement possible. Critical race theory (CRT) is useful for this analysis.

CRT addresses race as more than phenotypes or differences in outward appearance. It understands race as a real phenomenon that affects and informs

---

1. I place an asterisk after "New" to draw attention to the supersessionist undertones of the term "New Testament" that has historically been used to denigrate and relativize the Hebrew Bible (the so-called Old Testament), Jewish scriptures, and Jewish religious traditions more broadly.

institutions, structures, and multiple aspects of society. It is real in the way that various interests of elites, particularly those racialized as white, converge to preserve resources for one group of people and prohibit others from accessing those resources. CRT also helps to show how certain groups of people are structurally determined to not receive justice, fair housing, and equitable education through judicial, economic, and political structures. Such issues are structural, meaning that they are more complicated than one person negatively viewing another. They involve systems and structures designed to preserve power networks and hierarchized relationships. CRT understands racialization functioning as a process that tells stories contrived against marginalized people to bolster dominant, exploitative narratives. This process manifests itself against certain people in the United States, particularly Black and other racially minoritized people.

CRT is relevant for studying race and ethnicity as sociopolitical processes in the world around the New Testament. It provides an opportunity to rethink the types of logics and human classificatory systems that separate people and rationalize enslavement and subjugation. That insight invites us to consider race as more than a concept linked to phenotype or outward appearance only. The type of racialization that undergirded the European chattel slave system was a distinct process derived from ancient Greco-Roman processes, but by looking at the two together we can clearly see the types of processes that were at work in justifying the logics of enslavement.

To better understand how racialization functioned as a process in ancient times, it is important to note that religious, legal, and economic spheres were not clearly delineated (which is not totally different from contemporary overlaps). To expose how racialization functioned in ancient enslavement, I invite us to use the "ABCs" as a way to think about how ancient enslavement and racialization worked together. "A" is for "assemblage," which is a set of factors that are combined to portray aspects and characteristics of individuals and groups. Such features include tropes, stereotypes, and mythological narratives used in ancient thinking to create the racial and ethnic identities of enslaved people. This section will set the table for those that follow by demonstrating the significance of considering racializing assemblages in antiquity, which can then be applied to ancient Roman enslavement. "B" will engage "blackness" and ethnopolitical color symbolism. This section will juxtapose contemporary uses of blackness to fund the logic of African enslavement against older ethnopolitical invective raised against Egyptian and African bodies. "C" will explore how enslaved people were a feature of ancient imperial "conquest." The "D" is for "diaspora"; the Roman imperial project involved displacing indigenous people, which often included capturing humans, turning them into enslaved people of the new dominators, and at times involved forcibly relocating them to work. In this way, diaspora equates to instability and vulnerability. "E" and "F" are the "economic" and "family" aspects that contributed to how racialization was constructed in antiquity. From this perspective, enslavement itself could function as a type of racialization through natal alienation—that is, enslaved people who were taken from their homeland to work for others in other places were also often compelled to speak another language than their original language, and they were brought into different household structures and forced to become parts of different families. These categories will expose how racialization functions as a tool that strengthens, supports, and enables enslavement and similar processes that dominate and subject humans. The categories are especially useful for analyzing the first and second centuries, when the texts that composed the New Testament were first articulated to audiences.

A: Assemblages

Assemblages are useful for thinking about race in antiquity because societies use various means to separate and class human beings. "Assemblage" here refers to a collection of traits and features that people use to distinguish one group of people from another group. Alexander Weheliye defines racializing assemblages as "a set of sociopolitical processes of differentiation and hierarchization, which are projected onto the putatively biological human body."[2] Such features include, but are not limited to, where one is born, their biological kinship, and their native language. Although phenotypic differences or language differences are often components of the assemblages of ethnicity, race, or nationality in antiquity and now, they are only aspects of a larger portfolio of assemblages. Considering other types of differences, especially sociopolitical processes, give us an opportunity to think through how these aspects along with others are used to classify humans. The types of sociopolitical processes that contribute to racializing assemblages include but are not limited to laws, collective myths, pseudoscience, and logics that reinforce hierarchizing humans. For example, collective myths often contribute to how people understand themselves as related to gods who share their race and ethnicity, especially through stories that recount origins or founding narratives.

2. Alexander G. Weheliye, *Habeas Viscus: Racializing Assemblages, Biopolitics, and Black Feminist Theories of the Human* (Durham, NC: Duke University Press, 2014), 3.

Such myths impact how people understand what unites them, who opposes them, and who they oppose. Processes used for assemblages like legal status and collective myth-making are also embedded in the Greek words often used to depict race and ethnicity, and they are more fraught than their English counterparts entail or portray.

One example of how Greek words reflect ancient sociopolitical processes is the word *genos*, which is often translated as "race." This term provides insight into how societies and people combine multiple components to form assemblages that racialize. *Genos* refers to a group, class, or set of people, so it is a term that is used to classify. In contemporary usages, it is the Greek equivalent of the Latin term *genus,* used in the classification of organisms in biology (remember the taxonomy "kingdom, phylum, class, order, family, genus, species"). Furthermore, *genos* was the term adopted to describe the hereditary information passed from one generation to the next called "genes." Hence, each group in a family line is a "generation." This term seems to simply mean the passing of genetic material. We must remember, however, that ancient people had much less sophisticated understandings of biology. Some people even considered themselves to share *genos* or genetic material with gods, which helps demonstrate that *genos* is more complicated than tracing one's paternal lineage (not to mention, people groups varied in using patrilineal and matrilineal means to count descent). One's *genos* was significant for determining one's value in society. Such notions have persisted into more modern times. This appears in terms like "eugenics," which literally means "good race" and captures a type of pseudoscience that presents one *genos* as better than another and concludes that inferior races need to be dominated or exterminated. Placing the contemporary next to the ancient demonstrates how "race" and even "gene" are aspects of societies' projects of hierarchizing humans and justifying enslavement.

Similar to *genos* and race, *ethnos* (the Greek word behind "ethnicity") is difficult to map onto the contemporary term. The contemporary term "ethnicity" applies to a group of people sharing common cultural background or ancestry. Although culture itself is nearly impossible to define, among other features it incorporates shared language and rituals. In some ways, these aspects are also relevant for antiquity.

Ethnos also has another meaning, especially its plural *ethne*, which is often translated as "nations." Throughout the New Testament, the term refers to people who are not Jewish. In this way, Jews are juxtaposed against the *ethnē* or "nations." *Ethnē* is also rendered as "gentile." That term, however, is merely the Latin "*gentilis*," which means "tribe, family, nation." It is important here to note that "nation" and "nationality" are not useful words with which to think about what *ethnē* completely means, especially in antiquity. First, the modern notion of the nation-state with its fixed borders did not exist. Second, "nation" comes from the Latin *natio*, which ultimately refers to one's birth. Although not completely disconnected from place and land, the term is not limited to geographical confines, which makes it a flexible category term. One's *ethnos* could include the people among whom one was born, and it could also be a marker of where one was not from (e.g., neither from Judea nor from Jewish people or culture). Romans also used the term *ethnē* to describe the various peoples that they conquered. (I discuss this more in the section on conquest and diaspora below.)

Even in antiquity, race (*genos*) and ethnicity (*ethnos*) were not self-evident. The terms both portray processes of separating humans into categories. They also portray a similar, if not the same, process as racialization. These terms mark places where ancient notions of race and ethnicity are contested. Ancient people defined, described, wielded, and resisted difference just as contemporary societies have. The preceding word studies help to demonstrate how an analysis of racializing assemblages functions as a valuable lens for interrogating ancient social structures like the power networks that legitimated enslavement.

B: Blackness

We turn now to "B" to analyze blackness and ethnopolitical color symbolism's connections to ancient enslavement practices in the Roman Empire. Some of the anti-Black sentiments that fueled chattel slavery were rooted in what Benjamin Isaac has called proto-racism.[3] "Proto-racism" is a term that captures how ancient people, including Romans and Greeks, levied negative portrayals and disparaging ideas against various people in antiquity. Contemporary anti-Black racism is a product of Western European imaginations of superiority that fueled colonial expansion and its exploitative enterprises. In many ways, both Greeks and Romans considered themselves the center of the world. For example, the largest body of water they navigated was called the Mediterranean Sea, which literally means "the middle of the earth." People in the Roman Empire, especially the super elite, considered skin color as an aspect of people's character. People who lived far to the north of them, includ-

3. Benjamin H. Isaac, *The Invention of Racism in Classical Antiquity* (Princeton: Princeton University Press, 2004), 1–14.

ing Scythians, were viewed as too white due to cold temperatures. The dark-skinned, curly haired Ethiopians to their south were phenotypically described as such because of the warm climate. Of course, in this framework the olive skin tone of the Greeks and Romans sat at a happy medium between these two extremes. Such descriptions of Scythians and Ethiopians could seem neutral, and even sometimes flattering, as in Homer's positive portrayal of Ethiopians. Frequently, however, these portrayals of ethnic differences were the product of what has been called ethnopolitical invective.[4] One aspect of ethnopolitical invective is color symbolism, which relates certain colors, especially black, to negative omens. Plutarch, the second-century historian and priest at Delphi, even wrote that people should avoid "blackened men" (Plutarch, *The Education of Children* 17).

Color symbolism was not only about rendering people as inferior for servitude, but it was a component of a broader assemblage that portrayed darker-skinned people as deceptive, mischievous, and prone to subjugation. This assemblage animated Roman and Egyptian relations whereby Egyptians were not only disparaged for their skin color that linked them phenotypically with Ethiopians, but various Roman elites through the second century CE also viewed the religious and worshiping practices of Egyptians as deplorable, particularly their worship of deities with animal features. The Romans were, therefore, able to justify the domination and subjugation of the Egyptians.

Another example of how ancient writers in the Roman Empire thought about people in or around Ethiopia is the story of the Ethiopian eunuch in the Acts of the Apostles (Acts 8:26–40). The eunuch is most likely enslaved as a court official to the Candace, ruler of Ethiopia. On one level, this character represents a culmination of Jesus's programmatic instructions at the beginning of the book where he directs the apostles to be his witnesses to the ends of the earth (Acts 1:8). Ethiopia, for some ancient people, could very well have felt like the end of the earth. On another level, the eunuch is still in service to someone, the Candace, and he encounters Philip outside of the city. He is literally an outsider. Acts does not center this blackened character and instead buries this character under another person's story who also represents the Jesus movement extending to the end of earth, Cornelius. I intentionally use the term "bury" because Acts tells Cornelius's story twice (Acts 10:1–11:18). The Ethiopian eunuch, who is the only Ethiopian to speak in Luke-Acts, is enslaved and is literally and literarily marginalized.

4. See Gay Byron, *Symbolic Blackness and Ethnic Difference in Early Christian Literature* (New York: Routledge, 2002).

Figure 8.1. *The Baptism of the Eunuch.* Oil painting by Rembrandt van Rijn. 1626.

Also lumped together with Ethiopians were people of Cyrene in North Africa. As we turn to Cyrene, our consideration of ethnopolitical invective becomes even more valuable for a study of the New Testament and enslavement. At the crucifixion of Jesus, Simon from Cyrene is compelled, according to Synoptic Gospel accounts, to assist Jesus in carrying his cross (Mark 15:21; Matt 27:32; Luke 23:26). It is not clear why this particular person was conscripted to carry Jesus's cross for or with him. One strong possibility is his skin color or his phenotypical features. How might a Roman soldier perceive someone from that region of Africa? In Acts 6, the writer portrays a synagogue of freed people, Libertines, from Cyrene, which at least implies that the text and the early audience would have perceived a connection between enslaved people and formerly enslaved people in North Africa, especially Cyrene.

Looking back to Simon of Cyrene, it is worth noting that the punishment of crucifixion also connects ethnopolitical concerns with enslavement, because crucifixion itself was a type of capital punishment reserved for enslaved people and those considered bandits or thugs. Simon from North Africa is arrested to assist in an enslaved person's punishment. Furthermore, this scene can expose that even in antiquity living in a darker-skinned body resulted in different treatment from society. Those with darker skin bore what Jennifer Glancy calls "a whippable body," that is, a body that could be forced to experience physical punishments from which elite persons were protected.[5] In this way, blackness could function as not only a marker of negative omens but also a sign of low status and punishability. Again, this is not to say that ancient enslavement used racial difference and skin color in the absolute same ways as more contemporary chattel slavery. Rather, this example highlights how ethnic differences as portrayed through skin color, worship, and language were used to demonstrate that darker-skinned people were vulnerable to discrimination, physical punishment, and enslavement.

This is particularly relevant when we consider how many people would have encountered folks from different places because those people were enslaved. The enslaved would have been kidnapped or brought from different places as prisoners of war. Therefore, many peoples' experiences with foreigners and others from different places were mitigated through the lens of enslavement. Enslavement was a component and direct corollary to conquest and diaspora, two terms that are important for both contextualizing the New Testament, and for thinking about ancient enslavement more broadly.

5. Jennifer A. Glancy, *Corporal Knowledge: Early Christian Bodies* (New York: Oxford University Press, 2010), 24–47.

C and D: Conquest and Diaspora

Roman imperial enslavement and later colonial European enslavement share similarities in how they employed conquest and diaspora as components of the assemblages that hierarchized people and fueled their logics for enslavement. One reason why many pause when making comparisons between Roman enslavement practices and Western European and American enslavement practices is the targeted nature of the more contemporary practice of enslavement. In the more contemporary version, the primary group of people who were kidnapped, purchased, and forced into slavery were people from the African continent. Lumping people enslaved from the continent of Africa together renders invisible how the contemporary project of enslavement was indeed diverse. The enslaved came from different regions across the western coast of Africa, and although many shared dark skin, they brought with them a wealth of languages, religious practices, and understandings of deities. The project of imperialism, which directly leads to diaspora, works to homogenize minoritized people in the service of promulgating a "normal" existence.

Although enslavement practices across the Roman Empire were not targeted toward one racial group, one feature of many enslaved people in Roman antiquity was that they had been conquered and displaced by the imperial expansion project. Romans dominated and conquered entire groups of people, and as a result many were captured or depicted as enslaved. A great example of this is a frieze from Aphrodisias in modern-day Turkey. This archaeological masterpiece depicts scenes of various Roman figures, including emperors, conquering various peoples (*ethnē*) from across the empire. This is especially interesting for considering how the New Testament primarily uses *ethnē* to depict non-Jewish people, because in the frieze from Aphrodisias Jewish people (*Ioudaioi*) are considered *ethnē* or among the "nations."

Various peoples and groups, through military conquest, were indebted to the Roman Empire. Rome forced those people to pay taxes and surveilled them with militarized police. Romans monopolized violence, especially capital punishment against citizens and wealthy, free noncitizen residents. Due to the Roman Empire's militaristic exploits and its capture of vanquished peoples and soldiers, a major feature of the slave apparatus in the empire would have been slave markets filled with people from different places, with different practices, speaking different languages. Such people were perceived as foreigners. Their status is directly connected to the perception that they were negative and enslaveable with punishable bodies. Ultimately, differences, including

Figure 8.2. A frieze from the Sebasteon in Aphrodisias in Asia Minor (modern-day Turkey), showcasing a Roman soldier attacking a woman who represents Britannia. This scene signifies Rome's subjugation and occupation of Britain. First century CE.

racial and ethnic, made people vulnerable to the mechanisms of a ubiquitous slavocracy. It is worth noting that enslavement was also a form of punishment that could be meted out to low-status people. Even lower-level local courts could impose enslavement on people of low status without oversight

Figure 8.3. A frieze from the Sebasteon in Aphrodisias in Asia Minor (modern-day Turkey) showcasing the Roman Emperor Nero attacking a woman representing Armenia. This scene graphically depicted Rome's subjugation of Armenia. First century CE.

from the governor. Among the people of low status would be those who were ethnically different or racially otherized.

The differentness of some foreign enslaved people in new places fueled types of xenophobia that allowed for officials and elites to portray them as deserving of mistreatment. The Roman historian Livy, in his report of the Bacchanalia Affair, shows how rhetoric that portrayed groups and individuals as foreigners authorized officials to arrest and target groups for challenging Roman *mores* or traditions (*The History of Rome* 39.15–19). Also, the Roman satirist Juvenal depicts a foreign, possibly enslaved, Jewish high priestess in Rome as dubious and mischievous (*Satires* 6.542–547). A component of the assemblage of the enslaved in Roman antiquity was that they were people from other places and their difference made it more rational for them to be enslaved.

The empire's expansion brought people together under the banner of Rome, and people often lived a diasporic life away from their homeland. Many of the enslaved were taken from the place where their native tongue was spoken and from where their traditions were practiced. This means that they and other displaced people would have to survive and make meaning in these new places. Often their exoticness and difference in religious experience and skills gained them value in their enslavers' eyes. Two examples are worth noting here: (1) some enslaved people could write; and (2) some enslaved people operated as religious experts for their enslavers. One significant feature of Roman imperial literature is that, although many texts are attributed to elites, they were only made possible by enslaved people managing the other affairs of the elite "authors." In many cases, it was the enslaved people who wrote down the actual texts.[6]

Enslaved religious experts' skills and exoticness could sometimes work to the benefit of enslaved people, and they could use their skills for their enslavers. An example of this phenomenon is the enslaved girl with a Pythian spirit in Acts 16. Her owners turn a profit from her prophesying until Paul exorcises the spirit that empowers her to prophesy, and then she disappears from the text. It is not clear where she is from, perhaps Delphi, but what is clear is that her religious prophesying is profitable to her enslavers. This example also demonstrates how, when those skills could no longer be used in service of the enslavers and elite, the enslaved could swiftly become victims of assemblages that dehumanized people, rendered them invisible, and made them subject to punishment.

Among the enslaved were conquered people and prisoners of war, and there were people without status or without resources who could very easily find themselves in financial trouble and be sold into enslavement. Also, those who found themselves in criminal trouble could find themselves in punitive slavery. Therefore, part of the racial and ethnic assemblages that functioned

6. See Candida Moss, *God's Ghostwriters: Enslaved Christians and the Making of the Bible* (New York: Little, Brown, 2024).

to support Roman logics of enslavement included the militarized aspects of conquest. This connection to conquest also acknowledges the very closely connected consequence of imperial military conquest: diaspora.

E and F: Economics and Family

The "E" and "F" of racializing assemblages in the ancient world engaged notions of economics and family. For a modern Western person, the collusion of family and economics could seem strange. Etymologically, the connection is clearer. The Greek components that make up the word "economics" are *oikos*, which means "house" or "home," and *nomos*, which means "law." Together, economics is the law or the rule of the house. The Roman *oikos* was about business as much as it was about family. The Latin word behind family, *familia*, includes within its semantic range both the household and especially a household of enslaved people. This helps to highlight how the ancient household included enslaved families; put another way, the families of enslavers incorporated enslaved families. The New Testament incorporates enslaved people into families in multiple places, including Rhoda as part of Mary's family in Acts 12:12–17 and the mention of households being baptized in various texts (Lydia: Acts 16:11–15; the Philippian jailer: Acts 16:31–34; Stephanas: 1 Cor 1:16; 16:15–18). Foundational to Roman households, especially after Caesar Augustus's legal reforms, were the notions of order and hierarchy, especially kyriarchy. Kyriarchy is a type of

Figure 8.4. Funerary bust of an enslaved boy, Martial, who died when he was two years old. 100–115 CE.

patriarchy that not only acknowledges the domination of men over women, but also recognizes the subjugation of enslaved people to their masters (*kyrioi*), who might be women (see chapter 9, "Gender and Sexuality").

The family structure that included enslaved people in the New Testament is most obvious in what have been termed the "household codes," which appear in Ephesians, Colossians, and the pastoral letters (see chapter 12, "Household Codes"). One common feature of those texts is that without skipping a breath the writers move from describing the role and authority of the father or master of the house, known as the *paterfamilias,* to the wife, then to the children, and then to the enslaved people. These texts demonstrate how widespread such an understanding of family was. This is not to say that it was the only available option, but it was certainly one, and a pernicious one at that.

Attention to family structures provides even more context for ancient enslaved people, who functioned as more than chattel per se. Enslaved people had a variety of skills, which afforded them various opportunities in the household, especially in super-elite households. In such households, enslaved people could have positions of running the entire house, including its finances. They could also be charged with managing other enslaved people, a position known as the *oikonomos*—or, quite literally, "economist." In these ways, the term "economics" is extremely relevant.

The enslaved were from different families, but their slave status brought them to be a part of another family, the enslaver's family. Recognizing that enslaved people were a part of another family exposes how enslaved people formed and resisted ancient understandings of ethnicity and race. As discussed before, the terms "ethnicity" and "race" and "nation" are all connected to the idea of where one is born. Enslaved people very well could be slaving in a home where the language was different, the religious practices were different, and other customs like cuisine were different from the place(s) where they were born. Due to enslaved people not being considered full humans, they in some ways acquired their enslavers' ethnicity but not fully. Part of being an enslaved person was to not have the status that came with having freedom and citizenship. Again, enslaved people had no real status at all, but that did not negate their experiences of religion and ethnicity discussed above.

In antiquity, enslaved people did not come from just one ancestral background (this was also the case for people enslaved from across the continent of Africa and brought to the United States). Enslaved status, however, led to hybrid racialization, a type of racialization simultaneously connected to where they were from and to the race of their captors or enslavers. This might seem difficult for a contemporary person to understand, but consider the hybrid identity called "African American." The term attempts to pay homage to two disparate yet connected identities. That term still does not capture how flexible ethnicity in antiquity was, because in the contemporary world race and ethnicity appear more fixed.

An example of how family lineage is not as fixed as it may seem and certainly was not so in antiquity is the idea of adoption. Adoption, both in antiquity and in current times, brought somebody who was born into a different family into the family lineage of other people. Adopting someone into a family is and was more than a legal process. In antiquity, it was connected to bringing that person into the official lineage of the adopter, which included changing names, sometimes learning a new language, and worshiping new gods. Recall that nationality and race were connected to the place where one is born, and adoption involved the adoptee performing as if they were born in a different place to different people. Adoption was not a secondary type of family connection. It was real, especially in societies that relied on patriarchal lineage.[7] Often even without officially doing so, the father would have to claim or adopt a woman's child by making a sacrifice. I offer these reflections on adoption to demonstrate how one's ethnicity in antiquity was not just about language or phenotype, but it was also about how one was brought into a family.

Ancient understandings of race and ethnicity included people having the opportunity to become part of different families or to share a different lineage through achievement. Here, achievement means commitment to a particular set of philosophical principles or conversion to worship a different deity. People could become a part of different families, not just in terms of religion, although the religious, economic, and social were all integrated. By becoming a part of a different worshiping community, drawing one's identity from a different god, or subscribing to the teachings of a different thinker, the person in effect acquired a different genealogy. Enslaved people had to negotiate multiple types of families simultaneously. Perhaps this can shed light on the letter to Philemon. In that letter, Paul recommends that Philemon receive Onesimus as a brother (Phlm 16). Note the familial language. This familial language could signal that he wants Onesimus's position in the racial hierarchy to change, and would mean Onesimus goes from being enslaved to being Philemon's brother.[8] I do not, however, wish to use this example to suggest that Paul is advocating the abolition of slavery, but to examine how family language gets used as a tool to legitimate, resist, and expand enslavement, especially as a discourse.

Family language can often euphemize violent power relations, especially when it comes to the enslaved. In the United States antebellum South, many

7. For more on this lineage, see Caroline Johnson Hodge, *If Sons, Then Heirs: A Study of Kinship and Ethnicity in the Letters of Paul* (New York: Oxford University Press, 2007), 29–31.
8. See Matthew V. Johnson, James A. Noel, and Demetrius K. Williams, eds., *Onesimus: Our Brother: Reading Religion, Race, and Culture in Philemon* (Minneapolis: Fortress, 2012).

enslavers considered their enslaved people as part of the family through a form of paternalism. This form of paternalism shares similarities with Roman notions. Enslaved people were a part of the family but permanently in a lower caste and thus minoritized. I want to draw attention to the term "minoritized," because it captures the process of perpetually treating humans as children regardless of their age, such as a white teenager calling a seventy-year-old Black man "boy" or a sixty-five-year-old Latina woman "girl." A similar scene occurs in Acts 16:16 when the enslaved person is referred to as a *paidiskē*, which is often translated as "slave girl," but the term could very well be applied to someone at any age. Another example comes again from Philemon, where Paul calls Onesimus, presumably a grown man, his "child" (Phlm 10). Roman families included enslaved people, so some people were valued more than others, and the enslaved were rendered as perpetual children forever under the control of someone's mastery. Even as a free child would grow up and eventually become an enslaver or at least a full adult, their pedagogue or enslaved teacher would always remain subservient and in the position of a child.

The minoritization of enslaved people within the family also impacted how enslaved sexual relationships were fraught or even overlooked. A component of racialization was to render enslaved people as genderless. In the above-mentioned household codes, there are instructions for fathers, husbands, and wives, but children and enslaved people are not differentiated by gender. These codes are a corollary to more modern practices of enslavement that incorporated (among their assemblage of the enslaved) the fetishization or diminishing of enslaved people's sexuality. These projects demonstrate how families, especially ancient families and societies that enslaved people, categorized humans. Part of the categorization separated people, even in the home. The processes of racialization also functioned as the operating logic of larger spheres, including the city, state, and empire. The family as an economic unit and as a microcosm of the larger Roman Empire shows how enslaved people were rendered as nonhuman, minoritized, and even mere objects. This was all part of a family.

Conclusion

Ancient enslavement varied significantly from more contemporary versions of enslavement, but it was similarly embedded in power networks that legitimated its existence. Although race functioned differently diachronically, racializing assemblages are eerily present and display similarities in both systems. Color symbolism and ethnopolitical invective played a role to varying degrees in justifying enslavement. Conquest and diaspora sit at the heart of logics that necessitate enslavement and create the vulnerable groups who generate the pool of enslaveable people. The family and its business in elite households functioned as a microcosm of the larger empire that operated as the emperor's household with enslaved people included. These insights about racialization and ethnicity in antiquity are important for studying the New Testament, especially in terms of enslavement. Often enslavement in the New Testament is ignored or viewed as radically different than more modern practices. By analyzing racialization and power networks, however, astute readers can see damning similarities—damning for what contemporary societies condoned and damning for what the New Testament condoned. Considering race in terms of power networks and a host of factors that delimit people's access to full humanity is not only a contemporary problem, but it is one that extends into antiquity, and if we are not careful, will persist in perpetuity.

Discussion Questions

1. Consider the "ABCs" analogy concerning race and ethnicity in the New Testament. If you were to add one more letter to this list, what would it be? What would it stand for?

2. Read closely the story of the Ethiopian eunuch found in Acts 8:26–40. In addition to race and ethnicity, in what other ways is this enslaved character marginalized?

3. This chapter has outlined the ways that race and ethnicity are entangled with slavery in the New Testament. Is this ideology still pervasive within contemporary society and/or Christian communities? If so, how do we resist these ideologies so that they will not "persist in perpetuity"?

Further Reading

Buell, Denise K. *Why This New Race? Ethnic Reasoning in Early Christianity.* New York: Columbia University Press, 2005.

Byron, Gay. *Symbolic Blackness and Ethnic Difference in Early Christian Literature.* New York: Routledge, 2002.

Delgado, Richard, and Jean Stefancic, *Critical Race Theory: An Introduction.* New York: New York University Press, 2012.

Glancy, Jennifer A. *Corporal Knowledge: Early Christian Bodies.* New York: Oxford University Press, 2010.

Johnson, Matthew V., James A. Noel, Demetrius K. Williams, eds. *Onesimus Our*

Brother: Reading Religion, Race, and Culture in Philemon. Minneapolis: Fortress, 2012.

Smith, Mitzi, Angela Parker, and Ericka Dunbar, eds. *Bitter the Chastening Rod: Africana Biblical Interpretation after* Stony the Road We Trod *in the Age of BLM, SayHerName, and MeToo.* Lanham, MD: Lexington Books, 2022.

Williams, Jeremy L. *Criminalization in Acts of the Apostles: Race, Rhetoric, and the Prosecution of an Early Christian Movement.* New York: Cambridge University Press, 2023.

9   *Gender and Sexuality*

CHRISTY COBB

The story of Peter denying Jesus three times is one that is familiar to most Christians. In all four Gospels, Jesus predicts that Peter, one of his closest disciples, would betray him before the rooster crows. Later, Gospel writers include a scene after the arrest of Jesus where Peter is in a courtyard outside the house of the Jewish high priest. While he is sitting there, three people approach him to ask if he is a disciple of Jesus. All three times, Peter adamantly denies knowing Jesus. Then, a rooster crows, solidifying Jesus's prophecy that Peter would deny him (Matt 26:69–75; Mark 14:66–72; Luke 22:54–62; John 18:15–18, 25–27). What many readers of the Gospels do not notice in this familiar story is that one of Peter's questioners is an enslaved woman. In Matthew's version, two of Peter's questioners are enslaved women.

This story provides an example of the ways that gender and slavery are overlooked within New Testament texts. Both are ever-present; however, both are often glossed over, hidden from our sight. Noticing enslaved characters requires a close reading of the text. In this scene, for example, translation is our first problem. Our English translations of enslaved characters further erase slavery (see chapter 1, "The Language of 'Enslavement' in the New Testament"). The enslaved female character who questions Peter is translated as "female servant" in Matthew, Mark, and Luke in the NRSVue. The use of the title "servant" softens the implications of slavery in this scene, and some readers are not clear about the status of this questioner. In John, this questioner is described as a "woman," erasing her enslaved status altogether.

To be clear, the first person to question Peter in all four Gospels is an enslaved woman. She is enslaved *to* the high priest, a person in a powerful position in Jerusalem. She was working in his household, without pay, when she encountered Peter. But the texts differ slightly concerning her role. In the Synoptic Gospels (Matthew, Mark, and Luke), she is outside in the courtyard of the house when she sees Peter. In John, however, she is "the woman who guarded the gate" (John 18:16) and then is simply "woman" (John 18:17). Without knowledge of Greek, readers of John's Gospel would have no reason to assume that the first questioner of Peter is enslaved. In Greek, however, it is clear that the woman is enslaved, as the first word (*tē thyrōrō*) indicates a "doorkeeper," a job reserved for enslaved persons. The second Greek word used to describe this character is *paidiskē*, as it is in the other three Gospels, which is used for enslaved women who worked in domestic spaces (see chapter 1, "The Language of 'Enslavement' in the New Testament").[1]

To read this passage with attention to both gender and status, readers can apply a *hermeneutic of suspicion*. This reading strategy, outlined for New Testament scholarship by Elisabeth Schüssler Fiorenza, proposes that readers should be asking hard questions of the text with regard to marginalized characters. The texts of the New Testament were written within the context of a slave society. Slavery was pervasive and an integral part of domestic, political, economic, and religious life. Similarly, the Greco-Roman world was a patriarchal, male-centered space. We must read closely, against the grain of the text, to locate the ways that gender and slavery are functioning. We must fill in the gaps of the text where information is lacking as we explore slavery, gender, and sexuality in the New Testament.

In the story of Peter's denial, reading against the grain leads to the observation that the first questioner is an enslaved woman working in the house of the Jewish high priest. As the high priest was one of the most important leaders in Jerusalem, he would have had a large house that would have required many enslaved workers to function. Perhaps this woman was one of the domestic workers whose job it was to cook, clean, and welcome guests into the house. While the text does not tell us more about this person's daily life, we can fill in the gaps using historical information about slavery as well as our imagination. It is likely that this enslaved woman was born in this house, a child of another enslaved woman living there. She might have spent her entire life in this elite space, forced to work long hours even as a young child in service to her enslaver.

1. For analysis of other enslaved women in Luke and Acts, see Christy Cobb, *Slavery, Gender, Truth, and Power in Luke-Acts and Other Ancient Narratives* (London: Palgrave Macmillan, 2019).

This chapter explores the connections between gender, slavery, and sexuality in the New Testament and its ancient contexts. Enslaved women, like Peter's questioner, are found throughout biblical texts, yet are often overlooked. We will consider the ways that gender affected the lives of enslaved persons in antiquity and will then apply this information to several enslaved characters from the New Testament and other early Christian texts. Aspects that we will explore in this chapter include gender and status, enslaved female characters, relationships with enslavers, sexual violence, and prostitution.

Gender and Status

In the ancient world, gender identity was presented as a sliding scale of masculinity and femininity. The ideal gender was a privileged free male; thus, masculinity was the model for gendered behavior. Gender was illustrated by behavior. The ideal male presented himself as active, powerful, intelligent, and free of emotion. Men were empowered in a number of realms in society, including the political, legal, and economic spheres. In terms of family relationships, the father was understood as the head of the household. Everyone in the family was subordinate to him, including free women, children, and enslaved persons (see chapter 12, "Household Codes"). Enslaved men in the household, therefore, were assumed to have feminine characteristics of passivity, submissiveness, and lack of virtue. This meant that sometimes enslaved men were viewed as feminine. To be gendered as female in antiquity was to be contrasted with masculinity. Ideal women were passive, submissive, and quiet. If a person was too emotional, they were often described using feminine language—regardless of their preferred gender expression. Free women were also expected to be sexually chaste. While men in antiquity could be sexually active (for example, hiring sex laborers or having sex with their female enslaved workers), free women in antiquity were not to be open to sexual advances. Their bodies were to be protected and presented as sexually unavailable except to their husbands. Enslaved women, however, did not enjoy this same protection or presentation.

Most enslaved persons, ideologically, were located outside of this gendered view. Because they were not viewed as full humans, for example, in legal and philosophical documents (see chapter 3, "Enslavement in the Roman World"), they were viewed as *beneath* gender. In practice, however, enslaved persons were gendered in a number of ways. That is, the ideological and philosophical world did not easily translate into daily life. Classicist Allison Glazebrook describes this dynamic well when she writes: "The slave's experience may appear

Figure 9.1. Funerary monument depicting a standing elite woman, Lampron of Stymphalos, and an enslaved female attendant holding a jewelry box and a fan. 125–100 BCE.

somewhat genderless, external to ancient constructions of gender."[2] Therefore, free persons were the usual referent when understanding the differences between men and women in antiquity. This is exemplified through the language used for an enslaved person. For example, the word *pais* in Greek means "child" but was also frequently used for an enslaved person of any age. This was a strategy to infantilize an enslaved person and also was an ever-present reminder that enslaved persons were not viewed as full humans. Instead, they depended upon the enslaver and, like children, were not counted as men or women.

Gender identity was probably something enslaved people themselves cared about, according to Glazebrook. Denying their gender identity or misidentifying them could be considered part of the degradation of their status. It is clear in literature that enslaved persons were viewed as male and female through the jobs they were often given and through their relationships with their enslavers. While theoretically male and female enslaved persons were not gendered or femininely gendered, in practice there were many differences. One way this is clear is through labor and the jobs for which enslaved persons were trained. On large estates, female enslaved workers were given domestic tasks, such as cooking, cleaning, washing, helping their female

2. See Allison Glazebrook, "Gender and Slavery," in *The Oxford Handbook of Greek and Roman Slaveries*, ed. Stephen Hodkinson, Marc Kleijwegt, and Kostas Vlassopoulos (Oxford: Oxford University Press, 2017), 15.

enslavers, serving the free people in the house, and working with children. They were often wet nurses and nannies, taking care of the young children in the house. Many enslaved women and girls worked as spinners, weavers, seamstresses, or as a personal attendant to a female enslaver.

One way that enslaved women and free women were markedly different was through the presentation and assumption of virtue. Enslaved women were often used as bodies that protected the body of the free woman. For example, an enslaved woman would run errands for her female enslaver, which allowed the free woman to remain protected inside the house. The purity of free women was valued over that of the enslaved woman. For example, the funerary monument in figure 9.1 depicts a free elite woman alongside an enslaved female worker who is holding a jewelry box. In this scene, the enslaved woman is portrayed in order to illustrate the beauty and wealth of her enslaver, enhancing her virtue as well.

On the other hand, male enslaved workers were often assigned manual labor, working in the fields on various agricultural tasks, tending to animals, performing tasks in workshops and on construction projects, or working in the mines. This difficult work was brutal and harmful to the bodies of enslaved men; treated as chattel, enslaved workers who were assigned to these positions also experienced corporeal punishment and violence, such as being placed in shackles and chains. Some male enslaved workers were trusted with managerial roles and specialized tasks in the areas of accounting and business. In the domestic sphere, a male enslaved worker might serve as a manager of the other enslaved workers inside the house.

Figure 9.2. Terracotta drinking cup made by an enslaved worker named Rodo in the workshop of P. Cornelius. Circa 5–40 CE.

At the same time, an enslaved man in a domestic space would often work in multigendered contexts. He might also work as the doorkeeper, although enslaved women could serve this role as well (see Rhoda in Acts 12:12; see also chapter 11, "Literary Constructions and Stereotypes of Slavery"). Specialized work that involved training was usually reserved for male enslaved workers. Paul's scribe for his letter to Rome, Tertius of Iconium, for example, is male (Rom 16:22). There are examples of male enslaved workers who served as the teachers and escorts for the free children in the household (as *paedagogi*). Some enslaved women were trained as scribes and managers alongside men, but a majority of the prestigious positions reserved for enslaved workers were given to men.[3]

Geographical location might also affect the jobs and roles that an enslaved person was given. On a rural estate that may have had a small number of enslaved workers in the household, both men and women worked together in labor, especially in agricultural settings. Male and female enslaved workers might also work together in the kitchen to get a large meal ready for a gathering; during harvest time, all enslaved workers would be in the fields. In some households, it was necessary even for the free people in the house to work in the fields, or households employed day laborers to help as well (free people who were paid a small wage for working in the field). Thus, the social status of the enslaver's family also had an effect on the jobs of enslaved persons.

Enslaved Female Characters

In the New Testament, there are a few clearly identified enslaved female characters, including the questioner of Peter, mentioned above; Rhoda (Acts 12); and the enslaved fortune teller (Acts 16). Paul uses the figure of Hagar (Gal 4) as a metaphorical example in his letter to the Galatians. Paul also names a few other women who could be enslaved, such as Euodia and Syntyche (Phil 4:2–3). Junia, an apostle who is named by Paul in Romans 16:7, could also be enslaved or have been previously enslaved.[4] Chloe, named in 1 Corinthians 1:10, is also a woman who could have been a manumitted enslaved woman who is now an enslaver, as Mitzi Smith has recently argued.[5] Additionally, several parables include "male and female slaves," which indicates that the scenarios should be pictured as including enslaved men and women. Moreover, some women are described using words that suggest enslavement, such as Mary, in Luke 2 (see chapter 10, "Metaphors of Enslavement"), and the "whore" (or the enslaved sex laborer) of Babylon, whom I discuss below.

3. See Candida Moss, *God's Ghostwriters: Enslaved Christians and the Making of the Bible* (New York: Little, Brown, 2024).

4. This is an argument made by Bernadette Brooten, personal correspondence, March 2024.

5. Mitzi J. Smith, *Chloe and Her People: A Womanist Critical Dialogue with First Corinthians* (Eugene, OR: Cascade Books, 2023).

While this is a very short list, reading against the grain allows numerous other enslaved women to emerge from between the lines in the New Testament. For example, as mentioned above, enslaved women were often in charge of domestic tasks such as cooking, cleaning, and preparing for guests. When we read about the Last Supper, then, we should imagine that enslaved women prepared the meal that the disciples ate.[6] Maybe they were even present during the meal, waiting by the table to refill wine glasses, take away empty dishes, and bring out more food when necessary. When Paul visits a house in Acts or as mentioned in his letters, we can imagine that an enslaved woman greeted him and offered him something to drink upon arrival. When Jesus goes into a house to heal someone (i.e., the paralyzed man in Capernaum in Matt 9:1–8; Mark 2:1–12; and Luke 5:17–26), he likely encountered an enslaved woman, who was perhaps inside watching the children while she prepared a meal. Ultimately, enslaved women can be found everywhere within the biblical text if one knows where to look.

Relationships with Enslavers

Another way that gender surfaces in relation to enslavement is through the precarious relationships that enslaved persons had with their enslavers. Enslaved women could work as personal attendants for their enslaver, which meant being in close proximity to their enslavers at all times. These enslaved women would help with dressing, bathing, hairstyle, errands, and any other tasks needed on a daily basis. Ancient literature even depicts these relationships between female enslavers and their enslaved female attendants as intimate at times. These texts suggest that the female enslaver would trust her enslaved attendant with her innermost thoughts and secrets. While some of these relationships were depicted in the text and artwork as kind, we should read these with suspicion, as they were mostly written and described by free male writers and so are told through the lens of the enslaver.[7] How might a trusted female attendant have felt in this type of situation? Likely, she would have recognized the precarity of the relationship and known that one mistake could mean physical punishment or other repercussions. While the female

---

6. Christy Cobb, "Preparing and Sharing the Table: The Invisibility of Women and Enslaved Domestic Workers in Luke's Last Supper," *Review and Expositor* 117 (2020): 555–59.

7. Bernadette Brooten, "Early Christian Enslaved Families (First to Fourth Century)," in *Children and Family in Late Antiquity: Life, Death and Interaction*, ed. Christian Laes, Katarina Mustakallio, and Ville Vuolanto (Leuven: Peeters, 2015), 111–34.

enslaver might have trusted her attendant, the enslaved worker would have likely not been able to return that trust or intimacy, due to the hierarchical nature of their relationship.

One example of this close relationship is found in the Acts of Thomas, an early Christian apocryphal narrative that features Thomas, one of Jesus's disciples. In this text, a woman named Mygdonia is a wealthy woman who converts to Christianity. When she does so, her husband, Carish, is extremely upset, especially when Mygdonia tells him that she has decided to be celibate as a part of her religious commitment to Christianity. One night, things get heated between the married couple, and Mygdonia leaves their bedroom, naked, and goes to the room of her enslaved worker, Marcia, who is called a "nurse" in the narrative. As a nurse, Marcia could have raised Mygdonia and taken care of her as a young child, possibly even breastfeeding her and functioning as a maternal presence for her. In this moment of fear and anger, Mygdonia chooses to find solace in Marcia, and the text indicates that Mygdonia slept in her bed that night (Acts of Thomas 98:6).

These female–female relationships are depicted as intimate, trusting, and even familial in our ancient texts. Historical relationships between enslavers and enslaved workers might have included some of these aspects. Yet, one should also be cautious when reading descriptions of these relationships because of the power imbalance always present between an enslaver and an enslaved worker. A term for the hierarchy present in this relationship between a woman and another woman is *kyriarchy*. This word, coined by Elisabeth Schüssler Fiorenza, is reminiscent of the word "patriarchy" except that it is formed from the Greek word *kyrios*, which means "enslaver" or "lord." Thus, it exposes the multiple layers of power that are present within systems of slavery.[8] Kyriarchy describes the many factors inherent in relationships of domination, including class, race, and ethnicity. In the above example, Mygdonia and Marcia are depicted as intimately connected. This might have been true for some historical relationships between women, both enslaved and free. Yet also the ever-present power differential of slavery always casts a shadow onto these close relationships and reveals the kyriarchy within them.

Similarly, ancient literature depicts intimate relationships that develop between male enslavers and their female enslaved workers. Occasionally, a male

---

8. For a more in-depth discussion of the term, see Elisabeth Schüssler Fiorenza, *Wisdom Ways: Introducing Feminist Biblical Interpretation* (Maryknoll, NY: Orbis, 2001), 108–9, 118–24; and Elisabeth Schüssler Fiorenza, *But She Said: Feminist Practices of Biblical Interpretation* (Boston: Beacon, 1992), 115–17, 122–25.

enslaver would choose to free (or manumit) his enslaved worker in order to marry her. We find evidence of these relationships on ancient funerary monuments and within manumission records where the previously enslaved wife is depicted alongside the free husband (see chapter 3, "Enslavement in the Roman World," and chapter 6, "Manumission"). Some of these relationships might also have developed in authentic ways, yet I caution readers to remember the kyriarchy present in these descriptions too. If the relationship started (as most did) while the woman was still enslaved, she might not have had autonomy in her part of the relationship. Further, the offer of freedom might have been tempting for the enslaved woman, so it is difficult

Figure 9.3. Funerary monument depicting a seated elite woman, Sbardia, and an enslaved female attendant holding a fan. Circa 50 BCE.

to know whether she wanted to marry her enslaver or whether she simply desired freedom. The opening example in chapter 3 on Roman enslavement provides an example of a relationship between a male enslaver and his manumitted wife that exposes the possible problems in this type of marriage.

Sexual Violence

An additional aspect of an enslaved person's life was the possibility of sexual violence. Both female and male enslaved bodies were susceptible to sexual harassment and violence; we can assume that both male and female enslaved persons were raped by their enslavers and by other free people as well. Female enslaved workers were often forced into sex with their male enslavers in the hopes that they would get pregnant and then produce more slaves for their enslavers. In this way, female enslaved bodies were even more susceptible to sexual violence and exploitation. Children of enslaved mothers in antiquity were born enslaved. This use of enslaved women resulted in a larger population of enslaved persons. "House-born" enslaved persons were often depicted as more valuable in the economics of a slave society.

Enslaved female bodies, even those of young girls, were used for pregnancy and also for nursing children in the household. After an enslaved woman was able to produce milk, her body was able to be used, continuously, for feeding both her own children and the free children in the house. Thus, an enslaved woman's body was useful for enslavers in a number of ways: sexually, for producing new slaves, and even as a source of food. We can imagine that Peter's questioner has already experienced this difficult part of the life of an enslaved woman. She might also be young; the Greek word *paidiskē* can also mean "child." Perhaps, even as a young girl, she knows that this is a part of her life that she will have to endure.

Ultimately, in the New Testament we do not find a direct condemnation of the sexual use of enslaved persons by free persons. Thus, when we read a passage about an enslaved person, we should consider the possibility that this person could have been sexually exploited or raped by a free person—maybe even their own enslaver. For one example of the clear sexual exploitation of an enslaved woman, we turn to an early Christian text from the second or third century CE, the Acts of Andrew. In this narrative, the free elite Christian woman—Maximilla—decides that she wants to stop having sex with her husband (Aegeates) as a result of her conversion to Christianity. She forces her enslaved worker, Euclia, to have sex with him instead, ultimately coordinating the continued rape of her enslaved worker.[9] Following Maximilla's orders, Euclia masquerades as the free woman and has sex with Aegeates for eight months before the charade is discovered. When Aegeates finds out what has been happening—that he was sleeping with the enslaved Euclia and not his wife—he tortures and mutilates Euclia and leaves her body outside to die (Acts of Andrew 16–22).

As Bernadette Brooten observes: "Slavery and freedom are both deeply embedded within the Acts of Andrew and yet are also invisible—hidden in plain sight."[10] Maximilla, who is free, is able to protect her purity and gender identity

---

9. Christy Cobb, "Euclia's Story: Coordinated Sexual Assault, Violence, and Willfulness in the *Acts of Andrew*," in *Sex, Violence, and Early Christian Texts*, ed. Christy Cobb and Eric Vanden Eykel (Lanham, MD: Lexington Books, 2022), 37–52.

10. Bernadette J. Brooten, "Gender and Slavery in the Acts of Andrew," in *Ancient Chris-

through the sexual use of Euclia, who is enslaved. The two women appear interchangeable within the text. Euclia dresses up as her enslaver and apparently even fools Maximilla's own husband, Aegeates. This illustrates the slippery nature of enslavement and freedom in the world of antiquity. Yet, the enslaved woman is the only person in this scenario who is brutally punished for the charade; she is tortured and killed by Aegeates for her part in the deception. Maximilla remains unharmed; her body is not sexually violated. She is, ultimately, the ideal pure Christian woman. As Bernadette Brooten argues in her analysis of this scene: "The Acts of Andrew, which enjoyed widespread circulation over a broad geographical region for centuries, surely inspired women to follow their vision of the ascetic holy life. That vision may have even included using enslaved women as sexual surrogates."[11] The story of Mygdonia and Marcia, mentioned above in the Acts of Thomas, functions in similar ways. Mygdonia runs to Marcia's room in order to protect her free body from sex. These stories from early Christianity illustrate the ways in which enslaved persons were gendered and sexualized and solidify the argument made above that the New Testament does not offer a clear condemnation of the sexual use of enslaved persons.

Prostitution

While the sexual availability of enslaved persons was a given to their enslavers, some also worked as sex laborers. In both Greek and Roman culture, sex laborers (prostitutes) were assumed to be enslaved. This aspect of slavery intricately connects to the sexual availability of enslaved persons; the enslaved body, male or female, was available for sex without question. Sex laborers in the Greco-Roman world could be male or female, but a majority were women. In major cities, sex laborers could be found in brothels, but in smaller towns and regions they might work in a tavern or an inn. Ancient literature depicts these spaces as dark and filthy, yet recent work on the archaeological remains of the brothel at Pompeii by the classicist Sarah Levin-Richardson has challenged that view. While some brothels might have been dreary, others, such as the one in Pompeii, might have been lively. Within them, sex laborers found ways to subtly resist their situation and status, talking with one another and sharing information about clients.[12]

---

tian Apocrypha: Marginalized Texts in Early Christianity, ed. Outi Lehtipuu and Silke Petersen (Atlanta: SBL Press, 2022), 165–86, here 166.

11. Brooten, "Gender and Slavery," 185–86.

12. Sarah Levin-Richardson, *The Brothel of Pompeii: Sex, Class, and Gender at the Margins of Roman Society* (Cambridge: Cambridge University Press, 2019).

Figure 9.4. Fresco of an erotic scene from the purpose-built brothel in Pompeii, Italy.

Figure 9.5. A stone bed used by a sex laborer from the purpose-built brothel in Pompeii, Italy.

The Greek word *pornē* (plural: *pornai*) can refer to a person who works in a brothel or to an enslaved sex laborer. This term "sex laborer" is a replacement for the term "prostitute," which has developed negative connotations tied only to the laborers themselves.[13] The alternate modern term "sex worker" assumes chosen agency in this vocation. In antiquity, most sex laborers were able to choose this vocation; some free women did participate in the world of exchanging sex for money. Thus, "sex laborer" as a label is an attempt to remove the moral judgment on prostitution while recognizing that many ancient people in this line of work did not choose it.

Paul, in particular, has much to say about prostitution in his first letter to the Corinthians. In 1 Corinthians 6:9, for example, Paul lists "sex laborers" (*pornoi*; masculine plural) among others who he deems "sexually immoral." This word could indicate male sex laborers but also could indicate men who purchase the services of a sex laborer (regardless of the sex/gender of the laborer). Paul is clear about his thoughts on this: "None of these will inherit the kingdom of God" (1 Cor 6:10). A few verses later, Paul more clearly condemns those who purchase sex with a sex laborer when he writes: "Do you not know that whoever is united to a prostitute (*pornē*) becomes one body with her for it is said, 'The two shall be one flesh'" (1 Cor 6:16). This section (1 Cor 6:12–20) has been interpreted broadly to condemn all types of so-called deviant sex, yet the language of slavery within it has been flagged less often. To be clear, when Paul notes that those who have sex with a *pornē* are then united with her body, this indicates that the client, who is assumed to be free, would then also be metaphorically enslaved.

On the other hand, Matthew 21:31–32 indicates that sex laborers (*pornai*; feminine plural) hold a higher status than Jesus's interlocutors. In this section of Matthew, Jesus has just told his followers a parable about two sons (Matt 21:28–32) who the father tells to go and work in the vineyard. The first one says he will not go but then goes to work anyway; the second son says that he will go and work but then does not. After telling this parable, Jesus asks: "Which of the two did the will of his father?" (Matt 21:31). The disciples answer that it is the first son. Then Jesus responds by saying that "tax collectors and sex laborers are going into the kingdom of God ahead of you" (Matt 21:32). There are various ways to interpret this passage, but for the sake of this chapter note that Jesus is using these sex laborers (*pornai*) as an example of an immoral

---

13. Serena Witzke, "Harlots, Tarts, and Hussies? A Problem of Terminology for Sex Labor in Roman Comedy," *Helios* 42 (2015): 7–27; Allison Glazebrook, *Sexual Labor in the Athenian Courts* (Austin: University of Texas Press, 2021).

person (like the tax collector) who has chosen to believe in him. However, he is then depicting sex laborers as better than the disciples. What is not clear in the translation of this verse is whether "sex laborers" indicate enslaved persons or those who are forced into the work of prostitution.

Paul certainly condemns *porneia*, a word often translated as "sexual immorality" and that indicates sexual acts that were deemed unacceptable. However, as Jennifer Glancy has pointed out, this word and its implied morality might not have included a person having sex with their enslaved workers (whether male or female).[14] Glancy suggests that Paul might have even approved of a person using an enslaved person for sex in order to avoid sexual immorality. In 1 Thessalonians 4:3–5, Paul writes: "For this is the will of God, your sanctification: that you should abstain from sexual immorality (*porneia*); that each one of you know how to control your own body (*skeuos*) in holiness and honor, not with lustful passion like the gentiles who do not know God." In this passage, the word translated as "body" (*skeuos*) is also occasionally translated as "vessel" (*skeuos*). Some scholars suggest that here Paul means that male readers should "control their own wife." However, Glancy notes that *skeuos* would "not be a flattering term to apply to a wife."[15] For this reason, Glancy argues that *skeuos* should be translated instead as "utensil" or "object" instead. It is used throughout Greco-Roman literature to refer to enslaved persons and in some cases even implies chattel slavery.[16] If Glancy is correct in her interpretation of this verse, Paul is suggesting that his readers use enslaved persons as a way to avoid sexual immorality by having sex with them.

For one final possible example of an enslaved sex laborer, we turn to the book of Revelation. In Revelation 17–19, a character who represents an oppressive city (likely Rome) is called "Babylon" and is referred to as the "great whore." This word in the Greek is *pornē*, and it clearly implies a sex laborer (Rev 17:1, 5, 15–16; 19:2). While it is not clear in the translations of this passage, historically this *pornē* would have likely been assumed to be enslaved and possibly also connected to a brothel. This passage is also used as a metaphor for the city of Rome (see chapter 10, "Metaphors of Enslavement"). The identification of Rome with a sex laborer deeply insults Rome and its empire, even as that identification depends on the sex laborer's own degraded reputation. In Revelation 17:5, the writer notes that the name "Babylon, the great, mother

14. Jennifer A. Glancy, "The Sexual Use of Slaves: A Response to Kyle Harper on Jewish and Christian Porneia," *Journal of Biblical Literature* 134 (2015): 215–29, here 215.

15. Jennifer A. Glancy, "Slavery and Sexual Availability," in *The Oxford Handbook of New Testament, Gender, and Sexuality*, ed. Benjamin H. Dunning (Oxford: Oxford University Press, 2019), 627–44.

16. Glancy, "Slavery and Sexual Availability."

of sex laborers and of earth's abominations" was inscribed on her forehead. This could be referring to the ancient practice of tattooing an enslaved person's forehead, an action that was forced upon some enslaved persons in antiquity. Tattoos, especially when placed on the forehead, were a way of marking an enslaver's possession. This adds to the violence done to an enslaved person, here representing a female enslaved sex laborer.

Utilizing a postcolonial womanist interpretive lens, Shanell Smith suggests that, even though the author of Revelation depicts this enslaved woman in negative ways, using strategies such as a hermeneutic of suspicion or reading through the lens of kyriarchy can illuminate alternative readings. Focusing on the experiences of African American women, Smith reveals the "beautiful complexity" of the woman of Babylon.[17] Thus, Smith sees both the invective hurled when calling this character "the whore of Babylon" and the vulnerability of the character as an enslaved *pornē*.

Conclusion

Enslavement for women and girls was extra complicated, whether represented in the New Testament, living in the Roman Empire, or being a part of late antique Christian communities. While one might think that free women would be kinder and gentler when it comes to enslaving others, significant evidence tells us otherwise. Women were enslavers, and many of them likely treated their enslaved workers, male or female, harshly. Further, as we read with a hermeneutic of suspicion as well as with a focus on kyriarchy present in the text, it becomes clear that enslaved women were susceptible to violence—both bodily and sexual—and that women who were both Christian and enslavers actively participated in this violence.

Ideologies of gender, sexuality, and violence against enslaved persons continued into the period that saw the formation of early Christian communities. When returning to the stories in the New Testament, such as that of the enslaved female worker who questioned Peter, this treatment of enslaved persons can be read back into the text. Kyriarchal structures are ever present within our biblical stories; gendered and sexual violence can be found there too, although it is not always obvious within traditional translations and/or traditional interpretations. Ultimately, attention to issues of gender and sexuality is vital to an understanding of the contexts of slavery that help us interpret the New Testament. These ideologies did not disappear after the solidification

---

17. See Shanell T. Smith, *Woman Babylon and the Marks of Empire: Reading Revelation with a Postcolonial Womanist Hermeneutics of Ambiveilence* (Minneapolis: Fortress, 2014).

of Christianity. Instead, these views of gender, slavery, and sexuality continue to be pervasive and remain in aspects of Christianity today (see chapter 15, "Modern Slavery, the Bible, and Slow-Down Ethics").

Discussion Questions

1. Return to the story of Peter's denial. After reading this chapter, how can you reimagine the life of the enslaved woman who is the first questioner of Peter?
2. Ideologies of gender, sexuality, and slavery have persisted throughout the history of Christianity and still remain today. How and where do you see these ideologies functioning in your own communities?
3. Consider the argument that Paul—in 1 Thessalonians 4:3–5—was suggesting that his readers avoid sexual immorality through the sexual use of enslaved persons. Take a look at this passage, including the Greek words discussed. Do you agree with this interpretation? Why or why not?

Further Reading

Briggs, Sheila. "Slavery and Gender." Pages 171–92 in *On the Cutting Edge: The Study of Women in Biblical Worlds: Essays in Honor of Elisabeth Schüssler Fiorenza*. Edited by Jane Schaberg, Alice Bach, and Esther Fuchs. New York: Continuum, 2004.

Brooten, Bernadette J. "Gender and Slavery in the Acts of Andrew." Pages 165–86 in *Ancient Christian Apocrypha: Marginalized Texts in Early Christianity*. Edited by Outi Lehtipuu and Silke Petersen. Atlanta: SBL Press, 2022.

Cobb, Christy. *Slavery, Gender, Truth, and Power in Luke-Acts and Other Ancient Narratives*. London: Palgrave Macmillan, 2019.

Glancy, Jennifer A., and Stephen D. Moore. "How Typical a Roman Prostitute Is Revelation's 'Great Whore'?," *Journal of Biblical Literature* 130, no. 3 (2011): 551–69.

Glazebrook, Allison. "Gender and Slavery." Pages 1–23 in *The Oxford Handbook of Greek and Roman Slaveries*. Edited by Stephen Hodkinson, Marc Kleijwegt, and Kostas Vlassopoulos. Oxford: Oxford University Press, 2017.

Smith, Shanell T. *Woman Babylon and the Marks of Empire: Reading Revelation with a Postcolonial Womanist Hermeneutics of Ambiveilence*. Minneapolis: Fortress, 2014.

10   *Metaphors of Enslavement*

MARIANNE BJELLAND KARTZOW

The apostle Paul opens his letter to the Romans by introducing himself as a "slave of Christ Jesus" (Rom 1:1). Although the Greek term he uses is the standard for slave (*doulos*), many translators choose "servant" instead. But readers might wonder: In what way is Paul a slave? What function does the slavery metaphor have in the New Testament? How is the ancient slavery institution influencing the metaphorical usage of slavery in various early Christian texts?

Paul is not the only one who was a "slave," however. In the Gospel of Luke, the evangelist has Mary calling herself a slave (*doulē*) of the Lord, twice (Luke 1:38, 48). Once again, readers might wonder: What difference does it make when a woman employs the slavery metaphor? Or when a slave is called a slave of God? These examples suggest that metaphorical slavery is as diverse as real slavery. It is not merely God or Christ Jesus under whom the early Christians could be enslaved. It is possible also to be slaves under sin, death, or other powers (John 8:34; Rom 6:12; Tit 3:3; 2 Pet 2:19). We need to study each text in detail to be able to identify how metaphorical usages of slavery relate to slavery as an overall institution.

In this chapter, we will look at the slavery metaphor from many different perspectives. With examples from both the Pauline letters and the Gospels, it becomes clear the potential meanings of this metaphor have huge consequences for meaning-making. It matters who employs the metaphor. It matters what context it is used in. It is not always clear what the metaphor means, since metaphors, like other types of figurative speech, add specialized dimensions to plain speech. We, as readers or hearers, need to fill in, imagine, or connotate in certain directions. We do this with the help of clues in the literary and cultural context. But still, it is up to the interpreter to determine what a metaphor means—that is, we do not get a clear message from the word *doulos* itself. Should the metaphor mean "servant" or "slave"? What about the context indicates a metaphorical slave?

Slavery Metaphors in the New Testament and Other First-Century Sources

Many interpreters of the New Testament have tried to understand the background and purpose of the slavery metaphor. Slaves are used figuratively in the sayings and parables of Jesus,[1] and in Jewish literature and documents from the first century CE, slavery holds symbolic significance. Within these sources (which include the New Testament), four uses of slavery metaphors emerge: the religious, the psychological, the social, and the political usage, highlighting the many different functions of the metaphor.[2]

The slavery metaphor appears in the Pauline letters with some frequency as well. Yet, slavery metaphors, because of the nature of metaphors more generally, have multiple meanings depending on the perspective one takes toward the text.[3] Some readers have been primarily concerned with the origin of the Pauline metaphor. Others focus on how members of first-century Pauline communities would have understood Paul's "slave of Christ" metaphor.[4] For example, enslaved members of the Christ communities in Rome may have understood Paul's "slave of Christ" metaphor as a prophetic identification with their subjugated positions within the Roman Empire.[5]

Imagining the Reality of Enslavement

It is obvious that slave imagery plays an important role in early Christian discourse. To understand how such images function, we have to move beyond the "either-metaphor-or-social-reality" distinction. Within the socio-

1. Jennifer A. Glancy, *Slavery in Early Christianity*, 2nd ed. (Minneapolis: Fortress, 2024), 151–92.

2. See also Catherine Hezser, *Jewish Slavery in Antiquity* (Oxford: Oxford University, 2005), 324–79.

3. See John Byron, *Recent Research on Paul and Slavery* (Sheffield, UK: Phoenix, 2008).

4. See Marianne Bjelland Kartzow, *The Slave Metaphor and Gendered Enslavement in Early Christian Discourse: Double Trouble Embodied* (New York: Routledge, 2018).

5. See Byron, *Recent Research on Paul and Slavery*.

economic, cultural, gendered, and embodied context of the first centuries, various authors use slavery as a metaphor to describe relationships between God, Christ, and the believers or other powers. These metaphors, indeed, pose some ethical challenges when slavery is the referent for metaphorical theological reasoning—especially when inhumane structures remain unchallenged. Elizabeth Castelli shows this in her discussion of slavery in Pauline letters: "The use of social relations to make a theological point is successful to the degree that the metaphor reinscribes the social relation, rather than calling it into question."[6]

In relation to slavery in early Christian texts, the complex tension between metaphor and social reality is undertheorized. A metaphor can be so much more than an innocent figure of thought or speech, since it involves bodies, relationships, life stories, and memory in complex ways. Over the last ten years or so, researchers, activists, and human rights organizations have started to talk about slavery and legacies of enslavement as huge challenges with worldwide consequences (see chapter 15, "Modern Slavery, the Bible, and Slow-Down Ethics"). This new awareness invites historians and religious scholars to direct their attention to the ideological roots and ramifications of slavery. Slavery is an ancient institution—older than the Bible—with parallels in later cultures and on different continents. New ways of practicing and conceptualizing slavery build on old ways. Historically, slavery has been an ongoing process of both recovering past practices and inventing new ones. Biblical texts and other religious texts, with their canonical status in religion and culture, have had both brutal and liberating effects.

New Testament texts present slaves as characters in a multitude of genres, such as in the Gospels, the letters, or in the Acts of the Apostles. Slavery appears as a stock motif in the parables of Jesus (e.g., Matt 18:23–35; 24:45–51; Luke 12:42–48). Early Christian texts mirror the social hierarchy of enslaved and free persons (e.g., Col 3:22–4:1; Eph 6:6–9). Several texts also employ slavery metaphors as a title: "slave of Christ/God/the Lord" (e.g., Luke 1:38; Acts 16:17; Phil 1:1; Gal 1:10; Rom 1:1; Col 1:7; Titus 1:1). Some texts describe the relationship to sin or forces in the world (Gal 4:8–9) as slavery. Still others characterize the new relationship of the gentiles to God (1 Thess 1:9–10; Rom 6:15–23) as slavery. Let us look closer at some important texts in which slavery seems to be employed as a metaphor.

---

6. Elizabeth A. Castelli, "Romans," in *Searching the Scriptures*, vol. 2: *A Feminist Commentary*, ed. Elisabeth Schüssler Fiorenza (New York: Crossroad, 1994), 294.

"Don't Let It [Slavery] Trouble You!"

In one of his letters, the apostle Paul writes: "Were you a slave when you were called? Don't let it trouble you—although if you can gain your freedom, do so. For the one who was a slave when called to faith in the Lord is the Lord's freed person; similarly, the one who was free when called is Christ's slave" (1 Cor 7:21–22). In what way is real slavery imagined or reinscribed when slavery is used as a metaphor, as in this passage?

For a free person, to be called "Christ's slave" was an honor and normally did not affect his or her physical body, social status, or life conditions. Paul tells his fellow readers who were slaves when they were called to be part of the community not to worry anymore, since they are freed persons in the Lord. He replaces social reality with metaphor in a way that did not necessarily work in real life for real persons. Of course, real slavery could mean trouble for a "slave of the Lord."

Many studies have suggested that this Corinthian passage erases any concerns about a slave's real status, since what *really* counts is that they are all enslaved to Christ. All are now equal, since all are now slaves (of God). They are "the Lord's freedpersons," regardless of their social position. To this Pauline passage and this mainstream interpretation, we must ask: For whom and in what possible way was slave status "unimportant"? How did real slaves with real bodies understand this passage? How did real slaves feel about the fact that theological ideas were mixed up with slavery in metaphorical language? The paradox of slavery for "slaves of the Lord" who also were in fact enslaved could mean *double trouble*.[7]

Metaphors and Meaning-Making

Despite the fact that they lived in an environment where slavery was pervasive, most of the early Christian authors were never themselves enslaved, even as many of them call themselves "slaves of God" or "slaves of sin or lust" (see chapter 5, "Jews and Slavery"). When we read the texts they produced, we cannot look for the meaning of their metaphors solely in their language, argumentative figures, and theology. Slavery was not merely a thought figure, it was everyday reality for millions of men and women, children, and adults. Slaves embodied such texts, and they were part of these communities. They were among the first hearers/readers of these texts. How did their presence

7. See Kartzow, *Slave Metaphor*.

Figure 10.1. A funerary monument that depicts a young couple who were possibly prosperous freedpersons. Circa 13 BCE–5 CE.

influence the use and potential meaning of the slavery metaphor? How did
they conceptualize the slavery metaphor?

We do not know the answer to these questions. Metaphor theory suggests
that, in order to understand how metaphors function in a communication
process, we have to look at the interaction between body and culture and at
the life stories and shared cultural knowledge central to when people conceptualized metaphors.[8] Although slaves do not figure prominently in the sources,
they did of course also conceptualize metaphors.

We can read early Christian texts as representing part of a privileged discourse. Although some authors think of freedom or slavery as inner states, the
metaphor they choose to employ—that of slavery—takes its meaning from the
social environment in which physical bodies and human relationships were
determined by slavery structures.

Of course, slaves could be well cared for by their enslavers, and did sometimes
gain some sort of status and influence. Still, slavery was central to the politics, law,
and economy of the time. Slaves were owned bodies, available bodies, surrogate

8. For more on metaphors generally, see George Lakoff and Mark Johnson, *Metaphors
We Live By* (Chicago: University of Chicago Press, 1980).

bodies. Enslaved persons had to follow orders that made them sexually available—even for reproduction. They could be sold, hired, inherited, or shared. They had to obey, be silent, and do what the enslaver said. How could this brutal reality feed the seemingly harmless metaphor used so often in early Christian discourse? What does it mean that God is the enslaver in a metaphor that ties believers to such a brutal reality? If the enslaver had complete power over a slave's body, soul, and spirit, it would be hard to follow Paul's advice of "not being troubled."

The "Slavery" of Mary: Gender Matters

The Roman institution of slavery had specific implications for gender. Since slave bodies were sexually available property to their owners for their pleasure, for sale, or for reproductive purposes, enslaved women lived a different experience of slavery. In early Christian texts, several female characters are connected to slavery in metaphor and in social reality. How did gender potentially intersect with slavery in early Christian metaphors?

The story of Mary in Luke 1 demonstrates how complex slavery metaphors are in relation to gender and helps us see the interwoven nature of metaphors in Paul, Luke, and Genesis. In the scene where Mary is approached by God's angel to announce her pregnancy, she is called a slave (Luke 1:28). In the parallel story with Elizabeth, who also becomes pregnant in mysterious ways, and also delivers an important son, Elizabeth is never called a slave. Furthermore, the slavery metaphor used on Mary holds very different connotations from the one used on Simeon later in Luke 2:29. When Jesus is presented by his parents in the temple at eight days old, a righteous man called Simeon, who was looking forward to the consolation of Israel, calls God his master and himself a slave (Luke 2:29). He is a slave in different ways than Mary. We see this clearly when paying attention to gender.

The story of the Virgin Mary's pregnancy involves a dialogue between her and the angel of God, Gabriel, for the purpose of announcing that Mary will give birth to the son of God. In Luke 1:38, Mary's response to the angel's requesting her to accept this task has a standardized translation: "I am the *servant* (*doulē*) of God. Let it be with me according to your word." When as a pregnant woman she visits her relative Elizabeth, she sings a song with strong theological content (often called the Magnificat) about a God who protects the smallest and poorest among the people. This God has shown mercy toward her, so she offers her obedience to the Lord by calling herself "his slave" (*tēs doulēs autou*) in Luke 1:48. Both in her reply to the angel and in her song, Mary describes herself as enslaved.

In complex ways, Mary embodies the metaphor. She—and not her relative Elizabeth—is the slave of the Lord. Her young age, unmarried status, and reproductive capacity enable Mary to be a slave-like character, in contrast to the other pregnant woman, who as an older married and childless woman had different access to protection for her body, her reputation, and her integrity. Mary, however, lacks such protection and is far more vulnerable than Elizabeth. These two mothers-to-be are very different women in several ways, one resembling a female slave more than the other.

Mary the "slave" is also very different from Simeon the "slave" (Luke 2:29). As a prophet, Simeon receives Jesus as a baby in the temple. Simeon never offers his reproductive capital in service to his enslaver. He is old and has waited for salvation for a long time. A male slave's reproductivity was not so much of an issue. It was women whose value was based primarily on their body and their reproductive capabilities, due to men and women's different roles in childbearing. *Gender matters here.* Since metaphors always use reality to make sense, it is obvious that a metaphor employed on such very different characters as Mary and Simeon would mean very different things.

If a young woman is told to give birth to her enslaver's son and calls herself a slave of God, then she has less in common with Simeon and much more in common with other female slaves of the Jewish tradition. Narratives from the Hebrew Bible are essential if we are to understand New Testament conceptualizations of the slavery metaphor. But which stories are most relevant? The history of Israel recounts the stories of several prominent women who suffered from perhaps the greatest stigma and sign of disability of their time: they could not produce sons for their husbands. These women needed help from others to be socially and culturally accepted, to fulfill their gendered roles, and to be saved from social isolation and trauma. In a slave society, enslavers not only controlled the time and the working capacity of their slaves, they also owned their sexual and reproductive bodies. Enslaved mothers could give them sons or increase their property by childbirth.

The story of Abram and Sarai is probably the most well-known. The couple was old and had no sons to fulfill God's covenant promising them ample descendants. The solution lay in the slave girl Hagar from Egypt, whom Sarai made Abram "go in to," resulting in her pregnancy (Gen 16:4). Hagar was not only vulnerable as an enslaved woman, her Egyptian ethnic/national background also put her in a vulnerable position. However peacefully it started, the story ends with jealousy and conflict between the two women—both before and after Hagar gives birth to her child, Ishmael. After running away in Genesis 16, Hagar meets an angel and is the first one in the Hebrew Bible to give

God a name (Gen 16:13). When Sarai (by now renamed Sarah) herself gives birth to Isaac after divine intervention a few chapters later, Hagar and her son disappear into the wilderness (Gen 21:14–21).

Hagar, however, was not the only woman in the Hebrew Bible who worked as a reproductive slave. Later in Genesis, we hear that Laban gave Leah and Rachel two slave girls for the purpose of reproduction, Bilhah and Zilpah (Gen 29:24, 29). These enslaved women became a solution for Rachel and Leah to have more sons with Jacob and cure the stigma of barrenness. The enslaved mothers and their female enslavers are not unimportant women in the history of Israel. As mothers of patriarchs, Bilhah and Zilpah have different roles than Hagar, whose son Ishmael was born into another line, although the stories about them do have interesting parallels.

Mary did some of the same work as these reproductive female slaves in Genesis, Hagar, Bilhah, and Zilpah. Among them, however, it is only Hagar who is mentioned in the New Testament (Gal 4:21–31). Hagar (and Sarah) are employed as metaphors in a Pauline allegory wherein Paul uses the two mothers to discuss salvation and inclusion and exclusion. Hagar's role and function as slave and mother explains more abstract matters, when Paul argues that we are not like her and her son since we are free and part of the new covenant (Gal 4:22). She stands as a metaphor for outsiders of the other race. Here, Paul's metaphor depends on the social institution of slavery and its gendered and reproductive implications.

Several aspects of Hagar blend together, and her role as a female reproductive slave is used to draw boundaries between insiders and outsiders. In the letter to the Galatians, Paul uses the gendered and reproductive aspects of slavery to draw boundaries. His target is to explain the difference between us and them, and the abstract phenomenon of being under the law is explained by a more concrete phenomenon: the difference between slave-motherhood and wife-motherhood. He needs a thought figure where heritage and offspring play a role. Two versions of women and mothers, Sarah and Hagar as the first wife and the concubine-slave, respectively, function well. Here it is a specific female slave, well-known and named, who functions as a metaphor.

In the case of Mary in Luke 1, it is a male God who needs her reproductive capital. God plays the role of the barren female slave owners and their husbands in Genesis. Like those who for various reasons could not produce sons, God the father also needs help from a female slave to bear a son.

In contrast to Hagar, Zilpah, and Bilhah, however, Mary is approached by an angel before her pregnancy, and she is told exactly what will happen to her. She did not have much of a choice but is at least given some information in advance.

Figure 10.2. Byzantine medallion of the Virgin Mary. Circa 1100.

In contrast, the text reports of Hagar, Zilpah, and Bilhah state: "He went into her" (e.g., Gen 30:3). The power balance is also clear in the case of Mary: when she calls herself a slave, she seems to confirm that she considers the will of her God/master to be absolute. She behaves like a reproductive slave, offering the most valuable aspects of her female body in service to her enslaver.

Mary's words in Luke 1 enable several alternative interpretations, and deciding which interpretation to use is complicated. Perhaps the translation of *doulos* as metaphorical servant reflects the parallel stories of Mary and Elizabeth. In the passage from Luke, the context seems to be motherhood, pregnancy, and firstborn sons. Here Elizabeth and Mary are basically doing the same thing: offering their reproductive bodies to give birth to important sons, whom God needs to bring salvation to the world. Both are good servants of God doing what women in history have always been expected to do: give birth to healthy sons. They are good mothers, like the matriarch, or like all good mothers of the Roman Empire, who also gave birth to the next generation of loyal (male) citizens.

However, Elizabeth and Mary are also two very different women with different life stories and different bodily experiences: one is a married wife, old by age, sexually experienced from living many years with her husband, with a record of being a well-respected woman. Mary does not have all these advantages: she is young, unmarried, vulnerable, and a virgin. The role of wife is not hers yet. She looks more like a slave than Elizabeth does. The older woman is securely a man's wife; Mary is not. In that respect, Mary may resemble the female slaves of the Jewish tradition: she is an owned reproductive body doing what her enslaver asks. Here, Elizabeth resembles the proper matriarch, and Mary the slave girl. In contrast to the story of Sarah and Hagar, there is no rivalry between Elizabeth and Mary, although through this metaphor they may also be seen as one free woman and one enslaved woman.

What if Luke, by virtue of the slavery metaphor, is reinterpreting the Genesis story by constructing Mary's son to be the most important one, the son born of a slave woman? What if the Gospel presents a contrasting echo or a counter-story to the one about Sarah and Hagar, only now it is the son of the slave mother who becomes the most important one, not as patriarch but as Messiah? It is possible that some of the first hearers, including enslaved women among the Christ followers, constructed this meaning out of the story. Mary is the slave, yes, but the son of God could be borne by an enslaved mother. Like Hagar, who talked to an angel and named God, Mary in Luke is also more than a slave, as shown by her powerful song (Luke 1:46–55). This conceptualization clearly contrasts with how Paul retells the Sarah and Hagar story in Galatians, where the enslaved mother and her son are to be cast out (see Gal 4:21–31).

Further, Mary was not only a metaphorical slave, but she was enslaved *in her real body*.[9] To compare Mary the slave of God with Simeon, who holds the same title, presents a whole set of intersecting differences, the most important perhaps being that he is not at all doing a slave's reproductive work. Paul draws a different image of himself as a slave than Luke does with Mary, due to various intersections of gender, body, and culture. A man like Paul could use the slavery metaphor to think with, like a figure of thought or a rhetorical tool. When used by Luke on a young girl like Mary, however, being a woman of reproductive age who is asked to give birth to her master's son, the meta-

---

9. See also Mitzi Smith, "Abolitionist Messiah: A Man Named Jesus Born of a *Doulē*," in *Bitter the Chastening Rod: Africana Biblical Interpretation after* Stony the Road We Trod *in the Age of BLM, SayHerName, and MeToo*, ed. Mitzi J. Smith, Angela N. Parker, and Erica S. Dunbar Hill (Lanham, MD: Lexington Books, 2022), 53–70.

phor is "made real." This "realness" trades on the availability of Mary's meta-phorically enslaved body to do God's work. This contrasts sharply with Paul's self-identification. The fact that Paul uses the slavery metaphor so differently in reference to Hagar makes this contrast all the more important. Thus, we see free male writers use slavery metaphors in starkly gendered ways.

Because slaves were seen as surrogate bodies,[10] the reproductive work done by Mary in this Lukan text may open us up for new readings and receptions. A recent study read the story of Mary with low-caste surrogate mothers in India, coming up with the ambiguous concept of violent love to conceptu-alize Mary's role in this story alongside their own life experiences.[11] Such attempts to make sense of the Bible today and to analyze specific cases of bib-lical reception represent important contributions to the knowledge production connected to this text and to the meaning potential of the slavery metaphor. Mary's "slavery" seems to echo embodied and physical reproductive experi-ences very far from being metaphorical in our global world today.

Conclusion

What is the *double trouble* of the slavery metaphor? For an enslaved person, the slavery metaphor could not be separated from the embodied experience of punishment and forced sexual intercourse. Paul said slavery should not trouble the Corinthians since they were free in Christ Jesus (1 Cor 7:21–22), but for real slaves the slavery metaphor could give them additional trouble by reinforcing the real institution of slavery. We cannot continue categorizing early Christian slavery texts as either dealing with metaphorical or real slavery because the two inevitably intersect and reinforce each other.

"Slave of God," for example, is not an honorable and innocent title. The slavery metaphor is not merely a way of speaking—it is a way of using some people's vulnerable bodies and lives as source material to talk about abstract and concrete realities in God's world. As a paradox, a metaphor is a figure of speech that opens space for alternative meaning-production, misunderstanding, and creativity. To formulate Christian thought in the first centuries, slavery was needed. In many parts of the world today, these texts are considered holy, as part of sacred scriptures, or they form part of the cultural canon. How do we read all the various texts employing slavery metaphors? Should the texts be equipped with trigger warnings? Can we escape the problem by translating "slave" (*dou-*

10. See Glancy, *Slavery in Early Christianity.*
11. See Sharon Jacob, *Reading Mary alongside Indian Surrogate Mothers: Violent Love, Oppressive Liberation, and Infancy Narratives* (New York: Palgrave Macmillan, 2015).

Figure 10.3. A marble relief depicting captured men, collared at the neck, led in pairs. Circa 200 CE.

los) with "servant"? Or can these slavery metaphors offer some useful insights into the current discourse where modern slavery has become a new name for global injustice?

Further, when dealing with the slavery metaphor, gender matters. When Mary, the mother of Jesus, in the Gospel of Luke calls herself a slave of the Lord (Luke 1:38, 48), it has a significantly different meaning than when Paul in his letters uses exactly the same title for himself (see, e.g., Rom 1:1) or when old Simeon in the temple is called a slave of God (Luke 2:29). Mary imitates the behavior of other female slaves by producing a son for her enslaver. She is not only calling herself a slave, but she is acting like a young female slave—a well-known figure from the Hebrew Bible. In contrast, Paul or Simeon never offer their reproductive capital in service of the Lord, even as they both comment on the reproductive products of enslaved women.

However, there are similarities in the way Mary and these male figures are slaves: in the story, her character is given the prominent position of singing a song to foresee the destiny of her child, the son of God. She is a devoted servant of her Lord, like them, in her own way, influenced, among other dimensions, by gender and age. A twist on Mary's metaphorical slavery is to see how she, in particular, resembles the enslaved Hagar in Genesis. They are both reproductive slaves, and they both also interact with and talk to the divine. They overcome slavery and become prominent producers of theological insight. In this way, Luke is using the slavery metaphor very complexly. Mary is a slave, but she is also so much more than a slave.

As a result of Luke's use of this metaphor in this way, enslaved reality is not only reinscribed but also negotiated and transformed. Mary, the slave, is like both a real enslaved woman and a metaphorical slave, but this text also reveals a variety of alternatives on how to conceptualize her role and position. The ambiguity of her character is captured in the metaphor. For ancient hearers, with similar experiences, such as female slaves, this story about Mary may have had a very strong effect. She is the surrogate mother who reveals violent love.

Discussion Questions

1. What ethical dilemmas do "slave of God" or "slave of Christ" metaphors pose for interpreters of the New Testament today? What difference does gender make in how these dilemmas play out?

2. What role do ethnic or economic intersections play in shaping the meanings of enslavement metaphors? Look at Luke 17:7–10; Matt 24:45–51; and/ or Matt 18:21–35 for some examples.

3. How do metaphors of slavery both draw on our knowledge of ancient slavery and construct that knowledge at the same time? You may want to look at the parables in Matthew and Luke that include enslaved characters when answering this question.

Further Reading

Bryant, K. Edwin. *Paul and the Rise of the Slave: Death and Resurrection of the Oppressed in the Epistle to the Romans*. Boston: Brill, 2016.

Byron, John. *Recent Research on Paul and Slavery*. Sheffield, UK: Phoenix, 2008.

Glancy, Jennifer A. *Slavery in Early Christianity*. 2nd ed. Minneapolis: Fortress, 2024.

Harrill, J. Albert. *Slaves in the New Testament: Literary, Social, and Moral Dimensions*. Minneapolis: Fortress, 2006.

Jacob, Sharon. *Reading Mary alongside Indian Surrogate Mothers: Violent Love, Oppressive Liberation, and Infancy Narratives*. New York: Palgrave Macmillan, 2015.

Kartzow, Marianne Bjelland. *The Slave Metaphor and Gendered Enslavement in Early Christian Discourse: Double Trouble Embodied*. New York: Routledge, 2018.

11   *Literary Constructions and Stereotypes of Slavery*

Ancient Greek and Roman slaveholders constructed an image of their slaves as persons inferior to themselves. In their view, servile inferiority was across the board: moral, intellectual, and physical. This denigrating construction was not a true portrait but a conceptual framing of the servile character and behavior that reflected the interests of those who created it. This chapter looks at some important aspects of the construction, including literary stereotypes. The evidence in this chapter for the construction of the slave has been drawn from pagan Greek and Roman sources. The construction that emerges from these sources is nonetheless relevant to understanding the representation of slavery in the New Testament. Christians held slaves. They were acculturated in a society whose elite constructed servile inferiority. Power and privilege shaped the perceptions of Christian and pagan slaveholders alike. Although some Christians reacted against aspects of the denigrating construction of slaves, Christian texts reveal that many perpetuated and promoted it. But first, let us look at some general points about the construction of slaves:

1. The construction did ideological work for the slaveholders, rationalizing slavery as a system and justifying the enslavement of particular people.
2. Greek and Roman slaveholders were also defining themselves through their construction of slaves. The slave was not only their moral inferior but also their moral opposite. The slave was untrustworthy, the free person told the truth. The slave was either a coward or a violent brute, the free man possessed manly courage. The female slave's sexual accessibility contrasted with a free woman's sexual modesty.

3. The denigrating construction of slaves was shaped by the central dynamic of the slaveholder–enslaved person relationship. Slaveholders aimed to dominate their slaves, to use their power to bend slaves to their will. Enslaved persons tried to manage as best they could under domination, either through submission or strategies such as avoidance and resistance. Thus, when an enslaved person submitted after a beating, the slaveholder saw a person who, like a dumb beast, responded to force rather than reason. When the enslaver caught a slave in a lie, he saw a person who was innately dishonest, rather than one who feared the consequences of telling the truth.

4. The tension between slaveholders and enslaved persons was present in both Greek and Roman slavery. For this reason, Greek and Roman enslavers had similar constructions of the slave despite important differences in their practice of slavery. In addition, the denigrating construction of the slave persisted over time, evidenced in texts as early as Homer's *Odyssey* in the 700s BCE and continuing long after the advent and spread of Christianity.

A Person and a Possession

At the heart of Greek and Roman slavery was a contradiction: the enslaved person was both a person and a possession, a thing (see chapter 3, "Enslavement in the Roman World"). Law categorized the slave as a form of property, no less than possessions such as real estate, material objects, and animals. As property, enslaved persons were exceptionally fungible. That is, their owners found many ways to use them. Enslaved persons were sold, resold, inherited, given as gifts, and used as payment for debts—they were made to do all kinds of work. They were employed, for example, as farm workers, artisans, domestic servants, sex workers, clerks, and managers (see chapter 7, "Slave Labor and Trade"). As was the case with other forms of property, enslaved persons were also subject to good or bad treatment. Enslaved persons who, for whatever reason, incurred the slaveholder's displeasure or anger ran the risk of harsh physical punishment, even torture and death, and laws generally offered them scant protection.

Their status as property facilitated the assimilation of enslaved persons to nonhuman property by discounting their possession of intrinsically human qualities such as the ability to reason and engage in moral discernment. In addition, what a person in slavery wanted for herself, a facet of her autonomy as a human being, was irrelevant: the slave was there to enact the will of the master, not her own. The discounting of these human characteristics aligned with the characterization of the slave as a body fit for work, an idea reflected in ordinary language. A common Greek word for slave, *andropodon*, was formed by analogy to *tetrapodon*, that is, a body that was "man-footed," as opposed to four-footed.

With the contradiction between human and possession at its core, the construction of the slave could not be a coherent system of ideas. Slaveholders discounted the humanity of their human property but depended on the human intellect and judgment of their slaves for the system to work. Many enslaved persons worked at jobs that required significant levels of skill, intelligence, and personal responsibility, such as teachers, artisans, doctors, administrators, and business agents. The fourth-century BCE philosopher Aristotle acknowledges the contradiction in categorizing the slave as "a sort of living [literally, 'ensouled'] possession." More precisely, slaves were among the tools required for living the good life (*Politics* 1.1253b). By categorizing slaves as "tools," Aristotle discounts their human possession of an autonomous will. The philosopher would then blunt the contradiction between human and tool in positing the existence of the "slave in nature," that is, a person fit to be used as a tool because his soul is defective, sharing in reason only to the extent he can perceive it, but not possessing it on his own (*Politics* 1.1254b). Aristotle's theory of natural slavery attempts to give philosophical grounding to the social denigration of slaves. While not all ancient slaveholders accepted his hypothesis regarding the natural slave's defective soul, many shared the prejudice that motivated it.

Negative Constructions and Stereotypes

The prejudice that discounted the human moral and intellectual capacities of slaves served to distinguish them from free persons, who were inspired by moral and intellectual ideals. The contrast is illustrated in Aristophanes's Greek comedy *Wealth*, performed in 388 BCE. A character who is a slaveholder enumerates to the character "Wealth" (that is, wealth personified as a god) things that one may have enough of —in contrast to wealth, of which there never can be enough. When the slaveholder notes the possibility of having enough love, his slave, who is present, interjects with the possibility of having enough bread. The contrast is expanded with the slaveholder imagining a sufficiency of things that nourish the soul and his slave imagining a sufficiency of food, that is, things that nourish the body: enough of the arts versus enough snack food; enough honor versus enough cake; enough manliness versus enough figs; enough ambition versus enough barley bread; enough craft in war versus enough lentil soup (*Wealth* 187–193). The humor of the passage was grounded in the audience's recognition of the stereotypical contrast between the idealism of the master and the "pragmatism" of the slave, who is a mere body, able only to think of food.

However, slaves were not only amoral bodies motivated by physical pleasure and pain—they were actively immoral. This aspect of the stereotype is referenced in Plautus's Roman comedy *Amphitruo*, a drama about adultery produced early in the second century BCE. Plautus incorporates a Greek myth into the play. In the myth, Jupiter, the king of the gods, desired a mortal woman, Alcumena, the wife of King Amphitruo. The god assumes the exact physical appearance of Alcumena's husband to sleep with her. In Plautus's treatment of the myth, the god Mercury assists his father, Jupiter, in the deception. As Jupiter has transformed himself into a replica of Amphitruo, so does Mercury become Amphitruo's attendant, a slave named Sosia. Early in the play, while Jupiter, disguised as Amphitruo, is in bed with Alcumena, Mercury (disguised as Sosia) stands on guard outside the palace. The real Sosia comes on stage, sent by the real Amphitruo to announce his master's return. Mercury announces that he will drive off Sosia, the real slave, by acting like a real slave himself:

> Since I have taken on the appearance and the slave status of this man, it is fitting that I also take on his behavior and character. Therefore, I must be bad, clever, and sly and drive him off with his own weapon of wickedness. (Plautus, *Amphitruo* 266–299)

The god's self-conscious reflection on the character of slaves appeals to the prejudice of the slaveholders in the audience, for whom slaves were not only wicked (cf. Lat. *malitia*), but also cunning (*callidus*). The clever slave (*servus callidus*), a slave who uses his wit to trick his master, was a familiar literary stereotype, and Plautus's audience would have been amused by the incongruity of a god taking on this role.

A female version of the clever slave stereotype appears in Chariton's first-century CE Greek novel *Chaereas and Callirhoe*. Callirhoe, the noble-born heroine, has been enslaved after a series of melodramatic accidents. Like all heroines in Greek novels, she is incredibly beautiful. Dionysius, the man who bought her, will not rape Callirhoe, although he could as her enslaver. Instead, he employs one of his house-slaves, Plangon, to persuade the heroine to become his lover, promising Plangon her freedom if she is successful (see chapter 9, "Gender and Sexuality"). With freedom as her reward, Plangon eventually does succeed, but through calculated manipulation of the resourceless and cornered heroine. At a key moment in the process, the author comments:

Figure 11.1. Terracotta relief depicting a well-known ancient comedic scene that features an enslaved man taking refuge on an altar to avoid his enslaver's punishment. First century BCE–first century CE.

> Because she was a well-born young woman with no experience of the wickedness of slaves, Callirhoe had no suspicions regarding Plangon and her advice. (Chariton, *Chaereas and Callirhoe* 2.10.7)

In this aside, Chariton references both the clever slave stereotype and the construction of a moral contrast between slave and free.

Some slaves were assumed to be untrustworthy just as they were viewed as clever. The assumption of untrustworthiness helped enslavers explain a range of perceived servile behaviors: why their slaves were disobedient; why they lied or stole; why they ran away; why they were negligent in their work or shirked work altogether; and why, it seemed, slaves would try to get away with whatever they could. A passage from Columella's *On Agriculture* notes many behaviors associated with servile untrustworthiness. Columella lived in the first century CE. His *On Agriculture* is both an agricultural manual and a management handbook advising farm owners not only on agricultural production, for example, the cultivation and care of crops and livestock, but also on matters related to

Figure 11.2. Scene from a Roman mosaic in Algeria depicting possibly enslaved agriculture workers. First–second century CE.

those who did the work. One of the labor models familiar to Columella was one in which an estate owner entrusted the running of an estate to a manager, himself an enslaved person, who supervised a crew of his fellow slaves. As a rule, the enslaver would not be present but would inspect the estate to make sure the operation was being run properly. Columella advises the owner to avoid the slave-based labor model for a remote farm he cannot visit regularly, because

> slaves cause such farms a great deal of damage. They rent out the oxen and they do not feed them and the other animals well. They do not plow the fields properly. Their records overstate the amount of seed sown. Nor do they care for that which they have planted in the ground, so that it grows properly. And what they bring in for threshing they diminish by dishonesty or negligence. For either they themselves steal the grain or they do not keep it safe from other thieves. And they do not enter what is stored away in trustworthy accounts. (*On Agriculture* 1.7)

Columella describes here behaviors that involve various forms of lying, stealing, and negligence as typical of improperly supervised slaves and attributes these behaviors to the characteristic untrustworthiness of slaves. At the same time, depictions of hard-working enslaved workers often contrast sharply with this stereotype of negligent enslaved farm workers (see figure 11.2).

Roman legal experts were also concerned about servile untrustworthiness and negligence. Their concerns are preserved in the *Digest*, a compendium of Roman judicial opinions assembled in the 530s CE under the direction of the emperor Justinian. The first section of *Digest* 21 focuses on the rules regulating commercial transactions. Each year, an incoming official, the *curule aedile*, a magistrate in charge of markets, published these rules in the Edict of the Curule Aedile. Successive edicts repeated, with emendations and refinements, previous edicts. Through the edict, each magistrate aimed to prevent fraudulent sales and to define the conditions under which a sale might be nullified or its terms adjusted. While the *curule aedile* was concerned with all things that might be bought and sold, the language of the edict cited in the *Digest* focuses on the sale of slaves and the obligation of the seller to disclose defects in his human merchandise that might give a buyer grounds for legal action. Such defects are mostly physical in nature, for example, chronic disease. However, the edict also notes grounds for the magistrate's intervention in a seller's failure to disclose certain undesirable actions or behaviors, such as whether the person being sold had tried to run away, was a loiterer, was guilty of a capital offense, or was guilty of theft or the cause of other damage (for which loss the slaveholder was obligated either to provide compensation or surrender the slave). A seller also had to disclose whether an enslaved person had attempted suicide. After all, a slave who died by suicide was the ultimate example of untrustworthy property.

The selection of legal opinions that follows the text of the edict also focuses on slaves, discussing the sort of disease, defect, or undesirable behavior that might give a buyer grounds for complaint if not disclosed beforehand. These opinions are often of an academic nature, focusing on points of law, and may not reference actual instances of theft or damage caused by slaves, but rather the hypothetical consideration of the law involved. Nonetheless, hypothetical speculation is more useful if it is plausible. The extensiveness of the discussion suggests that Roman legal experts constructed slaves as criminal and negligent. Their assumption of servile wickedness is even present in the commentary on the sale of enslaved persons who had attempted self-harm. For example, the jurist Paulus (second and third centuries CE) attributed a suicide attempt either to the slave's bad character or the desire to avoid punishment for another crime:

> A slave attempts to commit suicide when he seeks death out of wickedness or evil ways or because of some crime that he has committed, but not when he is able no longer to bear his bodily pain. (*Digest* 21.1.43.4, trans. Watson)

An additional illustration of the construction of servile wickedness appears in a letter written by Pliny the Younger, a Roman imperial official and senator from the late first and early second centuries CE. Pliny collected and assembled in ten books over two hundred letters from his official and personal correspondence. These are formal and literary letters on a wide range of personal and official matters. *Letters* 3.14 describes the death of Larcius Macedo, a former high official, who in 108 CE was murdered by his slaves while in the bath. At the start of the letter, Pliny seems to attribute blame for the attack to Macedo himself, noting that he was an arrogant and cruel master. Pliny then recounts the attack in detail: a group of slaves savagely assaulted Macedo in his bath, pummeled him all over including, Pliny notes, his private parts, strangled him, and then threw him on the hot floor of the bath, apparently dead. After his attackers ran off, Macedo was revived by some "more faithful" slaves, but only to live just a few more days, long enough however to know most of his attackers had been caught and executed. Pliny concludes with a general observation:

> You see how much we are exposed to danger, insult, and mockery. And a man cannot feel safe because he is lenient and mild. Slaves murder masters because of their criminality not their capacity for reason. (*Letters* 3.14)

Pliny backs off from his suggestion that Macedo was murdered because he was a cruel master. Why? It may be that in recounting the details of the attack, Pliny reminds himself of his own vulnerability even though he was, in his own estimation, a mild master. Pliny's fear causes him to fall back on the construction of slaves as wicked and criminal, brutes without reason, incapable of loyalty even to a kind master.

Gender Stereotypes

Notions of gender, specifically, elite ideals regarding "male" and "female," also play a role in stereotyping enslaved persons (see chapter 9, "Gender and Sexuality"). Male slaves were constructed as cowards in contradiction to the construction of the slave as a criminal brute. However, Greek and Roman slaveholders' various justifications of slavery were flexible to the point of self-contradiction, a reflection of the contradiction inherent in the definition of the slave as both a human being and a possession. The concept of the cowardly slave may have comforted slaveholders like Pliny, who were conscious of their vulnerability to servile violence. This construction distinguished slaves from free men, who were expected to be physically courageous. Note that the Latin word for courage, *virtus*, is derived from *vir*, the word for a man. Real men were courageous. In contrast, Greek and Roman slaveholders routinely referred to male slaves, regardless of age, as "boys" (Gk. *paides* or Lat. *pueri*), implying that the adult male slave was not a real man.

In Achilles Tatius's second-century CE Greek novel, *Leucippe and Clitophon*, the protagonist narrator, a young man named Clitophon, relates an episode in which the slave Sosthenes, who had been keeping the heroine, Leucippe, under guard, learns that he is to be questioned in court under torture. This was the usual practice for slaves giving testimony. The slave, conceived as a body, was more likely to tell the truth to avoid physical pain. Thus, Sosthenes runs off. Clitophon notes:

> The saying is true, that fear wipes out the memory. For Sosthenes in his shock forgot everything at hand and did not lock the door to Leucippe's room. Indeed, the whole nation of slaves are terrible cowards in matters that involve fear. (*Leucippe and Clitophon* 7.10)

Enslavement in the Greek and Roman world was not reserved for any particular ethnic group or nationality. Thus, when Clitophon references slaves as a distinct people or nation (*genos*), he naturalizes a socially constructed group and character trait (see chapter 8, "Race and Ethnicity"). This passage is also interesting in Clitophon's observation that Sosthenes forgot to lock the door to the room where Leucippe was being held captive and allowed her to escape, another example of an enslaver noting servile negligence.

This ideology that posited a distinction between brave free men and cowardly slaves persisted in military practices, too. Although slaves were excluded from service, in emergencies they were recruited to serve, often with the promise of freedom in return for their service. The ideological importance of such exclusion is apparent in an exchange of letters between the emperor Trajan and Pliny the Younger, who in 110 CE began serving as imperial administrator in the province of Bithynia (in modern Turkey). Pliny consults with the emperor regarding two army recruits who had been discovered to be slaves. The emperor advises him that if the slaves had been drafted or presented as substitutes, they are not at fault. But if they had volunteered, they would need to be put to death (*Letters* 10.29–30). It is significant that Pliny here consults Trajan not just as emperor but as "the founder and upholder of military discipline." In this context, the Latin word for discipline, *disciplina*, refers to the science of war both as a body of knowledge and as a set of ideological doctrines in which slaves should not have a share. It was important to distinguish the obedience of the soldier, a reflection of courage, from the obedience of the slave, a reflection of subjection.

The exclusion of slaves from military service may also have been motivated by a reluctance to provide slaves with weapons. Armed slave rebellions were rare in antiquity and were always brutally repressed. One such rebellion occurred in Sicily in the late 130s BCE. The historian Diodorus Siculus, writing in the first century BCE, records an episode in which the armed slaves themselves refer to the stereotyping of slaves as cowards but turn the stereotype back on the Roman soldiers they were fighting. While besieging a city, the rebel slaves taunted the Roman defenders within the walls, declaring that they, the Romans, were the slaves running away from danger, not the actual slaves in rebellion (*Library of History* 35.2.46).

As courage distinguished free men from cowardly slaves, so did sexual modesty distinguish free girls and women from female slaves. Respectable free women were expected to remain virgins before marriage and maintain sexual fidelity during marriage. There was no such expectation for free men. Regardless of their marital status, free men could compel sex with enslaved persons they owned (including enslaved males, most often boys) or with slaves belonging to other slaveholders (so long as the owner consented). In theory, free women were off-limits (see chapter 9, "Gender and Sexuality"). The sexual availability of enslaved women generated still more stereotypes. The terms of the double standard are laid out in Plautus's comedy *Curculio*, which was performed around 200 BCE. Standing outside a brothel, a slave attendant advises his amorous young master to stay away from citizen women and boys, but that there is no prohibition against visiting an enslaved prostitute:

> No one will keep you from here or forbid you from
> buying what is openly on sale if you have the money.
> No one will prohibit you from walking on a public street.
> So long as your path does not stray into a field that has been
>   fenced off,
> so long as you keep away from a bride, a widow, a maiden,
> a young man and boys of free birth, make love where you will.
>
> (*Curculio* 33–38)

157

When Plautus was writing, the punishment of adultery was a private matter. A law passed in 18 BCE during the reign of Augustus made adultery a criminal offence. However, the new law did not impact the existing double standard. A man who had sex with a slave, male or female, did not commit adultery.

The slave required to provide sex had little if any power to give or withhold consent (see chapter 9, "Gender and Sexuality"). It has been argued that because she was obeying her master's command the slave employed in sex work did not incur the same degree of shame that would have been attached to an adulterous wife. Nonetheless, slaves did not entirely escape the degradation associated with sex work. In the late first and early second centuries CE, Plutarch, a priest of Apollo at Delphi and a Roman citizen, in an essay on marriage advises the wife not to be aggrieved or angry if her husband should go astray in some way with a hired party girl or one of his slave girls. Rather, the wife should reason that he was sharing his drunken behavior, his lack of self-control, and the violence of his sex drive with another woman because he respected his wife (*Moralia* 140B). The degradation of the enslaved woman functions to protect and enhance the honor of the citizen wife.

Despite her lack of real agency, the sexually accessible female slave was constructed as sexually willing. This stereotype of the wanton slave girl appears in an anecdote found in Plutarch's biography of the Roman general and political leader Marcus Licinius Crassus. In 87 BCE, Crassus, still a young man, was forced to flee Rome after a setback in his political fortunes. He escaped to Spain and lay low, hiding in a cave on the Mediterranean shore. The owner of the land was a friend and provided Crassus with all his material needs. In addition, the friend catered to Crassus's pleasure as a young man, sending two pretty enslaved women to the cave. They came upon Crassus in the cave and, as they had been ordered, said they were "seeking a master who was hiding there." The women remained his companions for the rest of Crassus's time in hiding. Plutarch concludes the anecdote with a report from a historian writing in the time of Augustus, who had met one of the two slaves, by that time an old woman, and often heard her recollect the incident, "eagerly recounting it in detail" (*Life of Crassus* 5). The anecdote notes that the young women were instructed to be "willing," ordered, as they were, to say they were "seeking a master," constructing a fantasy for Crassus that sex was their idea. The note concluding the anecdote signals the eager desire that Plutarch and his readers imagined in the young women through the eagerness of the old slave's memory of sex with Crassus.[1]

1. Katharine P. D. Huemoeller, "Voices from the Cave: An Enslaved Woman as a Source in Plutarch's *Life of Crassus*," Society for Classical Studies, New Orleans, January 7, 2023.

Plutarch's advice that wives look the other way if their husbands had sex with slaves suggests that such advice was necessary, that not all wives looked the other way. This is the case in an episode in Xenophon of Ephesus's *Ephesian Tale*, a Greek novel from the early first century CE. The heroine Anthia has become the slave of Polyidus, a Roman imperial official in Egypt, who wants to make her his slave-mistress. Polyidus's jealous wife, Rhenaea, gets Anthia alone and attacks her as a threat to her marriage:

> She said, "You wicked woman. You're scheming against my marriage. It's no use to you that Polyidus thinks you're pretty. You won't get any benefit from your beauty. You probably were able to seduce criminals and sleep with lots of drunk young men. But you won't ever harm Rhenaea's marriage and get away with it." (*Ephesian Tale* 5.5.3)

Xenophon's virtuous heroine is, in fact, blameless. Nonetheless, in Anthia's presumed sexual accessibility, Rhenaea sees a female version of the wicked and criminal slave, that is, a scheming and sexually wanton slave girl.

Positive Constructions and Stereotypes

Greek and Roman slaveholders also constructed an ideal of a good slave. Such slaves were loyal, obedient, and industrious in their work, even in the absence of the master. Examples of this stereotype appear in both visual and textual sources. Figure 11.2 above may depict idealized "good" slaves through the images of men hard at the work of plowing and sowing. Another example comes from Roman comedy. These plays frequently staged a comic version of the good slave in the stereotype of "the running slave" (*servus currens*). These characters are depicted running on stage to deliver important news to their masters. In their eagerness, running slaves are the opposite of negligent slaves. However, rather than being an object of admiration, a running slave is the target of mockery—a buffoon who is self-important with such big news. But even serious versions of the good slave were belittling, diminishing the slave in relation to the master. A third version of the good slave stereotype is found in ancient Greek art, which often represented enslaved persons on a smaller scale than the enslaver—a case of literal diminishment. For example, a relief sculpture on a Greek grave stele dating from about 390 BCE depicts an enslaved woman adoringly attending her deceased mistress (see figure 11.3).[2]

---

2. See Kelly Wrenhaven, *Reconstructing the Slave: The Image of the Slave in Ancient Greece* (London: Bristol Classical Press, 2012), 101–7, for related images.

Figure 11.3. Marble funerary monument of a standing elite woman next to an enslaved woman holding a jewelry box. Circa 400–390 BCE.

The tall figure on the left wearing a long tunic, called a *chitōn*, and over it a mantle, represents the deceased slaveholder. A personal attendant, her slave, stands in front of her, a woman much shorter than her mistress and wearing only a *chitōn*. She holds a box and appears to gaze up at the face of her mistress, who seemingly looks beyond her. The relief idealizes the master–slave relationship from the point of view of the slaveholder. The good slave stands in faithful attendance on her mistress and holds a jewelry or cosmetics box, emphasizing the beauty of her mistress. Her smaller stature signals the greater social importance of her deceased owner. The contrast in gazes may reinforce this idea: the enslaver is more important to the slave than the slave is to the enslaver.

Homer's *Odyssey* provides the earliest representation of the good slave stereotype in the Greek and Latin literary tradition. Odysseus's pig herder, Eumaeus, remained loyal for all twenty years of his master's absence. He himself had been born to noble parents but was kidnapped as a child and sold to Odysseus's father. When Odysseus finally returns home, disguised as a beggar, he stays with Eumaeus. The swineherd laments his absent master, not knowing the real identity of his humble guest: Eumaeus longs for his master, even more than he longs for his homeland and for the mother and father from whom he had been taken as a child (*Odyssey* 14.137–144). As a good slave, Eumaeus has come to place more importance on his identity as Odysseus's slave than on his birth identity, diminishing himself as a person in his own right.

This displacement of identity is observed in variations on the good slave stereotype. For example, an enslaved cook should replace his own sense of taste with that of the enslaver. Thus, the late-first-century CE Roman poet Martial wrote: "Skill alone is not enough for a cook. I don't want his tastebuds to be slaves: a cook ought to possess the palate of his master" (*Epigrams* 14.220). Good slaves might even take their emotional cues from their masters. Thus, Sosia, the slave in Plautus's *Amphitruo*, expresses his happiness in response to an apparent reconciliation between his master and his wife, asserting that a good slave "should take his cues from his masters, match his expression to theirs. He should be sad if his masters are sad, and mirthful if they are happy" (*Amphitruo* 957–961). The idealized good slave is not only a tool ready to enact the master's will, but an extension of the master's very thoughts and feelings, a diminished person in the suppression or erasure of his own will and personal autonomy.

Reading against the Grain

It is possible to read these texts against the grain, that is, contrary to the agenda and ideology of their slaveholding authors. One way to read against the grain is to consider the representations of enslaved persons in the broader context of the texts in which they appear. While chosen to illustrate aspects of the slaveholder's construction of the slave, the same selections can obscure the complexity of a text that is open to more nuanced reading. For example, Clitophon, the narrator of Achilles Tatius's novel, affirms the construction of slaves as cowards. A reading of the novel as a whole, however, reveals that Clitophon himself is a terrible coward. The broader context suggests that the novel itself, as opposed to the internal narrator, questions, rather than affirms, the stereotype. One may also read against the grain by imagining the situation reflected in the text from the point of view of a person degraded as a slave. A stereotypical lazy slave, for example, may not be existentially lazy, but unmotivated to work unless forced. So may an enslaved person performing sex work be motivated not by innate sexual immorality, but by coercion and necessity. The stereotypical lying slave may not be dishonest by nature, but wary of the consequences of telling the truth. In reading these texts, we should question the judgments of their slaveholding creators rather than accept them at face value.

Discussion Questions

1. Where do pagan Greek and Roman constructions and stereotypes of enslaved persons appear in the New Testament?

2. Do New Testament texts affirm or question these constructions and stereotypes?

3. When reading the New Testament, what strategies are available for reading slaveholders' constructions and stereotypes "against the grain" in addition to the ones noted in the chapter?

Further Reading

DuBois, Page. *Slaves and Other Objects*. Chicago: University of Chicago Press, 2003.

Hunt, Peter. *Slaves, Warfare, and Ideology in the Greek Historians*. New York: Cambridge University Press, 1998.

Perry, Matthew J. *Gender, Manumission, and the Roman Freedwoman*. Cambridge: Cambridge University Press, 2014.

Thalmann, William G. *The Swineherd and the Bow: Representations of Class in the Odyssey*. Ithaca, NY: Cornell University Press, 1998.

Wrenhaven, Kelly. *Reconstructing the Slave: The Image of the Slave in Ancient Greece*. London: Bristol Classical Press, 2012.

12   *Household Codes*

KATHERINE A. SHANER

The person depicted in figure 12.1 is only about six inches tall (about 15 cm). She can be found on an ancient wall, about five feet (1.5 meters) from the floor. She is painted directly into the plaster, carefully posed in an easy stance. She continuously offers delicious treats to anyone who walks past her, but few do. The room where she presides is tucked into the back corners of a luxury condominium complex in Roman-era Ephesus (modern-day western Turkey). Likely, this person depicts an enslaved woman. She is simply dressed, attentively standing, graciously offering a tray to the viewer. She is also represented in a solitary scene; the rest of the wall is simply white plaster. She represents an obedient, happy enslaved worker—the kind slave owners in the Roman world idealized. But her presence is also a reminder of many of the contradictions an enslaved woman would face in that time. For example, her stance gives her the appearance of someone who is contentedly obedient in her work. But to whom does she owe that obedience? Her enslaver? Her father? Her husband? What if each gives contradictory commands? And what about her sense of self and ability to make decisions about her own life and body? How does her easy stance of obedience mask the difficult contradictions among the primary relationships in her life?

In the coming pages, we will explore how families, households, and imperial politics all intertwine with the possibilities for this enslaved woman's experiences. By looking at how families are organized in the Greek and Roman world, we can begin to see idealized enslaver-perspective forms of family organization as they benefited the powerful, the wealthy, and the free in society at the expense of enslaved people and their families. These idealized forms of or-

Figure 12.1. Close-up of fresco, likely featuring an enslaved woman holding a platter. From the west wall of Terrace House 2, apartment 4, room 14c, in Ephesus.

ganization are sometimes called "household codes," a term defined later in this chapter. Such idealized enslaver-perspective forms of family and household organization were impossible to put into common, practical use, especially for enslaved members of them. These idealized forms of family and household organization were also not the only ways that ancient people thought about the organization of communities or the existence of enslaved people within them. The perspective we take as readers changes the way we see the everyday lives of enslaved people and their families.

What Is a "Household"?

Greek and Roman concepts of family and its organization were often quite different from the modern nuclear family. Greek does not have a word that means exactly the same thing as "family" in English. The word *genos* is sometimes translated as "family," although it denotes a tribe, a familial lineage rather than a nuclear family. Likewise, the word *oikos* is sometimes translated as "family," but it more often refers to a physical house, or the concept of a household. This concept of household is a common one in the historical context of the New Testament because it signals the complex relationships among a group of people whose employment, religious practices, social status, and even dwelling place are intertwined with a single person or couple who are in charge of the whole thing. We see this kind of household represented often in the New Testament. For example, Lydia in Acts 16:11–16 is baptized along with her household. Since she worked in the purple cloth trade, she was likely well-off. Acts does not mention a spouse or children. Even if she had neither, her household would have probably included enslaved people, employees, adopted children, adult siblings, business partners, and/or parents as part of her *oikos* ("household").[1]

In ancient households, we can recognize many of the relationships that exist today. Mother, father, daughter, son, sister, brother, and child are all relationships that existed in the ancient world. While modern readers often romanticize these relationships as having close emotional ties, these relationships also existed within strong power networks. We see this most clearly when we add in other relationships that were considered part of the family system, namely, enslaver (*despotēs / kyria / kyrios*), slave (*doulē / doulos*), and freedper-

---

1. See Katherine A. Shaner, "Family Structures: New Testament," in *Oxford Encyclopedia of the Bible and Gender Studies*, ed. Julia M. O'Brien (Oxford: Oxford University Press, 2014), 217–22.

son (*eleutherē / eleutheros*). While slaves within the ancient household could be parents, had siblings, and were children, the conditions of their enslavement meant that these relationships were never the primary ones that influenced their lives. Their enslavers (those who claimed and enforced ownership over them) or even their former enslavers frequently held enormous power over them (see chapter 6, "Manumission").

Household relationships were often organized in political structures that attempted to ensure the existence of clear power lines. These power lines were highly gendered in addition to their attention to slave and free status. Husbands were in charge of their wives, fathers in charge of their children, masters in charge of their slaves, and lords in charge of their business clients. Yet even in antiquity, this kind of household organization appears in texts as an idealized form of household organization rather than descriptions of how people experienced these relationships. The woman on the wall in Ephesus, for example, was someone's daughter as well as someone's enslaved child. She may have been someone's wife as well as someone's enslaved domestic worker. Whose authority was primary for her day-to-day life? Her father's, her husband's, or her enslaver's? What if her father and her enslaver were the same person? Or her husband and her enslaver were the same person?

Greek and Roman Household Ideals

The term "household codes" goes back to Martin Luther and the Protestant Reformation in the sixteenth century. It was used to identify lists of domestic and societal duties. Such lists had existed long before Luther coined the term. Household codes were found in ancient philosophical treatises and "best practices" manuals throughout the ancient Greek and Roman world. Aristotle (384–322 BCE) is generally recognized as the first to use the structure that is found in the New Testament. In his book about political organization (*Politics*), he lays out what he considers the best kind of mutual governance for a city: deliberation among those consenting to be governed. We know this as democracy. Aristotle sees a need, however, to define both the smallest unit of governance—a city (*polis*)—and the smallest unit of the governed—a household (*oikos*). Each household sends one person to the deliberative body of the city. That person, for Aristotle, should be the free male citizen whose responsibility is to run the household. By that, Aristotle means the householder should be skilled at marriage, reproduction (literally child-making), and mastery. In other words, the people who participate in governing a city should be good at *oikonomia* or household management (the root of our contemporary word "economics"). Aristotle writes:

> Household management falls into departments corresponding to the parts
> of which the household in its turn is composed; and the household in its
> perfect form consists of slaves and freemen. The investigation of everything
> should begin with its smallest parts, and the primary and smallest parts of
> the household are master and slave, husband and wife, father and children.
> (*Politics* 1.1253b.3–8)

Notice that enslaved and formerly enslaved people define a household in
Aristotle's ideal. They are specifically named as part of the "perfect form." This
is evidence of how slavery is structurally embedded within ancient household
ideals as well as ancient understandings of democratic governance.

In Aristotle's ideal, the householder (a free, property-owning man) is capable of virtuous reasoning, rational thinking, and deliberative speech, since he
will have to negotiate governance among his peers. Aristotle, however, has to
argue that every other member of the household by nature lacks these skills
or has deficiencies in them. Women have less rational thought than men.
Children's reasoning is not yet developed. Slaves have only enough rational
thought to follow their enslaver's orders. In fact, Aristotle argues that slaves are
simply extensions or tools of their masters by nature (*Politics* 1.1259b.22–25).
While Aristotle concedes that not everyone agrees with him in his assessment
of women, children, and especially slaves, these three relationships became a
central focal point for creating hierarchical social expectations in other aspects of ancient life. Aristotle's free citizen male, who is the caretaker of all
three inferior kinds of people, becomes the paradigm for full personhood in
ancient (and even more modern) discourses. Seen through Aristotle's ideal,
our fresco woman is not, in fact, capable of independent living—her serving
stance suggests that such service is her ideal role.

Aristotle's philosophy was developed in the fourth century BCE, several
centuries before the New Testament was written. But his influence continued
to be quite strong well into the first and second centuries CE. Roman imperial
supporters found his ideal household structure quite useful for consolidating
power. Everyone living in the Empire counted as members of the emperor's
household. This shift was especially prominent as Augustus came to power
and the Roman Republic became the Roman Empire. Making the Empire
a household, however, did not dissolve existing households. Each existing
household became a constituent member of the emperor's household. Arius
Didymus, a stoic philosopher who was a close advisor of Emperor Augustus,
is credited with synthesizing Aristotle's household management ideal into this
useful tool for imperial political structures. In his summary, he strengthens the
hierarchical relationships between the same pairs (husband/wife, master/slave,

father/children) and emphasizes the authority of the free male over women, children, and slaves. He writes: "The man has the rule of this household by nature" (Stobaeus, *Eclogues* 2.149.5–6).[2] Didymus emphasizes the inevitability of this structure through an appeal to nature as the source of a free man's authority. Yet this assertion about the natural authority of free men needs still more reinforcement. It is not enough for a free man to be naturally a ruler. In addition, enslaved people were depicted as part of two categories, "either a slave by nature (strong in body for service, but stupid and unable to live by himself, for whom slavery is beneficial) or a slave by law" (Stobaeus, *Eclogues* 2.149.1–3). If free men are by nature authoritative, enslaved people must by nature be the opposite in Didymus's ideal. He continues: "For the deliberative faculty in a woman is inferior, in children it does not yet exist, and in the case of slaves, it is completely absent" (Stobaeus, *Eclogues* 2.149.6–8).

Both Aristotle and Didymus imagine a household teeming with slaves, those who work in domestic service and those who work in trade, industrial workshops, and agricultural production. Their ideal formation for the governing citizen is not just free men, but free men with significant wealth. In the case of Didymus, the emperor is the governing citizen *par excellence* because he is imagined as the *paterfamilias* for the whole empire. That is, the emperor is head of a household that encompasses everyone living within the imperial borders, including enslaved people. To return to the possibilities for the serving woman on the wall, seen through Didymus's understanding of Aristotle, she is doubly enslaved both to her immediate owner and, by extension and within the larger system of the empire, to the emperor.

New Testament Household Codes

Three separate household codes appear in the New Testament in Colossians 3:18–4:1; Ephesians 5:21–6:9; and 1 Peter 2:13–3:7. In 1 Timothy and Titus 2:3–10, we see similar instructions about creating clear free male lines of authority. All of these texts, with the exception of 1 Peter, fall into Paul's legacy. While Colossians is disputed, Ephesians, 1 Timothy, and Titus are all considered pseudepigraphical, that is, written in Paul's name by his followers after

---

2. The Greek text of Didymus's *Epitome*, excerpted by Stobaeus, is found in Curt Wachsmuth and Otto Hense's edition of Stobaeus, *Anthologium* II (Berlin: Weidmann, 1958). The translation provided here is from David Balch, "Household Codes," in *Greco-Roman Literature in the New Testament*, ed. David Aune (Atlanta: Society of Biblical Literature, 1988), 25–50, here 40–45.

his death. The New Testament household codes draw on the ancient rhetoric discussed above as well as Paul's earlier undisputed letters to create a clear patriarchal structure for household relationships. Often the New Testament household codes attempt to clarify an unclear portion of Paul's previous letters. We will look at that idea in the next section.

Let us look more closely at Colossians 3:18–4:1, the oldest of the household codes in the New Testament and likely the source for the one in Ephesians 5:21–6:9. I will assume, for this discussion, that neither were uniquely written by Paul because of their late date and because of their connections to Aristotle and Didymus. Colossians and Ephesians are very similar in how they address the same three pairs of household relationships as Aristotle and Didymus: husbands and wives, fathers and children, enslavers and enslaved. The writer of Colossians speaks directly to wives or women (the Greek word *gynaikes* could mean either) in Colossians 3:18, directing them to "order yourselves under" (*hypotassō*) husbands. The Greek verb *hypotassō* as it is used here carries some very particular connotations. First, it is in the imperative mood, meaning that it is giving a direct command, "do this." Second, it is in the middle voice, which is something we do not have in English grammar. The middle is a reflexive voice, meaning the subject of the sentence (wives or women) is doing the action to themselves. Third, *hypotassō* is a verb used in military stories to mean "marshal" or bring a group of soldiers to order themselves under a commanding officer. Thus, the writer of Colossians tells wives or women to "order themselves under the command of husbands or men" (Col 3:18) in the same way soldiers might order themselves under a commanding officer. Colossians does command husbands or men (*andres*) to love (*agapate*) their women/wives and not to "be exasperated" by or "vex themselves" (*pikrainō*) with their women (Col 3:19). While many commentators have argued that these two commands demonstrate equitable reciprocity—to subordinate oneself for women and to love without being exasperated for men—the power differential implied with women's subordination and their potential merely to exasperate men assumes that women have little or no authority in the relationship.

Why hover over relationships between men and women in a chapter about enslaved people? Because the dynamic around gender is gentle in comparison to that outlined between enslavers and their enslaved people. In Colossians 3:22, the writer directly commands enslaved people to obey (*hypakuoō*) their masters (*kyrioi*) according to the flesh in everything. The writer specifies that enslaved people should "hyper-listen" to their enslavers, who are called *kyrioi*, the same word used as Jesus's title of "Lord." This is a different action than subordinating oneself to a social or military order that may imply some conversation about collective action. Enslaved people are commanded to be obedient in all things—a verb and qualifying phrase that has no room for resistance, question, or even discussion. Colossians continues to connect enslaved obedience to obedience to Jesus as *kyrios* through Colossians 3:22–25, suggesting that the enslaved person who is obedient to their human *kyrios* will find that their "slaving" (*douleuō*) serves the *kyrios* Christ (Col 3:24). Colossians 3:25 continues suggesting that wrongdoing—that is, disobedience—will be paid back to the enslaved person through divine judgment. Finally, in Colossians 4:1 the author addresses "the lords" (*kyrioi*) or enslavers directly, reminding them they also have a *kyrios* in heaven.

Many interpreters have pointed out the differences between Aristotle, Didymus, and the New Testament versions of household codes. Using Colossians and its related text, Ephesians, some have pointed out that both enslaved people and enslavers are addressed directly, something none of the household codes found outside of the New Testament do. These interpreters then suggest that New Testament household codes show a moderation that is not present in Greek or Roman versions of the social order. They conclude that Christians are more moderate and kinder to enslaved people and women than those who live by the Greek or Roman social order. Some suggest that Christian theological teachings around mercy and justice motivate Christians to soften the harsh hierarchy of the codes. Yet neither Aristotle nor Didymus speak directly to enslaved people about their own enslavement, nor give advice directly to enslaved people about their own conduct. Both seem to be speaking to free, male, relatively privileged audiences rather than those who are ideally subordinated to them. Moreover, in the New Testament household codes the instructions to enslavers are neither warnings nor commands but reminders of enslavers' metaphorical enslavement—enslavement that holds few of the implications of legal enslavement (see also chapter 10, "Metaphors of Enslavement").[3]

Some interpreters have suggested that the reciprocations in Colossians and Ephesians even show an abolitionist sensibility in the Christian texts. Yet the instructions to enslaved members of the household of God in 1 Peter 2:13–3:7 directly speak to the opposite dynamic. In 1 Peter 2:13, the writer begins not with the male head of the household but with an admonition to honor the emperor. This list of duties is explicitly political from the beginning. The very next address is to enslaved people and suggests not only obedience, but also acceptance of violence and suffering as part of the relationship with one's en-

---

3. See also Katherine A. Shaner, "Slaves of the Gods or Enslaved to the Gods? Enslaved Labour and the βασιλεία τοῦ θεοῦ," *Religion in the Roman Empire* 10, no. 1 (2024): 107–26.

Figure 12.2. Funerary relief of Zabdibol that also depicts his son, Mokimu, and his two daughters, Tadmur and Alayyat. Second–third century CE.

slaver: "For it is to your credit if, being aware of God, you endure pain while suffering unjustly. If you endure when you are beaten for doing wrong, where is the credit in that?" (1 Pet 2:19–20). The text continues that this endurance is part of an enslaved person's calling because Christ also suffered for them.

The text goes on to admonish wives to accept the authority of husbands and for husbands to care for their wives as "the weaker sex" (1 Pet 3:1–8). Some interpreters suggest that these instructions are less about ensuring the power structure of imperial households that was in place and more about surviving the reality of suffering that was a common experience for enslaved people in the Christ-following community.[4] If we think through this perspective with our fresco woman, several questions arise. What kind of suffering might she be masking in order to stand so quietly and calmly? What does her enslaver understand about her suffering, especially if they have inflicted it? But we would also do well to take into account the ways we see her through her enslaver's

---

4. See Shively Smith, *Strangers to Family Diaspora and 1 Peter's Invention of God's Household* (Waco, TX: Baylor University Press, 2016).

eyes rather than her own. Her calm, dignified stance may mask some of her suffering, but for an enslaver whose hand produced such suffering, her dignity may be subtle defiance. She is still a person in the world, capable of kindness even in the face of unjust brutality.

Creating further difficulties in interpreting both the Greek and Roman and New Testament household codes is the fact that the genre generally essential- izes persons and roles. Women/wives seem to be clearly defined, even though enslaved women and women who are not married to *the* head of the household have no clear place in the codes. Enslaved people, though having parents and possibly partners, seem to have no need of such relationships in these codes. In fact, as we have seen elsewhere, enslaved persons' social positionality at the bot- tom of kyriarchal systems and their sexual availability to their masters feminizes them, further marginalizing enslaved men (see chapter 9, "Gender and Sexual- ity"). The New Testament household codes directly tell children to obey parents. Yet for enslaved children, such obedience is ambiguous at best. An enslaved child likely decided often between obedience to their master and obedience to a parent. Understanding the intersectional nature of the household codes illu- minates the ways in which the codes attempt to impose imperial social relation- ships on a community for whom such structures are much more complicated in their everyday interactions (see chapter 14, "Ethics of Interpretation").

Imagining a Different World

Sometimes historians and interpreters rightly point out that in the ancient world slavery was a pervasive social system. You could not live in the ancient Greek and Roman world without encountering enslaved people or traces of their work. Further, some historians argue that because slavery was so embed- ded in the fabric of everyday life, most people—including Christ followers— could not conceive of its abolition. While it is true there was no widespread, organized, politically powerful movement toward abolition, opposition to enslavement and ideologies of abolition were available in the ancient world. Some Christ followers participated in this opposition, and some did not. The household codes show us those who did not, and the codes became a kind of guidebook for slavery in the Western Hemisphere in the modern period.[5] But other evidence shows us, by reading against the grain of texts, that there was opposition to slavery in the Greek and Roman eras.

5. See Sylvester Johnson, "The Bible, Slavery, and the Problem of Authority," in *Beyond Slavery: Overcoming Its Religious and Sexual Legacies*, ed. Bernadette J. Brooten (New York: Palgrave Macmillan, 2010), 231–48.

One piece of evidence comes from Aristotle's own argument in *Politics*. Like a good philosopher, Aristotle addresses the arguments of those with whom he disagrees. In the process, though, savvy readers can begin to understand what the arguments against Aristotle might be. He notes that some of his opponents "maintain that for one person to be another person's master is contrary to nature, because it is only convention that makes the one a slave and the other a free person and there is no difference between them by nature, and that therefore it is unjust, for it is based on force" (*Politics* 1.1253b.20–23). Here, Aristotle represents his critics as those who see slavery as unjust (contrary to nature), without clear rationale (only convention), and violent (based on force). While Aristotle is clear that *he* does not agree with this position, the fact he must represent it means that ideas about the problematic nature of slavery were circulating in his world.

Within the New Testament, Galatians 3:28, sometimes known as the "baptismal formula," contains an imagination about the erasure of slave and free status: "There is no longer Jew or Greek, there is no longer slave or free, there is no longer male and female; for all of you are one in Christ." This statement contains the possibility that slave and free status do not matter for whoever is "in Christ." At the same time, most readers assume that in this statement slavery is what goes away rather than freedom. Thus, all slaves "in Christ" become free. Yet Paul, in the next chapter uses a metaphor of slave and free to criticize the Galatians' choices around religious practice (Gal 4:21–5:1). By using this metaphor, the possibilities of abolition disappear (see chapter 10, "Metaphors of Enslavement"). Nonetheless, some early Christ followers likely tried to implement the erasure of free and slave status within their communities. The household codes respond quite directly and clearly against the material freedom that Galatians 3:28 suggests. Why? Later communities likely needed to reinforce both gender and slave/free hierarchies because some early Christ followers understood material freedom as not just a possibility but the rule for those "in Christ."

Paul repeats this sensibility in 1 Corinthians 12:13 when he argues that the Spirit makes Christ followers one body "Jews or Greeks, slaves or free." Yet earlier in the letter, Paul suggests that those who joined the community "in Christ" as enslaved people should remain in that position (1 Cor 7:21–24) and suggests that everyone who is "in Christ" should recognize God as either their enslaver (if they are legally free) or as their metaphorical former enslaver (if they are legally enslaved). Even in antiquity, these passages were confusing. Should enslaved people try to gain their freedom? Some Christians living about fifty years after Paul's letter to the Corinthians understood their own vocation as manumitting slaves. Ignatius, a bishop in the early second century CE, wrote about this practice in a letter to his bishop-friend Polycarp. After suggesting that Polycarp teach his community to treat slaves well but avoid letting them be "puffed up,"

Figure 12.3. An iron collar meant for an enslaved person, with a bronze plate offering a reward to whoever returns the escaped enslaved worker to their enslaver, Zoninus. 4th–5th century CE.

Ignatius advises Polycarp not to allow slaves to request their freedom be paid for from funds common to the community (*To Polycarp* 4.2–3). While Ignatius is against neither slavery nor manumission, he reveals that the community has established practices that give enslaved members of the community a sense of ownership in it as well as the material possibility for manumission.

Might the serving woman on the wall also know about the possibilities for freedom, or even work behind the scenes to organize her fellow enslaved people and sympathetic free people around slavery's abolition? The possibility exists that she would know about critiques of slavery or would have been a leader in her own community around such critiques. At the same time, the fact that only a portrait of her as a compliant enslaved woman exists shows us that the texts and stories that have gained power in our historical studies actively curtail movements that may have gained her the freedom those she represents likely desired.

Why Household Codes Matter

How one orders a household or constitutes a family is a political decision. So often, we think about families and households as private matters, ones that have no bearing on the larger society. But exactly the opposite is true. What we have seen so far in this chapter is the complexity and multiplicity of ideals for managing, ordering, and governing households within larger civic systems. This ideal, however, has often been used for the purpose of keeping systems of domination in place, usually to the detriment of those with the least power. Thus, the New Testament household codes have been used to direct women in abusive marriages to remain, children to be "seen and not heard," and slaves to be obedient even in the face of torture and violence.

The household codes give authority to one, singular figure within a household system, whether that figure is a free male husband, father, and enslaver; the emperor; or God. In the process, complex relationships for anyone other than the single authority disappear. While the singular authority figure can hold multiple roles within this ideal system, no one else can. This ideal household structure, when applied as a system of practice, is only comprehensible to free male citizens. Enslaved women would not be mothers to their children with the same kind of authority free mothers would have (see chapter 9, "Gender and Sexuality"). But free mothers would also not have authority over their children in the same way free fathers would. Enslaved children would not be able to honor their parents in the same way free children could. Enslaved partnered women with living parents would not be able to follow any of the ideals set forth in this system. While this may seem like an obvious problem with household codes, the lived experience of enslaved people in the first century CE created many variations on this dilemma, since they were ideologically tools of the household and relationally human beings within it. Making decisions about interpreting New Testament texts like the household codes is a complex process, one that requires not only the historical and literary contexts from previous chapters, but also an eye toward the ethics of interpretation (see chapter 14, "Ethics of Interpretation").

Indeed, these decisions are crucial for how we understand our companion through this chapter: the woman on the wall in Ephesus. If we decide that the household codes have no authority for her, are we suggesting that she is willingly remaining enslaved? Or are we saying that her enslavement is not that difficult? If we decide that the household codes describe her existence, then how might we imagine her life differently now? If we decide that what we know about her is veiled through the gaze of her enslaver's ideal serving woman, how might we imagine her self-representation differently? After all, her freedom is available to imagine—both in her time and in ours.

Discussion Questions

1. Think about your own family or household. What does it look like? How would you describe it to a stranger? Why does it matter which relationships are part of a family?

2. Read Titus 2:1–10 and compare it with the household codes discussed above. What similarities and differences do you see? Why might the similarities and differences matter for enslaved people?

3. What difference does the political context of the household codes make for understanding their ethical and/or theological importance today?

Further Reading

Brooten, Bernadette J. "Early Christian Enslaved Families (First to Fourth Century)." Pages 111–34 in *Children and Family in Late Antiquity: Life, Death and Interaction*. Edited by Christian Laes, Katarina Mustakallio, and Ville Vuolanto. Leuven: Peeters, 2015.

Cohen, Shaye, ed. *The Jewish Family in Antiquity*. Providence, RI: Brown Judaic Studies, 1993.

Johnson, Sylvester. "The Bible, Slavery, and the Problem of Authority." Pages 231–48 in *Beyond Slavery: Overcoming Its Religious and Sexual Legacies*. Edited by Bernadette J. Brooten. New York: Palgrave Macmillan, 2010.

Martin, Clarice J. "The *Haustafeln* (Household Codes) in African American Biblical Interpretation: 'Free Slaves' and 'Subordinate Women.'" Pages 206–31 in *Stony the Road We Trod: African American Biblical Interpretation*. Edited by Cain Hope Felder. Minneapolis: Fortress, 2021.

Shaner, Katherine A. "Family Structures: New Testament." Pages 217–22 in *Oxford Encyclopedia of the Bible and Gender Studies*. Edited by Julia M. O'Brien. Oxford University Press, 2014.

Smith, Mitzi J. *Chloe and Her People: A Womanist Critical Dialogue with First Corinthians*. Eugene, OR: Cascade Books, 2023.

Smith, Shively. *Strangers to Family Diaspora and 1 Peter's Invention of God's Household*. Waco, TX: Baylor University Press, 2016.

13   *Early Christian Slavery*

CHRIS L. DE WET

In the fourth century CE, Basil of Caesarea (ca. 330–379 CE), also called Basil "the Great," the bishop of Caesarea Mazaca in Cappadocia (in modern-day Turkey) and one of the famous Cappadocian Fathers, wrote the following in his treatise *On the Holy Spirit*:

> Sometimes, by a wise and inscrutable providence, worthless children are commanded by their father to serve their more intelligent brothers and sisters [as slaves; Gen 9:25–27, with reference to the so-called Curse of Ham]. Any upright person investigating the circumstances would realize that such situations bring much benefit and are not a sentence of condemnation for those involved. It is better for a person who lacks intelligence and self-control to become another's possession. Governed by his master's intelligence, he will become like a chariot driven by a skilled horseman, or a ship with a seasoned sailor at the tiller. (*On the Holy Spirit* 20.51)

Basil was one of the most influential theologians in the golden era of Christian theological development. And like most theologians of early Christianity, Basil relied on social institutions, like slavery, to better understand and explain the nature of Christian belief and practices. In the text cited above, Basil states that enslavement could be the will of God, since some persons are not able to master themselves, thus they are best suited to be mastered by others. His language almost sounds similar to Aristotle's ideas about natural slavery. In other words, slavery was used as a "thinking tool," or a *discourse*, by the first Christians to explain their understanding of the world, their God, and their

Figure 13.1. Ivory carving portraying Basil of Caesarea, John Chrysostom, and Gregory of Nazianzus. Circa 1500 CE.

fellow human beings. The discourse of slavery has been termed "doulology," from the Greek words *doulos* ("slave") and *logos* ("word" or "discourse"). Without doulology, the shape, form, and expressions of Christianity we see today would have been surprisingly different.

Early Christian thought was fundamentally shaped by late Roman enslaving ideologies and practices. For quite some time, though, it was thought that slavery was almost absent from late antiquity, and that the institution was slowly transforming into medieval serfdom. This view, however, has been repeatedly repudiated. We know, especially from the early Christian sources themselves, that slavery was present in Roman late antiquity. While most Christian churches today would totally denounce the abhorrent slaving practices we see in the late ancient world, the early church was rather ambiguous about slavery. We do not find one uniform response for or against slavery from early Christianity. Although they were critical about certain practices of slavery, such as using excessive violence against slaves or the sexual abuse of slaves, early Christians never wholly advocated for the abolition of slavery. The earliest Christians were enslavers, and many of them were enslaved.

We should therefore begin this chapter with the acknowledgment that there are a *variety* of early Christian responses and stances in relation to slavery, from accommodation to rejection, each stance being *complex, nuanced,* and bound to *contextual matters*. In this chapter, we will grapple with slavery alongside the Christian sources and try to showcase these varieties of early Christian thought and practice with regard to slavery. The best way to understand early Christian slavery is to discover it through the lens of early Christian biblical interpretation, theology, and social ethics. The aim is therefore, in a sense, to listen to the surviving voices of early Christians themselves and to hear what they say about slavery. We will begin with an analysis of how slavery featured and functioned in early Christian theological thought, and then trace how this may have shaped early Christian slaveholding principles and practices, especially regarding the treatment of slaves.

Early Christian Theological Understandings of Slavery

For the first Christians, scripture was the guiding force in the formulation of beliefs and practices. Even though, in the first four centuries CE, we do not have a formal canon or "Bible" as we have it today, the Hebrew Bible (especially its Greek translation, the Septuagint) and most of the writings later collected into the New Testament already held a great deal of authority and were used to regulate Christian life and behavior. Unfortunately, scripture itself does not give detailed guidelines about slavery. It seems Christians were less concerned about saying whether slavery was an evil or not, especially since slavery is almost never labeled as a "sin" in itself. Rather, they used slavery as a discourse to speak about other things. By discourse, I mean both metaphors and other figurative ways of speaking with and about slavery (see chapter 10, "Metaphors of Enslavement"). This is what we often find in the biblical writings themselves, and this approach to slavery persisted in early Christian thought.

Where did slavery come from, according to early Christian belief? Christian thought about sin and salvation was meticulously conceived in terms of slavery and freedom. Often, these concepts overlap and the complex layers of meaning these interconnected concepts attained affected Christian ideas about slavery. Let us return, for a moment, to Basil and the passage we read at the start of this chapter. The preceding section of that passage reads:

> Do they not realize that even among people, no one is a slave by nature? People are brought under the yoke of slavery either because they are captured in battle or else they sell themselves into slavery due to poverty, as the Egyptians became the slaves of Pharaoh. Sometimes, by a wise and inscrutable providence, worthless children are commanded by their father to serve their more intelligent brothers and sisters. (*On the Holy Spirit* 20.51)

As he develops his ideas about the Holy Spirit in this treatise, Basil develops his ideas about slavery in parallel. This is an important charactcristic of early Christian slavery: it was inextricably linked to doctrine, and when doctrine became immutable, the institution of slavery persisted through it.

Although Basil's ideas sound like Aristotle's notion of natural slavery, most early Christians did not accept the idea of natural slavery (for more on Aristotle's ideas of natural slavery, see chapter 12, "Household Codes"). Slavery was conceived of in social terms, which was characteristic of Roman thought. Thus, slavery is located in the broader social environment—not as an *inborn* or *inherent condition*—but as the *result* of something. People are not born slaves, they become slaves. Augustine explains:

> Slavery is the result of sin. And this is why we do not find the word "slave" in any part of Scripture until righteous Noah branded the sin of his son with this name. It is a name, therefore, introduced by sin and not by nature. The origin of the Latin word for slave is supposed to be found in the circumstance that those who by the law of war were liable to be killed were sometimes preserved by their victors and were hence called servants. And these circumstances could never have arisen save through sin. (*City of God* 19.15)

Although slavery is rarely conceived of as a sin in itself, it is commonly seen as the *result* of the sinful human condition. This theological presupposition locates slavery firmly in the realm of Christian social ethics. Why is this important in understanding early Christian slavery? It is important because early Christian views on slavery function within a conceptual network that also informs other social institutions, especially marriage and imperial governance.

Another fourth-century Christian author, John Chrysostom (ca. 347–407 CE), articulated the interconnectedness of social institutions thus:

> While their receiving government was the result of God's lovingkindness alone, then, their forfeiting government was the result of their indiffer-

ence: just as kings discharge from government those who disobey their commands, so too did God in the case of human beings, discharging them from government at that time. Now, it is necessary to explain today the great honor of another kind as well, which sin of its nature removed, and all the forms of slavery it introduced, like a kind of usurper with a variety of shackles shackling our nature in its various roles of government. (*Sermon 4 on Genesis* 1)

Chrysostom, like many other Christian thinkers of antiquity, believed social institutions served the purpose of governing human beings after the Fall. He explains further: "And from the beginning God made only one form of rule, appointing the man over the woman. But after that our kind ran aground in much disorder, so he appointed other forms of rule as well, those of slaveholders, and those of governors" (*Sermon 4 on Genesis* 1). Chrysostom here represents a common Christian view about the nature of social institutions. Like marriage, imperial governance, and slavery, social institutions were introduced to mitigate the effects of sin. They were introduced to bridle human beings, so to speak. We should carefully note the rhetoric. Marriage, imperial governance, and institutional slavery are all seen as forms of bondage or enslavement, "slaveries," in themselves. Institutional slavery, then, is just one of several slaveries introduced to manage the effects of sin. Slavery is therefore not a sin but a measure used by God to control sin. Basil's comment at the start of this chapter also plays into this thinking.

Why is it important to first grasp this theological positioning of slavery in early Christian thought? It is important because if we want to understand early Christian views and practices of enslavement, we should understand that slavery was seen as a necessary institution alongside others like marriage and imperial government—slavery was therefore part of an imperfect yet necessary social ecosystem. When we understand this principle, we also understand why other early Christian groups opposed slavery.

In the synodal letter from the fourth-century Synod of Gangra, we read of a Christian group that opposed slavery and (illegally) freed slaves—the so-called followers of Eustathius. In the third canon of the Synod, we read: "If anyone shall teach a slave, under pretext of piety, to despise his master and to run away from his service, and not to serve his own master with good-will and all honor, let him be anathema." It seems that some Eustathians encouraged enslaved persons to rebel against their enslavers. However, we also read that the Eustathians encouraged husbands and wives to leave one another and to pursue a life of celibacy, so as to further remove themselves from sin. Tertullian

Figure 13.2. Terracotta oil lamp depicting three enslaved workers carrying a large object, possibly an amphora. Circa 40–100 CE.

(160–240 CE) made similar accusations against the Marcionites, although we do not know whether the Marcionites really renounced slavery or if it this is only Tertullian's invective against a group he so despised. The canons and synodal letter of Gangra, as well as Tertullian's remarks about the Marcionites, are important since they represent instances of at least two Christian groups possibly adopting a practice close to what we might call abolition.

Even with the possibility of groups that opposed slavery, the matter is complex because of the social ecosystem in which Christian slavery operated. Did the Eustathians and Marcionites renounce slavery because they understood it to be evil in and of itself? Or did they renounce slavery as part of a broader rigorous ascetic program renouncing all forms of government that came as a result of sin, including marriage? Arguing from an ascetic perspective, many early Christian authors understood marriage as a type of "slavery" in which the husband and wife should submit to one another (cf. 1 Cor 7:4). Whatever their motives, ascetic or otherwise, the Eustathians may represent a group of Christians who were able to recognize the oppressive and even sinful nature of slavery. Thus, the common assumption that ancient thinkers did not abolish slavery because they were unable to think outside of their social context does not hold ground. Some Christian individuals and groups were able to envision a world without slavery, but sadly these groups were swiftly branded as heretics and anathematized by the "mainstream" church. From the earliest times, Christian theology was utilized to both affirm and renounce slavery as a social institution. It was the former ideology that gained the most momentum in the early church.

Then, we have one of the most famous Christian sermons denouncing slavery as an act of pride against God himself. Gregory of Nyssa (ca. 335–ca. 395 CE) was Basil of Caesarea's younger brother, and in a sermon on Ecclesiastes 2:7—which reads, "I bought male and female slaves and had slaves who were born in my house"—he states:

This man counts as his own what truly belongs to God and gives to the likes of himself the kind of power which makes him think that he can be the master of men and women. You are condemning to slavery human beings whose nature is free and characterized by free will. . . . Did the little notebook, the written agreement and the calculation in obols trick you into thinking that you could be master of the image of God? What utter folly! If the contract was lost, if the writing was eaten by moths, if a drop of water fell on it and washed it away, where is there any proof that you have a slave? Where is there anything that supports you in being a master? (*Homily 4 on Ecclesiastes* 1)

Gregory's sermon especially condemns the practice of buying and retaining slaves through the law. It is considered one of the first "seeds" of abolitionist thinking in early Christianity. But even this text is not without its complexities and problems. We have no evidence that Gregory put this rhetoric into practice, and he may have continued to own slaves for the rest of his life. The sermon still sees human rule and domination over the earth as appropriate, only that human beings may not own or dominate one another. Nevertheless, the sermon remains an important testimony to the varieties of early Christian discourse about slavery.

Augustine seems to have understood something at which Gregory hints: "For a Christian ought not to possess a slave in the same way as a horse or money: although it may happen that a horse is valued at a greater price than a slave, and some article of gold or silver at much more" (*Our Lord's Sermon on the Mount* 1.19.59). Augustine still allows for slave ownership but expresses a tension in professing to "own" human beings like other forms of property. Like many other Christian thinkers, Augustine does not go so far as Gregory or the Eustathians to denounce slavery in principle.

The early Christian "theologization" of slavery had another significant consequence. Along with positioning and approaching slavery in the broader network of social institutions, the early Christians frequently used slavery as a metaphor, often to explain the characteristics of Christian life and one's relationship to God (see chapter 10, "Metaphors of Enslavement"). The metaphor of slavery to God ran very deep in early Christian discourse, and we cannot deny that the proliferation of these types of discourses inevitably embedded institutional slavery deeper and more firmly into Christian thought and practice. At some points, the metaphor of the slavery to God became so potent that it is difficult to ascertain where the metaphor meets reality (see chapter 10, "Metaphors of Enslavement"). For example, an apocryphal text known as the

Acts of Thomas tells us about the disciple Judas Thomas, who is sold by Jesus as a slave to a merchant in order to go and preach the gospel in India. In this story, Thomas is both a slave of Christ and an institutional slave, and the distinction between these two identities is opaque at best.

The Acts of Thomas was one of the most influential texts in the development of early Christian monasticism, and in the next centuries we see the title "slave of God" or "slave of Christ" becoming more and more indicative of the identity of the Christian monk and ascetic. In Syrian Christian monasticism, "slave of Christ" functioned as a technical title for a monk. Slavery was an important metaphor for making sense of asceticism. The fourth-century Syriac Book of Steps, a manual for Christian monks, explains one of the main premises of a monk's identity using the metaphor of slavery:

> I will make my body a slave and discipline it and I will not allow it to clothe, put on shoes, feed, and refresh itself according to its own will. And I will not allow it to be honored whenever it wishes, not even to sleep with honor, but I will subdue it with hunger, thirst, and nakedness, vigil, weariness, asceticism, and emaciation, and with much fasting and prayer, with supplication and loud crying, with many bitter tears, and with lowliness, endurance, and patience. I will subdue myself in order to honor everyone as a slave and in order to stand before and greet everyone before me, bowing [my] head before everyone. . . . I will lead [my body] wherever it does not wish: to its despisers and those who are angry against it. Just as our Lord went to teach his crucifiers and despisers, I will make it visit as the slave of everyone, the slave of slaves, just as our Lord visited the evil and insolent ones who held him in contempt. (*Book of Steps* 29.1)

The body had to be a slave of the soul, and the soul always had to dominate the body and its passions. Paul's words in 1 Corinthians 9:27, declaring that one needs to subordinate the body like a slave, were strikingly influential in this regard. In Christian thought, therefore, the metaphor of slavery was not only used to make sense of one's relationship with God, but the very nature of human subjectivity, the relationship between the soul and the body, was conceptualized in terms of slavery. What is quite interesting in this regard is that it seems that early Christian ascetic practices such as fasting, vigils, chaining, and so on were directly shaped by slaveholding discourses and practices. This is a good example that demonstrates how slavery as discourse shaped early Christian rhetoric, identity, and religious practice.

Within the Christian metaphorical imagination, all human beings were seen to be the slaves of some master. If you were not a slave of God or Christ, you were inevitably a slave of sin and the passions. We have already seen that slavery was not considered to be a sin in itself but rather the result of sin. However, in early Christian thought being subject to sin was the worst form of slavery. John Chrysostom once again makes this point apparent:

> And how shall slavery be able to harm you? It is not slavery itself, beloved, that harms us; but the real slavery is that of sin. And if you are not a slave in this sense, be bold and rejoice. No one shall have power to do you any wrong, having the temper which cannot be enslaved. But if you are a slave to sin, even though you are ten thousand times free you have no good of your freedom. (*Homily 19 on 1 Corinthians* 6)

This type of rhetoric assumed that being an institutional slave was "better" than being a slave of sin. This metaphorical use of slavery removes the focus from the oppression of institutional slavery. The implication is that we should not worry about institutional slavery—that is not the "real" problem. The "real" problem and "real" slavery is sin. Furthermore, the freedom of salvation was paradoxically enslavement to Christ. Augustine called salvation in Christ *libera servitus*, "free slavery" (*City of God* 14.15; 19.15). Sadly, this type of thinking is a stumbling block to the abolitionist project since institutional slavery is downplayed. Thus, when we study the early Christian use of slavery as a metaphor, we should always ask what the social and political effects of such metaphors could have been.

In sum, early Christians responded variously against slavery. These authors never directly debated slavery as they did with some theological topics like the Trinity or the nature of Christ. Slavery was often used as a discourse to talk about other things. Thus, there is no uniform response against practices of enslavement. Although some may have been uncomfortable with the façade of Roman slaveholding as they perceived it, many Christians probably owned slaves. Our next question is to ask how they treated their slaves. Did Christian enslavers necessarily treat slaves differently?

Early Christian Views on the Treatment of Slaves

The first Christians owned slaves. Enslaved persons occupied the homes and house churches of the first Christians from the earliest days of the movement. As in Roman ideologies of enslavement, Christians also understood slaves as part of the wealth of an individual or family. Thus, Christian views on wealth and poverty also shaped slaveholding practices. We see this in some prescriptions about the number of persons one should enslave. Most Christian authors did not approve of a person enslaving large numbers of people. John Chrysostom, for example, tells his wealthy Constantinopolitan audience this:

> But there is no one who lays down their abundance. For as long as you have many slaves, and garments of silk, these things are all abundances. Nothing is indispensable or necessary, without which we are able to live; these things are superfluous and are simply add-ons. Let us then see, if you allow me, what we cannot live without. If we have only two slaves, we can live. For some live without slaves, what excuse do we have, if we are not satisfied with two? (*Homily 28 on Hebrews* 4)

Such an admonition to only own a handful of slaves, maybe between two and four, would have been perceived as rather radical advice by some of the wealthy patrons of the eastern imperial capital, some of whom may have had hundreds of slaves, or even over a thousand of them. Wealthy Christians wanting to pursue monastic life sometimes manumitted masses of enslaved workers.

For example, Melania the Younger manumitted thousands of slaves according to tradition, but such accounts of mass manumissions are complex, and questions arise about the accuracy of such accounts. How would such mass manumissions have practically been administered? What were the detrimental effects of such manumissions on enslaved persons themselves? Which slaves were manumitted, and which were retained? Melania took some enslaved persons with her to the monastery, and we do have accounts of monks themselves owning some slaves while pursuing the ascetic life.

Yet, it does seem that early Christian ideology positioned itself against mass slaveholding. Like Chrysostom, Basil of Caesarea was very uncomfortable with the excessive wealth of some landowners who owned multitudes of slaves (*Homily on the Martyrdom of Julitta* 1). He also believes that one should not use slaves for tasks that promote luxury. Whether most "regular" Christians, in turn, followed the advice is a matter of speculation. Implied in the reduction but not elimination of one's enslaved population is that enslaved workers were necessary for the most menial and shameful tasks, tasks not fit for a free person. Thus, reducing the number of slaves in households was not necessarily a positive move. The remaining slaves probably would have had a much harder life and would have lived under much more scrutiny. Additionally, Basil laments that the slaves of such rich people are "torn to pieces," which most likely refers to the whipping of slaves both on farms and in urban households (*Homily on the Rich Young Man* 2.6).

It has been shown that there were similarities between early Christian and Stoic views on the treatment of slaves. They especially agreed that slavery did not threaten one's soul, that enslavers should not treat their slaves badly and unfairly, and that slaves should still be submissive and obedient to their enslavers.

Basil and most other Christian authors were not against the punishment of slaves in principle, but they did oppose the excessively violent punishment of slaves, which was considered unlawful, shameful, and a result of a loss of self-control on the part of the enslaver. This was a very common view in early Christianity and Stoic philosophy. According to this view, enslavers were never to punish their slaves excessively and out of anger; otherwise, the enslaver appeared shameful and unruly. The most important principle of corporal punishment was that it should be administered with restraint. Christian writers like Basil and John Chrysostom recommend that enslavers should always keep moderation in mind in dealing with their slaves.

John Chrysostom warns his audience not to assume "that what was done to a slave will be forgiven by God, just because it was done to a slave" (*Homily 22 on Ephesians* 1). The use of excessive violence against slaves is strictly prohibited. Chrysostom is aware of secular laws that do not protect enslaved people from abuse, but in a rather Stoic way he believes that, according to the laws of God, all are equal. "But the law of the common Lord and Master of all, who does good to all on an equal level," explains Chrysostom, "and distributes the same privileges to all, knows no such difference" (*Homily 22 on Ephesians* 1). God is once again seen here as the enslaver of all. Although this rhetoric may appear positive, it is difficult to determine the extent to which these views made a practical difference in the lives of the enslaved.

The fact that this advice is so common in early Christian sources may mean that the physical abuse of slaves was commonplace, even with Christian enslavers. John Chrysostom emphasizes: "But you think that the whole race of slaves becomes unbearable when they are treated indulgently. Yes! I know that myself" (*Homily 15 on Ephesians* 2). Any form of discipline and corporal punishment had to be pedagogical for the slave and in the service of self-control. Punishment and reward had to be strategic. Chrysostom says that the female enslaver of the household could withhold food from her slaves if their work was not finished (*Homily on the Statues* 14.4). Already, the diet of enslaved workers was meager in Christian homes, and we hear that many ate only bread (*Homily 16 on 1 Timothy* 2).

Of course, slaves were also rewarded in numerous ways. Such "good" treatment was always to be answered with gratitude, although enslavers were

not expected to thank their slaves for their service. On this point, Chrysostom recalls Luke 17:9: "Do we thank our slaves when they serve us? Definitely not!" In a metaphor where Christ is the heavenly enslaver, Chrysostom notes that it is "the glory of the master to have grateful slaves," and it is "the glory of the master, if he should love his slaves so" (*Homily 2 on Philemon* 2). Christian enslavers did not have to show gratitude to their slaves, but enslaved workers always had to be grateful that their enslavers "loved" them and

Figure 13.3. A Roman iron shackle from Britain that was likely used to physically restrain enslaved persons.

treated them with care. We see here a disturbing paternalism, which intends to put the enslaver in a good light, while it emphasizes the enslaver's need of the slave, but never shows the dependence of the enslaver on the enslaved.

Christian enslavers were also responsible for managing the relationships of their enslaved workers, especially sexual relationships. One of the distinctive features of early Christian slavery was that Christian slaves were expected to have sexual modesty and shame. The sexual exploitation of slaves was harshly criticized, which leads us to believe that this did occur in Christian households. In Christian sexual ethics, the sexual abuse of a female slave was now included in the scope of sexual misconduct (*stuprum* in Latin; *phthora* in Greek) and adultery (*adulterium* or *moicheia* in Latin and Greek, respectively). John Chrysostom is once again a useful source in this regard. In a homily devoted to the problem of fornication and adultery (interpreting 1 Cor 7:2), Chrysostom states:

> We are not unaware that many people suppose "adultery" is only when a man defiles another man's wife. But I say if a man who has a wife carries on in a wicked and lascivious manner with a whore who works the streets,

a household slave, or some other woman who does not have a husband, such an act is adultery. Indeed, the accusation of adultery is confirmed not only by those who have been abused but even by the abusers themselves. So do not tell me now about the laws of the outside world that drag women who engage in adultery into court and require a public examination and punishment, but do not require a public examination and punishment for married men who defile themselves with their female slaves. Instead, I shall read to you the law of God that censures both the woman and the man alike and says this act is adultery. (*Homily on 1 Corinthians 7:2-4* 4)

The sphere of adultery is now expanded, and not only includes violating a married woman, but also an enslaved person. The sexual honor of slaves reflected back onto enslavers, and some enslaved persons in Christian homes could even be expected to remain virgins. Thus, we see another measure of sexual control and domination imposed on slaves, now in a mode that promoted Christian sexual ethics of self-control and sexual renunciation.

Just as a father had the right to determine who his children would marry, an enslaver had the final say regarding the relationships between his enslaved men and women. Basil writes in one of his letters: "It is a serious mistake, even for a slave girl, to bind herself in secret in marriage, and thus fill the house with shame and insult her master as a result of her own mischievous lifestyle" (Basil of Caesarea, *Epistle* 199.18). Enslavers were responsible for managing their slaves' personal relationships and always had to handle these relationships in such a way that they would not bring shame on the owner and his household.

Finally, the treatment and behavior of slaves in Christian contexts had to contribute to the positive image of Christianity. This was a principle that often preoccupied Christian discourse about slavery. The anonymous Latin Christian writer later known simply as Ambrosiaster (fl. 366–384 CE) gives us an interesting glimpse into this aspect of early Christian slavery. Ambrosiaster explains that Christian slaves who do not do good work dishonor God's name. "Paul exhorts slaves to serve their earthly masters in the fear of the Lord, so that it may appear that they deserve their freedom," he writes, and he believes that "Paul says this perhaps because he is afraid that a converted slave might be more and may become negligent when he does good deeds for his earthly master and thus disgraces the teaching of Christ" (*Commentary on 1 Corinthians* 7.21). He focuses here more on how the enslaved should behave than on how enslavers should treat their slaves. The implication is that if slaves behaved like free persons, they would be treated as if they were free, or at least deserved freedom—an idealism that was probably quite unrealistic.

Ambrosiaster saw this principle in practice in the case of Philemon and Onesimus. In his commentary on Paul's letter to Philemon, Onesimus is viewed as a slave of sin. Ambrosiaster assumes that Onesimus committed a crime against Philemon and fled. This assumption is complicated by the fact that Onesimus was enslaved to Philemon. These two aspects of Onesimus overlap to such an extent that a reader cannot separate the two, and this was precisely Ambrosiaster's aim. For Ambrosiaster, Onesimus's conversion was, so to speak, a deliverance from enslavement to sin and to Philemon, although nowhere in Paul's letter, or in Ambrosiaster's commentary on it, is it mentioned that Onesimus had to be manumitted. Ambrosiaster assumes that Philemon would treat Onesimus differently because of his conversion to Christianity. This is consistent with John Chrysostom's and Basil's views that disobedient, sinful slaves were to be treated harshly and punished severely. Like the Stoics, again, Ambrosiaster also appeals to the common humanity of the enslaved person and the slaveholder.

Many Christian authors were convinced that when slaves and enslavers converted to Christianity, they would be better in their respective roles. A Christian slave had to be better than the one who was not converted. We also see that Ambrosiaster advised slaves who owned their own slaves, a common phenomenon in Roman society, to treat these slaves well, just as they would want to be treated by their own masters (*Commentary on Ephesians* 6.5). In a rare case where slaves are directly addressed in a homily, John Chrysostom also states:

> For if you serve your master with good intentions, yet the cause of this service commences from your fear of God, so the one who serves with such great fear will receive the greater reward. For if a slave does not control his hand, or his undisciplined tongue, how will the Greek admire the doctrine that is among us? But if they see their slave, who has been taught the philosophy of Christ, showing more self-mastery than their own philosophers, and serving with all meekness and good intentions, he will admire the power of the gospel in every way. For the Greeks do not judge doctrines by the doctrine itself, but they make the practice and lifestyle the test of the doctrines. (John Chrysostom, *Homily 4 on Titus* 1)

Enslavers should not neglect to teach their slaves Christian virtue, since this could damage the reputation of the church. Thus, the conduct of enslaved Christians not only reflected honor or shame back onto the enslaver, but disobedient Christian slaves were seen as dishonoring the church itself. An obedient Christian slave would be a hallmark for outsiders. "For if the unbeliever sees slaves behaving imperiously on account of the faith," Chrysostom explains, "he will blaspheme, as if the doctrine caused insubordination. But when he sees that they are persuaded to be obedient, he will be more persuaded" (*Homily 4 on Titus* 1).

Ambrosiaster further elaborates on this issue: "The person who keeps to the measures of his service towards his earthly master is the one who serves God" (*Commentary on Ephesians* 6.6–7). Such a statement is, of course, very one-sided and clearly in favor of the enslavers. As with the other authors we have discussed in this chapter, we see that church writers such as Ambrosiaster considered the obedience of slaves to be central to Christian ethics. Ambrosiaster did use the concept of communal slavery to God to entice enslavers to treat their slaves fairly: "Earthly masters must acknowledge that God is the common Lord of all and must therefore only insist on the services that they themselves would be willing to do if it were asked of them" (*Commentary on Ephesians* 6.9).

Finally, the ordination of slaves and freedpersons into the clergy was widespread in early Christianity, although the traditional hierarchical structures of the church were not always in favor thereof. Gregory of Nazianzus (ca. 329–390 CE), for example, called such low-status clergy "heaven-bound dung beetles" (*Poem* 2.1.12). Nevertheless, we have ample evidence of enslaved leaders and clergy in early Christian communities. Monasteries could also have slaves, and it often happened that fugitive slaves fled to monasteries for asylum. Both these issues, the ordination of enslaved persons and monastic asylum for slaves, were strictly and restrictively regulated in early church policies.

Conclusion

In this examination of early Christian thought, we see how deeply slavery was embedded in early Christian theology and ethics. The actions of enslavers and enslaved people alike garnered much discussion. The treatment of slaves in early Christianity therefore produced a question about the dynamics of interpersonal relationships between individuals of various social statuses. Furthermore, the metaphor of slavery illuminated the relationship between God and the believer, a metaphor as influential as that of God as father and son. The way enslavers treated their slaves should reflect how God treated his slaves—there should be a symmetry of behavior patterns between God and enslavers. Thus, early Christian theological thought about slavery directly influenced how slavery was enacted in late antiquity.

Discussion Questions

1. Choose one of the early Christian writers mentioned in this chapter. In a small group, look them up and find basic information about them. Then,

using the chapter, outline their views on slavery. How would you present those views to your colleagues in your class?

2. What were the consequences for early Christians of creating theologies that draw on enslavement discourses? What are the consequences today for Christians drawing on enslavement discourses for theological meaning-making?

3. What is the relationship between practices of slavery and theologies that use enslavement discourses for early Christians? Why is this relationship important for us to think about today? How might we read against the grain of some early Christian enslavement discourses to understand how enslaved people could have experienced life among Christians in late antiquity?

Further Reading

Charles, Ronald. *The Silencing of Slaves in Early Jewish and Christian Texts*. London: Routledge, 2019.

Glancy, Jennifer A. *Slavery as Moral Problem in the Early Church and Today*. Minneapolis: Fortress, 2011.

———. *Slavery in Early Christianity*. 2nd ed. Minneapolis: Fortress, 2024.

Harper, Kyle. *Slavery in the Late Roman World, AD 275–425*. Cambridge: Cambridge University Press, 2011.

Ramelli, Ilaria L. E. *Social Justice and the Legitimacy of Slavery: The Role of Philosophical Asceticism from Ancient Judaism to Late Antiquity*. Oxford: Oxford University Press, 2016.

Rotman, Youval. *Byzantine Slavery and the Mediterranean World*. Translated by Jane Marie Todd. Cambridge, MA: Harvard University Press, 2009.

Shaner, Katherine A. *Enslaved Leadership in Early Christianity*. New York: Oxford University Press, 2018.

Wet, Chris L. de. *The Unbound God: Slavery and the Formation of Early Christian Thought*. London: Routledge, 2018.

Wet, Chris L. de, Maijastina Kahlos, and Ville Vuolanto, eds. *Slavery in the Late Antique World, 150–700 CE*. Cambridge: Cambridge University Press, 2022.

14   *Ethics of Interpretation*

MIDORI E. HARTMAN

Very often, it can be quite a challenge for students and readers to confront the reality of slavery in the Bible. The following two texts above are both included in the New Testament, yet present vastly different ideas regarding slavery:

> Urge slaves to be submissive to their masters in everything, to be pleasing, not talking back, not stealing, but showing complete and perfect fidelity, so that in everything they may be an ornament to the teaching of God our Savior. (Titus 2:9–10)

> There is no longer Jew or Greek; there is no longer slave or free; there is no longer male and female, for all of you are one in Christ Jesus. (Gal 3:28)

Titus suggests that enslaved people owe unquestioned obedience. Galatians suggests that enslaved status is not relevant for those who are "in Christ." It can be troubling to confront the reality that a text with so many stories about liberation from oppression (e.g., the Exodus story) can also contain texts commanding enslaved people to submit and obey their enslavers (see chapter 12, "Household Codes"). When facing this paradox, some readers may only want to read and use positive stories or to talk about enslavement only in indirect, metaphorical terms (see chapter 10, "Metaphors of Enslavement"). These are understandable responses; however, they cannot adequately address the uncomfortable historical reality of enslavement in the biblical world.

As careful readers of the Bible, we have an ethical obligation to acknowledge that enslavement was a foundational and accepted reality of ancient Near

Figure 14.1. Detail from the mosaic floor of the House of Dionysos in Paphos, Cyprus. Second–fourth century CE.

Eastern and Mediterranean societies. This means that the Bible will sometimes seem alien to our own modern sensibilities and desires as readers (see chapter 2, "Studying Slavery"). However, I suggest that we wrestle with this difficult reality and its implications throughout history by directly engaging enslavement passages of the Bible within their original contexts and by exploring how these same passages have been interpreted variously over time by subsequent generations.

Our exploration of enslavement as an ancient reality of the Bible becomes an important part of our interpretive toolkit because such context helps us to appreciate both how radically egalitarian biblical passages can be interpreted *and* how far we have come in the modern, post-slavery context. For example, we can consider how the erasure of various binaries such as the free–slave distinction in Galatians 3:28 above is part of the Jesus movement's offering of a new framework for living—a primary identity in Christ—over and above how the wider Mediterranean social world organized itself. So, while we must acknowledge overall that the earliest Jesus movement was not focused on the abolition of slavery (e.g., 1 Cor 7:21–24), it does contain the ideological seeds, such as Galatians 3:28, that would be used as scriptural support for later generations to abolish enslavement as a social institution in the modern world.

This chapter focuses on how we as readers of the Bible are called to wrestle with difficult enslavement passages by learning the ancient context of slavery and its relationship to ethnicity so we can understand biblical stories better and, equally as important, so we can confront the long impact of ancient enslavement on historical and living communities who center the Bible in their ethics. Since ethics are the societally developed moral principles by which actions are judged as right or wrong (just or unjust), then enslavement as a problematic human institution demands our continued ethical consideration because of its long impact on our world to this day. This can be seen through the legacy of Jim Crow as well as through global human trafficking (see chapter 15, "Modern Slavery, the Bible, and Slow-Down Ethics"). The Bible's role in this history cannot be ignored or downplayed.

Let us turn to two possible ethical approaches to use when reading difficult biblical passages on enslavement and ethnicity in the New Testament followed by a case study for each approach. These approaches are a starting point, but they cannot encompass all ethical ways of interpreting difficult passages of the Bible. The first approach for ethical interpretation I will introduce is "intersectionality." I will use Paul's retelling of the Sarah and Hagar story from Galatians 4 to illustrate the possibilities of this reading. The second approach for ethical interpretation that I will introduce is "centering enslaved persons." For this, I will turn to Paul's letter to Philemon as an example of centering the enslaved Onesimus in our analysis.

Intersectionality: Recognizing Power and Privileges within the Biblical Text

Intersectionality is a term that illustrates how a person's identity is not singular but contains many layers that can *either* empower *or* marginalize them depending upon how a given society views each layer of identity.[1] These layers of identity include, but are not limited to, gender, sexuality, class, ethnicity, nationality/citizenship, age, and disability. A given society's preference for certain layers of identity over others results in the discrimination or elevation of how

---

1. See Kimberlé Crenshaw, "Demarginalizing the Intersection of Race and Sex: A Black Feminist Critique of Antidiscrimination Doctrine, Feminist Theory and Antiracist Politics," *University of Chicago Legal Forum* (1989): 139–67.

a person may be viewed and treated. This approach allows us to identify and analyze these layers, which then helps us begin to recognize where power and privilege manifest in preferred layers of identity over others in a society. Thus, as a tool, intersectionality helps us consider how people are far more complex than the dominant layers of identity we might focus upon at first glance. This point is very important for us to remember in order to avoid becoming inattentive interpreters of the Bible who reinscribe hierarchical discrimination by only paying attention to more privileged layers of identity, such as elite status (see chapter 8, "Race and Ethnicity").

As an interpretive tool, intersectionality allows us to unpack the ways in which ancient enslavement in the Bible is deeply intertwined with many other aspects of identity, including ethnicity. When taking an intersectional approach to interpreting the Bible, we can recognize with intention that the text's rhetoric and characters are complex, nuanced, and ambiguous in ways that call us to pay attention to whom or what is being marginalized in the text's own bias concerning what is "ideal."[2] Thus, the use of intersectionality is an ethical way to read difficult enslavement passages in the Bible because it recognizes the reality of oppression within the biblical text. This, in turn, impacted subsequent generations of people who had to wrestle with enslavement and how the Bible both played a role in enslavement and was a tool of arguing for its resistance (i.e., modern abolitionist movements).

When intersectionality is used as a lens to study the Bible, it illuminates examples and rhetoric concerning hierarchical and dualistic binaries of categories that connect with identity construction, which helps us pick up on the implicit biases of the ancient social world. The prioritization and privileging of certain aspects is used to justify and reinscribe the status quo of the society that depends upon such binaries to organize their social worlds and ideologies. Even when our ancient texts complicate and question these dualistic categories, the texts still depend upon them for meaning in the first place.

Below is a broadly constructed and basic list of binaries representing the hierarchical and dualistic binaries that organized much of the ideologies of the social worlds of the ancient Near East and Mediterranean. The lefthand side were qualities most often considered ideal ("good"), and the righthand side were those often less idealized, less valued, or viewed as problematic ("bad") in the dominant rhetoric. Note that this list is an artificial construction, and

2. See Marianne Bjelland Kartzow, *The Slave Metaphor and Gendered Enslavement in Early Christian Discourse: Double Trouble Embodied* (New York: Routledge, 2018).

real life was often much more complex in practice, as seen in our discussion of intersectionality above:

EXAMPLE BINARY VALUES

"Good"	"Bad"
Self	Other
Free	Slave
Male	Female
Elite Class	Lower Class
Insider	Outsider
Human	Animal
Order	Chaos

Using this list, we can investigate how biblical passages construct their rhetoric and/or characters in alignment with or resistance to the binaries above. Intersectionality allows us to see how the rhetoric and characters of the Bible are complexly constructed according to the aims and goals of their textual authors, which also calls us to be aware of what presumptions we bring to the text as interpreters.

In what follows, I turn to a case study that invites an intersectional view of how gender, enslavement, and ethnicity come together in how we can approach a challenging biblical passage, namely Paul's allegorical use of Hagar (from Genesis) in Galatians 4.

Case Study: Wrestling with Paul's Allegory of Hagar and Sarah (Gal 4:21–31)

Around 53 CE, Paul wrote a letter to the communities that he established while he was recovering from an illness in the region of Galatia (Asia Minor), which is in modern-day Turkey. He was frustrated that they were persuaded by competing apostles who advocated that the Galatian gentiles had to practice Jewish customs to be part of the Jesus movement, most notably the act of circumcision (the cutting off the male foreskin), which was established as a custom when Abraham and God made a covenant in Genesis 17:9–14. This interpretation went against Paul's gospel vision, in which God made a separate path of salvation for the gentiles with the intervention of Jesus Christ, such that they did not need to uphold the law like Jews did for their salvation.

According to Paul, if a gentile participated in Jewish practices, this proved they did not understand the gospel and did not truly believe in their salvation through Jesus Christ.

Paul illustrates this point with a metaphor that introduces both enslavement and ethnicity into his argument. In Galatians 4:21–31, Paul allegorically reads two Hebrew Bible characters, Hagar and Sarah, to argue that gentile Christians are the offspring of Sarah (Isaac) and not Hagar (Ishmael):

> But what does the scripture say? "Drive out the enslaved woman and her child, for the child of the enslaved woman will not share the inheritance with the child of the free woman." So then, brothers and sisters, we are children, not of an enslaved woman but of the free woman. (Gal 4:30–31)

This allegorical interpretation is based upon Genesis 16:1–16, which states that Sarah (Sarai) was not able to bear children for Abraham (Abram), so she offers up her slave, Hagar the Egyptian, as a surrogate to produce a son, Ishmael. Sarah's jealousy leads her to punish Hagar, leading the enslaved woman to run away into the wilderness. An angel of the Lord commands her to return and submit to Sarah with the promise of many descendants (i.e., a lineage). In Genesis 17:1–8, God promises Abraham many descendants (a lineage) in the Promised Land (Canaan) if he takes up a sign of the covenant upon him and his line: circumcision. God promises that the elderly Sarah will bear him a son, Isaac, who will be honored with an everlasting covenant separate from the blessings given to Ishmael, the child of the enslaved Hagar. How should we interpret Paul's allegory of Hagar and Sarah so that we recognize the power and privilege of the biblical text in intersectional terms?

From an intersectional perspective, we should focus upon how the identity layers of these characters are used to marginalize or elevate a character in an unequal hierarchical social system. In my intersectional analysis, I have bolded the identities that align with the chart above, in order to show the way they are used within Paul's retelling of this story. Abraham as a Jewish **insider** and a **free male** chosen by God and promised a great lineage is the most privileged and prioritized character, which matches with expectations of the ancient patriarchal culture of Israel. Next in the hierarchy is Sarah, who is more marginalized than Abraham for being **female**, and thus is legally considered his property and happens to be unable to provide children for her husband. However, Sarah also has privilege, as she is **free**, an enslaver, and has a Jewish ethnicity. Within the Jewish-centric bias of the biblical text, Hagar is the most marginalized character by virtue of being **female**, having the status of **enslaved**, and having

Figure 14.2. Hagar. Marble statue by Edmonia Lewis. 1875.

an **outsider** ethnicity (Egyptian). The social marginalization of Hagar plays out not only in her being abused to produce offspring for Abraham when Sarah cannot, but also ideologically in the unequal divine promises and benefits given to the freeborn Isaac versus the slave-born Ishmael. With the tool of an intersectional perspective, we can complicate our alignment with the text's default identification with Abraham and Sarah as the progenitors of Judaism by seeing them as more complicated characters, not models for emulation. We are challenged to see how our own limitations might prevent us from identifying automatically with Hagar. We can also consider what it might take for us to see Abraham and Sarah as more ambiguous characters than how they have been treated in our religious traditions.

Informed by these insights from intersectionality and the original Genesis passage, we can turn to Paul's rhetorical use of Hagar and Sarah to inform the Galatian gentiles that they are part of the covenant through faith, and we can clearly see its limitations. Paul's interpretation of Genesis 16 hinges on the continued rhetorical use and abuse of an enslaved character to make a point of privilege for a select few, namely that the Galatians are "Isaac" (Sarah's child) in Paul's framework. Paul can use the women as a teachable allegory because while they would not be so familiar with the Torah itself, his gentile audience would desire to align with the free (Sarah) and not the enslaved (Hagar) given the ancient social values represented in the free–slave binary. In short, Paul's use of Hagar and Sarah is an example of how power and privilege ties to the ideology of freedom in the Bible.[3]

Nevertheless, Hagar's story does not end with Paul. Her experience has been reinterpreted as a source of empowerment, resisting dominant and automatic identification with Sarah and Abraham. For example, Delores S. Williams argues for the paralleling between the story of Hagar and the enslaved African American women's experience in the antebellum period in the United States, in which enslaved women were literal and metaphorical "surrogates" for the material and immaterial needs of their enslavers. Recognizing God as the source of Hagar's survival but *not* her liberation, Williams helps us to see that Hagar's liberation "finds its source in human initiative" to use God's provided resources of the "survival/quality-of-life tradition of African-American biblical appropriation" to survive enslavement.[4] In this way, Williams invites us "to see the Hagar-Sarah texts in the Bible from the position of the slave woman Hagar rather than from the perspective of the slave owners (Abraham and Sarah) and their culture."[5] This resists the default approach most Eurocentric interpretations have taken with the enslaved Hagar's story because of the implicit bias toward Sarah and Abraham as the progenitors of God's chosen people.[6]

In summary, thinking with an intersectional approach helps us name the power and the privilege of the worldviews of the biblical text. In doing so, it invites productive attention to the marginalized, such as the enslaved, as an act of resistance against dominant interpretations that cause marginalization.

3. See Christy Cobb, "Enslaved Women, Women Enslavers: Evidence of Kyriarchy in the New Testament," *Journal of Feminist Studies in Religion* 40, no. 1 (2024): 43–60.

4. Delores S. Williams, *Sisters in the Wilderness: The Challenge of Womanist God-Talk* (Maryknoll, NY: Orbis, 1993), 4–5.

5. Williams, *Sisters in the Wilderness*, 7.

6. See Nyasha Junior, *Reimagining Hagar: Blackness and the Bible* (New York: Oxford University Press, 2019).

If we accept that the biblical text privileges the biases of its authors' social worlds, then we are invited to point out the limitations of those biases. With such a perspective, we can approach Paul's allegorical use of Hagar's story as a problematic appropriation of enslavement that reflects his own rhetorical biases that marginalize the enslaved by rhetorically connecting the Galatians with Isaac. This leads us to another interrelated approach to take on in our interpretive toolkits, namely centering enslaved characters and populations.

Centering Enslaved Characters and Populations, Named or Otherwise

A major challenge we face as interpreters of the Bible is the lack of firsthand ancient accounts of the experience of enslavement from the perspective of the enslaved. In other words, we do not have their voices to learn directly from. Instead, we have the thoughts and perspectives of the free, manumitted, and enslavers' thoughts on the enslaved experience. This absence of the voices of the enslaved makes it challenging to write biblical history that accounts for their experiences in authentic ways. One productive way of addressing this absence is to read biblical texts alongside the personal accounts of the enslaved we have from modern slavery. For example, Mitzi J. Smith reimagines a dialogue between Chloe in 1 Corinthians 1:11 and Aunt Chloe in American abolitionist and suffragist Frances Watkins Harper's *Sketches of Southern Life*.[7] This comparative approach can provide us with the tools to engage in productive historical imagination of what the enslaved experience was like in antiquity. Another way scholars can approach the issue, which is the focus of this section, is to "center" marginalized characters in the Bible and to "decenter" the major characters.

The scholarly move to center the marginalized and decenter spotlighted biblical figures is a growing movement in the field of biblical studies. This can be seen as an ethical turn in interpretation because it addresses how the long history of biblical interpretation has replicated the textual marginalization of certain figures by the continued overfocus on more famous figures. The process of interpretation itself often says more about our own interests and limitations than what is fully represented in the biblical text itself, which is a point of connection we have already seen when thinking about the use of intersectionality. For example, while much scholarly ink has been spilt on the figure and ideas of Paul, the interpretive move to decenter him invites an

---

7. See Mitzi J. Smith, *Chloe and Her People: A Womanist Critical Dialogue with First Corinthians* (Eugene, OR: Cascade Books, 2023).

exploration into how it may help decolonize the subfield of Euro-American Pauline scholarship itself.[8] This is not to say we throw Paul out with the bathwater. Rather, we should raise up other figures who have been neglected or forgotten by generations of interpreters of the Bible, which may lead to novel and innovative insights that enrich our understanding of the text.

Thus, to center enslaved biblical characters is to resist their marginalization and erasure in the biblical text and our interpretations by "'reading from the margins,' that is, from a perspective of those who have been traditionally locked out of the dominant elite discourses and rhetorics."[9] Such an approach resists how enslavement has made it so that, as Saidiya Hartman, scholar of African American studies, notes, "the most universal definition of the slave is a stranger."[10] When we read difficult passages on enslavement in the Bible, we should look for how the enslaved are treated as strangers. We might then notice how the text invites us to resist that reading by making them more familiar, more readily raised in our memory. In other words, rather than strangers, how do we bring enslaved characters into our kinship circle of interpretation? This has implications for how we understand ethnicity in the Bible, especially the ways in which we can complicate how it is used as a set boundary marker between groups. In what follows, I turn to a case study that invites an intentional centering of Onesimus from Paul's letter to Philemon.

Case Study: Centering Onesimus (Letter to Philemon)

Around 55 CE, Paul wrote a personal letter to Philemon, the head of a community; Apphia, "our sister"; and Archippus, "our fellow soldier" (Phlm 1–2). Unlike Paul's other correspondence, this very short letter concerned personal relationship issues, and thus does not deal with issues of theology or the Jesus movement's relationship to Judaism, which may explain why it is not as popular as his other letters. In the letter, Paul appeals to Philemon on behalf of Onesimus, whom Paul met and converted to the Jesus movement while under

8. Melanie Johnson DeBaufre and Laura S. Nasrallah, "Beyond the Heroic Paul: Toward a Feminist and Decolonizing Approach to the Letters of Paul," in *The Colonized Apostle: Paul through Postcolonial Eyes*, ed. Christopher D. Stanley (Minneapolis: Fortress, 2011), 161–85.

9. Demetrius K. Williams, "Utility, Fraternity, and Reconciliation: Ancient Slavery as a Context for the Return of Onesimus," in *Onesimus: Our Brother: Reading Religion, Race, and Culture in Philemon*, ed. Matthew V. Johnson, James A. Noel, and Demetrius K. Williams (Minneapolis: Fortress, 2012), 12.

10. Saidiya Hartman, *Lose Your Mother: A Journey along the Atlantic Slave Route* (New York: Farrar, Straus and Giroux, 2006), 5.

house arrest (i.e., prison). Paul sends Onesimus back to Philemon with the letter in hopes of restoring the relationship between these two men:

> I am appealing to you [Philemon] for my child, Onesimus, whose father I have become during my imprisonment. Formerly he was useless to you, but now he is indeed useful to you and to me. I am sending him, that is, my own heart, back to you. . . . Perhaps this is the reason he was separated from you for a while, so that you might have him back for the long term, no longer as a slave [*doulos*] but more than a slave, a beloved brother—especially to me but how much more to you, both in the flesh and in the Lord. (Phlm 10–12, 15–16)

Now, in alignment with a traditional, more Paul-centric reading, we should take note that the letter tells us a great deal about Philemon, as a direct addressee, and Paul, as the author of the letter. We can see Philemon, as the head of his community (the "church in your [sing.] house," Phlm 2), is an elite individual but is also Paul's convert, so Paul has a great deal of sway over him because Philemon "owes" Paul for his own salvation (a kind of spiritual debt that should be paid off). Paul takes the time to address Philemon's love and faith as a brother in Christ (Phlm 4–7) before going directly to the more difficult part of the letter: Paul's plea for Onesimus (Phlm 8–21). In deference to this elite and influential man and patron, Paul cannot directly command Philemon to take the action he wishes for Onesimus, but he must try to persuade the other man to do "even more than I ask" (Phlm 21). In short, the first insight we observe from this exchange is that there is a questioning tension over who has the most power in the relationship between men with different kinds of authority (in society, in the Jesus movement). If all this can be said about both Paul and Philemon, then we are invited to consider what might be said about the most marginalized character in the letter, Onesimus. This is where centering enslaved biblical figures comes into play.

If we take on the intentional approach of centering our focus on Onesimus, we can use Paul's own letter to produce a sketch of the man in ways that challenge treating him as simply a tool in Paul's ministry. To do so is to address a problematic reality in our interpretive history of the Bible—that "biblical criticism in the West has assured and sustained Onesimus's silence and enslavement."[11] For example, in being called to find a kinship with Onesimus as the most marginal character of the letter, we resist default identification with

---

11. See Matthew V. Johnson, James A. Noel, and Demetrius K. Williams, eds., *Onesi-*

the elite and free as represented by Paul and Philemon. In short, it is an intervention that "bring[s] enslaved persons back into the historical narrative.¹²

Figure 14.3. Antislavery medallion. Circa 1787.

It is important to note here, while biblical interpreters have traditionally accepted that Onesimus was a runaway slave, this is not a universal interpretation.¹³ For example, some nineteenth-century American abolitionists argued that Philemon and Onesimus were quarreling siblings, thus making the slave language of the letter (Phlm 16's "no longer as a slave [*doulos*]") more metaphorical than literal. While such non-enslavement interpretations add differing nuances on how to receive and use this letter, for our purposes the traditional reading of Onesimus as a slave gives us the richest material with which to center the enslaved perspective. Even if we found evidence today that Onesimus was not enslaved, I would argue that his story still invites us to imagine the enslaved experience of early Christians by virtue of the long interpretive tradition that has viewed him within an enslavement context. To put it another way, for every "Onesimus" we have on record, there are innumerable erased voices of the enslaved in antiquity to justify our investigation of the marginalized experience of enslavement.

---

mus, Our Brother: Reading Religion, Race, and Culture in Philemon (Minneapolis: Fortress, 2012), 1.

12. Katherine A. Shaner, *Enslaved Leadership in Early Christianity* (New York: Oxford University Press, 2018), xiii.

13. For overviews of the various interpretations, see Johnson, Noel, and Williams, *Onesimus.*

One place to begin to center marginalized and enslaved characters is to consider names, if they are given. The name Onesimus affirms the understanding that he is an enslaved character. His name means "useful, profitable, beneficial" in ancient Greek, a point that resonates with how an enslaver and other free people would view him, namely by virtue of what he could provide for the enslaver. This overarching sense of Onesimus's "utility" to others in the letter (Philemon, Apphia, Archippus, Paul, the Jesus movement) is an invitation for us to step back and question how we approach marginalized biblical figures in similar terms of their utility for our own interpretive needs and biases we bring to the text. In our interpretative process, might we afford Onesimus the ability not to be "useful" to others but to simply "be" for himself and his own spiritual development? Might this not be a kind of gift of personal freedom?

Aside from Onesimus's name, we know he was brought into the Jesus movement by Paul. While we may assume the connection between Onesimus and Philemon would have necessitated exposure to the Jesus movement, it is Paul's confirmation of Onesimus's status as a "beloved brother" both in flesh (his body) and in the Lord (his spirit) that elevates him to this position (Phlm 16). This acceptance into the Jesus movement would not have meant an automatic material and external status change. A challenging reality of the earliest Jesus movement is that becoming part of it did not erase status or earthly difference, as witnessed in Paul's own phrasing for the enslaved to remain as they were when called (1 Cor 7:21–24). Rather, identity being first and foremost in Christ was supposed to overshadow the reality of material difference (see above-quoted Gal 3:28). This has implications for understanding issues of the relationship between ethnicity and enslavement because the Jesus movement provided a kind of universalizing identity that did not erase ethnicity and enslavement status but superseded them. In short, Onesimus's elevation into the Jesus movement as a member was an invitation for him to see himself beyond his status as being enslaved, perhaps even beyond his own ethnicity itself, whatever that may have been (a Greek name may or may not indicate his ethnicity; see chapter 8, "Race and Ethnicity").

Next, we can turn to the fact that Onesimus may have gone to Paul under conditions that may be deemed illegal in legal or civil terms. As stated above, the larger history of biblical interpretation presumes that Onesimus is a runaway slave, which was a crime in Roman law, even if there is nothing explicitly stated in the letter itself. Concerning civil law, there may be an implication in the letter that Onesimus took money or supplies, as well, because Paul promises to pay back whatever is owed (Phlm 18–19). This suggestion parallels with the ancient concept of a ransom, in which a person could be bought back from kidnappers. This has further connections with Christian concepts of redemption, namely liberation through payment, all of which ties back to larger theological ideas about Christ's redemption of humanity.

Since we do not know what action Philemon ultimately took in response to Paul's letter, it is important to engage in some historical imagination and debate the backstory of the letter. If we center Onesimus, first and foremost, by telling what we know about his story, most of us want the story to end with Onesimus's manumission (the legal act of freeing an enslaved person; see chapter 6, "Manumission"). If we lean into the fact that Paul calls Onesimus a "brother" in the flesh (body) and in the Lord (i.e., spirit; Phlm 16), we start to see a story about three free men who are working in the Jesus movement. By centering Onesimus, we must seriously consider what liberative possibilities the Jesus movement could have provided to the most marginalized members of the ancient world. Christians for whom Paul is an authoritative voice in their communities might hope that with Onesimus Paul is making the way for radical egalitarianism and liberation that affirms how they view Christianity or religion more broadly. While this reading is hopeful, we may remain disturbed over the fact that we can never truly know the outcome of Onesimus's story.

Yet, we must also recognize that this desire might not match up with reality, namely the impact of human nature and systems of power, especially when we consider the historically close relationship between modern enslavement and its justification through pro-enslavement interpretations of the Bible. We must wrestle with the fact that Paul told the enslaved to remain in whatever condition they were called to the Jesus movement (1 Cor 7:21–24), a call that begins to make sense when we consider Paul believed the Second Coming was coming immediately, so he would not be privy to the reality that an earthly concern such as enslavement would be a long-standing issue. Moreover, we may be disturbed by the idea that Paul may have been indicating that Philemon gave Onesimus over to Paul for continued services as a "benefit," which suggests Paul became Onesimus's enslaver (Phlm 13, 20). Pulling back, we are invited to contemplate how Paul might have been reinscribing the existing pro-enslavement social structures of the Roman Empire. This reading is pessimistic, and we may remain disturbed over the fact that we can never truly know the outcome of Onesimus's story.

In summary, when we center Onesimus and other such (potential) figures of enslavement in the Bible, we are invited to explore closely the perspectives and issues of ancient life of "people from the margins" (the enslaved, women, foreigners, etc.). These perspectives rarely make it to center stage in our approaches to the Bible because traditionally we have been led to focus only on main characters like Jesus and Paul for inspiration or on theological concerns as they relate to personal faith and doctrine. While there is much wisdom and insight to be found in such traditional focal points, we must also acknowledge that we can add much more depth to our understanding of the ancient world of the Jesus movement by intentionally centering marginalized figures and populations such as the enslaved.

Conclusion

This chapter has explored how to engage with and interpret difficult enslavement passages of the Bible as an act of ethical interpretation. We have discussed two ethical ways of approaching passages concerning enslavement and ethnicity in the Bible, namely an intersectional approach with a case study of Hagar in the letter to the Galatians and a centering of enslaved characters and populations approach with a case study of Onesimus in the letter to Philemon. These approaches can be used in your interpretive toolkit to wrestle with similarly difficult passages that highlight the realities of enslavement in the ancient social world as it is represented in the Bible.

Overall, this chapter's attention to ethical interpretive methods concerning enslavement and ethnicity helps us to see that ethnicity was still a crucial part of an enslaved person's identity and situation, even if it was not the main justification of their status as enslaved as with modern slavery. As we can see in the New Testament, becoming part of the Jesus movement invited an umbrella identity in Christ that superseded other status quo layers of identity, including ethnicity, yet this "inclusive" logic also required the reality of enslaved status and ethnic difference for the value of the Christian identity to have meaning for its audience. In other words, there can be no universalizing identity of being "one in Christ Jesus" (Gal 3:28) without the particulars of other identity layers in life to give that singular identity meaning, including ethnicity and enslavement status. This means that we are invited as interpreters of the Bible to give focused attention to the enslaved and enslavement in difficult biblical passages because they provide context for understanding how the earliest Jesus followers wrestled with a movement that argued for a radically different reality, even as it was contextualized by and developed within the status quo of the ancient Mediterranean world. We, too, must wrestle with the reality that the Bible, although a liberative text, was not outright demanding the abolition of enslavement. Nevertheless, we are witness to the roots of the ideas and stories that would come to be its justification.

Discussion Questions

1. Your friend says that they do not care about enslavement in the Bible because it is no longer a reality for people today. Why should this friend reconsider their stance considering what you have learned in this chapter?

2. Who are enslaved biblical figures or characters who you could center in your discussion? How would you persuade a skeptical person or group that this figure is just as (or maybe more) important to consider than the usual, dominant figures like Abraham, Jesus, Paul, etc.?

3. When reading biblical passages about enslavement, how are the enslaved represented? How do you identify the multiple layers of identity (gender, sexuality, class, ethnicity, nationality/citizenship, age, and disability) represented in them? How might you interpret them with an intersectional perspective?

Further Reading

Callahan, Allen. *Embassy of Onesimus: The Letter of Paul to Philemon.* Philadelphia: Trinity Press International, 1997.

Cobb, Christy. "Enslaved Women, Women Enslavers: Evidence of Kyriarchy in the New Testament." *Journal of Feminist Studies in Religion* 40, no. 1 (2024): 43–60.

Johnson, Matthew V., James A. Noel, and Demetrius K. Williams, eds. *Onesimus, Our Brother: Reading Religion, Race, and Culture in Philemon.* Minneapolis: Fortress, 2012.

Junior, Nyasha. *Reimagining Hagar: Blackness and the Bible.* New York: Oxford University Press, 2019.

Kartzow, Marianne Bjelland. *The Slave Metaphor and Gendered Enslavement in Early Christian Discourse: Double Trouble Embodied.* New York: Routledge, 2018.

Smith, Mitzi J. *Chloe and Her People: A Womanist Critical Dialogue with First Corinthians.* Eugene, OR: Cascade Books, 2023.

15   *Modern Slavery, the Bible, and Slow-Down Ethics*

YVONNE C. ZIMMERMAN

For a reliable moral quickie, human trafficking is an ideal topic. A moral quickie is a snap judgment. It is a hastily performed act of moral discernment that leaves the person performing it feeling self-satisfied and morally gratified. Human trafficking, also called modern slavery, is a perfect topic for a moral quickie because, for one, everyone agrees that human trafficking is wrong and should have no place in a just and equitable society. It is a moral no-brainer. Further, the fact of this agreement means that condemnation of human trafficking and modern slavery has all the trappings of a principled moral stance. Stating opposition to human trafficking looks and feels like moral clarity, and moral clarity feels really good. Being "against trafficking" allows people to experience themselves as socially engaged, morally principled, and standing unequivocally for social justice.

But what is it people are against when they oppose human trafficking or modern slavery? Who or what is it they seek to change in activism and advocacy on this issue? And what help—or hindrance—does the Bible provide? Now lest it seem like I might be implying human trafficking is not a serious moral issue (or set of issues), let me clarify that I agree that human trafficking and modern slavery are wrong. A commitment to the liberation and empowerment of all to pursue their well-being in communities of equity demands nothing less than such a condemnation. Simultaneously, if such a commitment is genuine, I believe that it demands much more than easy denunciations may lead us to believe.

Denunciations of human trafficking almost always target sex trafficking—specifically imagining the abduction and imprisonment of young and vulnerable cisgender girls or women by corrupt men who sell them for sex. These denunciations depict human trafficking as sexual slavery. Thus depicted, the commercial sex industry emerges as the primary culprit in perpetuating human trafficking. If sex was not bought and sold, human trafficking would cease—or so the logic goes. The reality here is somewhat more complicated. Across religious affiliation, political identity, relationship status, sexual orientation, gender identity, and almost every other sociodemographic marker, most American adults have never paid for sex in a direct fee-for-service transaction, and most never will. This means that a stance against the sale and purchase of sexual services as the crux of human trafficking is a stance that denounces the actions of others, problematizing *others'* behavior as the source of the problem. Meanwhile, the practical arrangements of our own lives as average, hard-working people and the values and moral commitments on which these arrangements are premised often go without moral scrutiny when human trafficking is denounced. We who do not buy sex get to experience ourselves as morally unproblematic and even virtuous.

But human trafficking is more than sex trafficking, and eliminating human trafficking and the exploitative conditions in which trafficking proliferates and thrives will require more than male sexual reform or abolishing commercial sex. The purpose of this chapter is to clarify how human trafficking is anything but a moral quickie. The method I use is a form of moral discernment and ethical decision-making that the Christian ethicist Marvin Ellison calls "slow-down ethics."[1] Slow-down ethics is not motivated by making grand declarations and does not treat complicated moral issues quickly and as being easily resolvable. This method recognizes that complicated moral issues usually cannot be settled quickly, so it asks us to be patient about figuring out how to feel, what to think, and, importantly, what to do. As Ellison explains, slow-down ethics asks us to pause among shades of gray and to sit with complicated issues so we might really understand and not simply react to them. In this practice of sitting with the issues, practitioners are encouraged to listen to and consider fresh and challenging perspectives on them. In other words, slow-down ethics asks practitioners to decelerate moral discernment and decision-making processes at precisely those points where, otherwise, we may just "go on instinct," relying on custom, tradition, or gut reaction. It allows as much space and time as we need to slowly focus our minds and consult our hearts. A benefit of this method is that slowing down moral discernment allows practitioners to make

---

1. Marvin M. Ellison, *Making Love Just: Sexual Ethics for Perplexing Times* (Minneapolis: Fortress, 2012), 3.

decisions guided by critical thinking rather than impulse. The space of this short chapter is not long enough to slow readers all the way down on the issue of human trafficking, let alone for people to figure out what to think, how to feel, and what to do. A much deeper and more time-consuming dive is necessary. Still, I hope to leave readers with enough of a sense of the complexity of the issue that they grasp why slowing down on the topic of human trafficking is necessary and why turning to scripture can be complicated as well.

Defining Terms

Modern slavery is an umbrella term for a wide range of compelled forms of labor and exploitative labor situations. Notably, the term *modern slavery* is not defined in law, but is used to refer to a range of specific legal concepts such as forced labor, human trafficking, debt bondage, and forced marriage. In this section, I define each of these terms briefly. Forced labor is defined in the International Labour Organization's 1930 Convention Concerning Forced or Compulsory Labor as "all work or service which is exacted from any person under the menace of any penalty and for which the said person has not offered himself [*sic*] voluntarily."[2] Similarly, US federal law defines human trafficking as the use of coercion, force, or fraud to obtain some type of labor.[3] The legal definition of debt bondage supplied by the 1956 Supplementary Convention on the Abolition of Slavery is rather complex and unwieldy, but essentially defines debt bondage as situations where persons are forced to work to pay off a debt.[4] The 2022 report *Global Estimates of Modern Slavery: Forced Labour and Forced Marriage* defines forced marriage as "situations where a person has been forced to marry without giving their consent."[5] In essence, the term *modern slavery*

2. International Labour Organization, Convention Concerning Forced or Compulsory Labor, 1930, no. 29 (June 28, 1930): Article 2.1.

3. Trafficking Victims Protection Act of 2000. Pub. L. 106–386, Section 103 8(b).

4. The formal definition of debt bondage is "the status or condition arising from a pledge by a debtor of his personal services or of those of a person under his control as security for a debt if the value of those services as reasonably assessed is not applied towards the liquidation of the debt or the length and nature of those services are not respectively limited and defined." United Nations, 1956 Supplementary Convention on the Abolition of Slavery, Article 1(a).

5. International Labour Organization, Walk Free, and International Organization for Migration, *Global Estimates of Modern Slavery: Forced Labour and Forced Marriage*, Geneva, 2022, 15. This report is available at https://www.ilo.org/wcmsp5/groups/public/---ed_norm/---ipec/documents/publication/wcms_854733.pdf.

Figure 15.1. A child laborer working at Globe Cotton Mill in Augusta, Georgia. Photograph taken by Lewis Wickes Hine. 1909.

denotes "situations of exploitation that a person cannot refuse or leave because of threats, violence, coercion, deception, and/or abuse of power."[6]

Since *modern slavery* has no formal legal definition, I prefer to use either *human trafficking* or *forced and exploited labor* for the pervasive and structured phenomena of exploited labor in the sociopolitical economic situation of late capitalism. When I use the term *human trafficking*, I am talking about the problem of severe labor exploitation. Specifically, I mean situations in which people have lost control of their lives such that they are paid nothing or next to nothing for their work and are not able to leave their situation without fear of violence to themselves or someone they love.[7] People who experience trafficking are not able to just walk away. This is common to all trafficking situations. The designation *human trafficking* means a person does not have

6. International Labour Organization, Walk Free, and International Organization for Migration, *Global Estimates of Modern Slavery*, 13.

7. See Letitia M. Campbell and Yvonne C. Zimmerman, "Christian Ethics and Human Trafficking Activism: Progressive Christianity and Social Critique," *Journal of the Society of Christian Ethics* 34 (2014): 145–72.

control over the terms and conditions of their employment. Rather, the person or group for whom they are working has all the control.

Addressing Misconceptions

Clarity about the meaning of terms is important because misconceptions about forced and exploited labor abound. Extensive interdisciplinary scholarship explores these misconceptions and attendant issues. Here, I focus on two of the most common mistaken beliefs about human trafficking: (1) human trafficking always entails sexual violation or commercial sexual exploitation; and (2) prostitution is human trafficking.

Contrary to popular belief, human trafficking is not just sex trafficking. US federal law defines human trafficking by the presence of fraud, force, or coercion. Every situation of human trafficking must have at least one of these elements. Now, coercion, force, and fraud certainly can be exercised around sex, and the 2022 *Global Estimates of Modern Slavery* report estimates that forced commercial sexual exploitation, or sex trafficking, accounts for only 23 percent of all instances of human trafficking.[8] Although human trafficking can (and often does) involve sexual violation, it is important to understand that sex is not a constituent element of a trafficking crime. What defines a situation as human trafficking is fraud, force, or coercion.

The most common type of human trafficking is forced labor. The labor sectors in which forced labor is most prevalent are services, manufacturing, construction, agriculture (excluding fishing), and domestic work. Also contrary to popular perception, forced labor is not a problem only in poor countries. More than half of all forced labor occurs in middle- or upper-income countries. Still, the labor sectors where human trafficking is most prevalent are ones that tend to be unregulated or under-regulated. In general, worker exploitation rises when there are weak legal protections for workers, or none at all.

Worldwide, migrant workers are particularly vulnerable to forced and exploitative labor practices. According to the same 2022 report, migrant workers experience forced labor at disproportionately higher rates than nonmigrant workers in the labor force. The book *Life Interrupted: Trafficking into Forced Labor in the United States* explores migrant workers' experiences of forced and exploited labor in the United States, revealing that exploitation of migrant

---

8. The facts and statistics about forced and exploited labor referenced in this chapter are from International Labour Organization, Walk Free, and International Organization for Migration, *Global Estimates of Modern Slavery*.

workers is not only widespread, but actually sustains parts of the US economy. Mirroring global trends, forced labor is especially prevalent in labor sectors with weak protections for workers, such as agriculture and domestic work. Other factors the book identifies as contributing to the exploitation of migrant workers include the pressing demand for workers to fill low-wage jobs; the insecurity of and, often, unsafe working conditions in these jobs; the disarray and dysfunction of the federal immigration system; ineffective labor laws; and migrants' fears of detection, detention, and deportation.[9] To be sure, situations that rise to the legal level of human trafficking are on the extreme end of the range of abuses migrant workers experience while working in the United States. Still, a distinct combination of factors that makes all migrant workers disproportionately vulnerable to abuse in the workplace is possible to identify. These factors are (1) the collective failure to create and enforce laws that adequately protect migrant workers from labor exploitation; (2) the systematic subjection of migrant workers to unfair and unethical employment practices; and (3) the use of fear and intimidation as tactics to dissuade migrant workers from exercising the meager rights they do have. This combination of factors not only makes migrant workers more vulnerable to workplace exploitation and abuse but increases the likelihood that the abuse migrant workers experience will rise to the legal level of human trafficking.

Adding to the misconception that human trafficking is always sex trafficking is the notion that prostitution is human trafficking. Prostitution refers to the exchange of sexual services for money or other items of value and is frequently associated with the exploitation of women. Except for limited areas in Nevada, prostitution is illegal in the United States. This makes commercial sexual exchanges part of the informal or underground economy and means that people who sell sex have few if any legal protections. Lacking protections as workers, people who sell sex are very vulnerable to exploitation and abuse by clients. For example, if a person who sells sex is not paid or is a victim of violence by a would-be client and approaches the police for help, they are as likely to be dismissed (as not a "real" victim) or even arrested (for the crime of prostitution or solicitation) as they are to be recognized and responded to as a legitimate victim of crime. Although forced and exploited labor is more prevalent in the "regular" labor market than it is in the commercial sex industry, part of the strong association of prostitution with human trafficking has to do with the exploitation and abuse workers face in *any* unregulated eco-

9. See Denise Brennan, *Life Interrupted: Trafficking into Forced Labor in the United States* (Durham, NC: Duke University Press, 2014).

nomic sector, especially if that sector is part of the shadow economy (see also chapter 9, "Gender and Sexuality," for differences with the ancient world).

Still, more than just associated with the possibility of human trafficking, commercial sex is routinely altogether *conflated* with human trafficking. Conflated, prostitution is regarded as automatically and de facto human trafficking. Furthermore, this conflation is only superficially rooted in concern about the human rights and dignity of workers. Its deeper roots are in a framework of Christian sexual morality in which sexual purity reads as moral virtue.

Prostitution has long been denounced as countering conventional standards of public decency and sexual morality. Late nineteenth- and early twentieth-century social purity movements that sought to eliminate prostitution and other sexual activities deemed incompatible with Christian morality particularly fueled these sentiments. It was during this period that the association of sexual purity with moral purity was indelibly forged. Gender and sexual propriety were central concerns of Christian morality in the Victorian era (late 1840s to 1900). Deeply concerned with when, with whom, and for what purposes people should have sex, the main legacy of Victorian-era Christian morality is contemporary Christian purity culture. Drawing on biblical interpretation, and Pauline letters in particular, as the authority for its sexual ethic, purity culture teaches that the only morally appropriate context for sex is "legal, monogamous marriage between a cisgender, heterosexual man and a cisgender, heterosexual woman for life."[10] Not all Christians ascribe to this restrictive sexual ethic, of course. For example, many are more comfortable with a less restrictive version of purity culture that, in addition to marriage, recognizes love and commitment as two conditions that also morally exonerate sex. Whether in its most restrictive or more permissive form, the influence of purity culture and its sexual ethics on US-American public and cultural life is significant.

Importantly, these versions of sexual morality share common ground in their rebuke of commercial sex. Commercial sex satisfies none of the conventionally recognized conditions (love, commitment, or legal heteromonogamous marriage) for morally exonerating sexual activity. As a result, commercial sex and prostitution are widely denounced as wrong and considered legitimate targets of moral condemnation. In combination with the strong association of human trafficking with sex trafficking, purity culture's condemnation of commercial sex and prostitution leads to the easy conflation of

10. Emily Joy Allison, #*Churchtoo: How Purity Culture Upholds Abuse and How to Find Healing* (Minneapolis: Broadleaf Books, 2021), 31.

Figure 15.2. A Blue Campaign human trafficking airport poster.

prostitution and human trafficking because they are seen as wrong for the same reason. Both are associated with immoral sex, defined as sexual activity isolated from the socially recognized conditions of love, commitment, or legal heteromonogamous marriage that morally absolve it. First Corinthians 6:12–20, for example, issues a particularly emphatic warning against sexually immoral behavior in which admonition against prostitution ("unit[ing] . . . with a prostitute") is central. To the extent that any real difference between prostitution and sex trafficking is retained in purity culture's conflation of them, it is that sex trafficking is acknowledged as a particularly egregious and extreme violation of the standards of sexual morality.

Human trafficking is, indeed, morally wrong. However, the flaw in purity culture's moral analysis of human trafficking is that it is not sexual immorality, or failure to comply with the criteria for morally permissible sex, that makes it so. The immorality of human trafficking does not stem from sex or sexuality. Returning to the definition of human trafficking presented at the beginning of this chapter clarifies this point. Human trafficking refers to severe labor exploitation, or situations in which people have lost control of their lives and are unable to leave their situation without fear of violence to themselves or someone they love. Therefore, what makes human trafficking wrong is that people are not paid fairly or adequately for the work they do (including, sometimes, sex work) and that they cannot leave their situation without fear of violence and harm. This definition clarifies that human trafficking is wrong because it involves economic exploitation (being paid nothing or next to nothing) and violence (the inability to leave or stop a situation without fear of harm to oneself or others). Even in situations of sex trafficking, the moral line is *still* economic exploitation and violence, not sexual immorality.

In summary, although people involved in prostitution sometimes experience human trafficking and, further, sometimes the violence experienced in forced labor is sexual violence, the larger point remains that the umbrella category of human trafficking is much broader than commercial sex and need not involve sexual harm. Across all its forms, the defining feature of modern slavery is the inability to refuse or leave an exploitative situation because of threats, violence, coercion, deception, and/or abuse of power. Centering force, fraud, and coercion as the defining features of human trafficking clarifies that the moral issues at stake in human trafficking are less about sex than they are about economics. Indeed, among the most significant factors exacerbating vulnerability to human trafficking are poverty and lack of access to money. Consequently, addressing the economic issues that make life precarious for poor people is the most pressing concern in preventing and ending human trafficking.

Exploring Ambivalence

As we slow down our moral analysis of trafficking, the importance of economic justice comes to the fore. Labor and work are central to economic justice (or the lack thereof) in the daily lives of everyday citizens the world over. In US-American culture, such a high value is placed on hard work that it is not a stretch to say that respect for hard work is a defining American value. The notion of a hard day's work as something to be proud of is as American as apple pie. Americans consider hard work intrinsically and unquestionably valuable, believing work to form people into mature, decent, and responsible citizens. Reflecting this belief, the general expectation in American culture is that adults should occupy themselves with some sort of labor, whether paid (in a job) or unpaid (as student, parent, or other caretaker). The crux of this work expectation is expressed in the familiar aphorism "He [*sic*] who does not work shall not eat."[11] The unyielding obligation to work is premised on the assumption that work is intrinsically good—good in itself, good for the person laboring, and good for the society and economy to which the benefits of labor accrue.

11. This is a New Testament aphorism from 2 Thess 3:10 that was cited by John Smith in 1609 to the colonists at Jamestown, Virginia.

Figure 15.3. Bronze ornament of Medusa from a chariot pole. First–second century CE.

At the same time, as highly as US-Americans value work, a marked moral ambivalence about labor imbues the culture. For one, many Americans are unaware of the prevalence of exploitation and abuse in the US labor economy. While vaguely aware of labor exploitation in other parts of the world, they resist the idea that exploited labor is a significant problem domestically in the US labor market. Yet, substantial parts of the US economy, including agribusiness, food production, apparel manufacturing, and construction, are undergirded by exploited labor.[12] Labor violations committed by trusted name-brand companies and retailers are routinely minimized or ignored. Corporate perpetrators of these violations sometimes are even praised for promoting efficiency and maintaining low labor costs.

In addition to reticence to accept how significant exploited labor is to the US economy, Americans are also unenthusiastic about engaging in collective moral reflection on the ethics of work. For example, questions concerning when, with whom, under what conditions, for what compensation, or for what purposes people should work rarely gain widespread traction. It is as if to question whether labor is intrinsically ennobling is faintly sacrilegious, or

12. See Brennan, *Life Interrupted.*

to call attention to the ways compelled or exploited work erodes the social bedrock implicitly attacks America or insults those who work hard. Instead of engaging why, under what conditions, and for what purposes people are morally justified in pursuing work, Americans are far more comfortable placing the moral burden on those seeking exemption from paid labor. The difficulty of qualifying for disability benefits and the meager benefits public assistance affords are two examples of this moral burden. Social exemption from work is granted only in the most extenuating circumstances (and often not at all), and those who seek such relief are often cordoned into a sort of second-class American citizenship behind "real" Americans who, honest and hard-working, earn a living through their labor.

The American ambivalence about labor is not confined to questions about who is or is not socially obligated to work. It also manifests around wages, or just compensation for work. The federal minimum wage, currently $7.25 per hour, is a rate of pay substantially below the hourly wage required to sustain an individual, let alone a family, at a dignified standard of living. Yet minimum wage is the actual rate of pay that many low wage workers in America earn and on which they are somehow expected to live. Given how highly Americans value work and the idea of a hard-working citizenry, we might expect a robust social outcry about this injustice. But not only are such protests muted, they are virtually nonexistent.

A significant source of the moral ambivalence around labor and work in US-American culture is that not only has it historically *accepted* forced labor, but it has also morally justified and *defended* it. Although many, especially white, Americans may prefer to forget this fact, chattel slavery was the law of the land in the United States until just 150 years ago. The institution of chattel slavery allowed people to be considered legal property that could be bought and sold. Being a slave was a permanent legal status, and so enslaved persons could expect a lifetime of being bought, owned, and sold. Crucially, not just anyone needed to worry about becoming enslaved. Chattel slavery was practiced as a race-based institution that enslaved indigenous people as well as those of African descent. From the sixteenth to the early nineteenth century, upward of 10 million enslaved Africans were transported across the Atlantic Ocean to the Americas in the transatlantic slave trade.

Christian theology and biblical interpretation were a key source of the racist ideas used to morally justify chattel slavery and the transatlantic slave trade. The racist theology of white supremacy taught that God created and ordained white people as the pinnacle of humanity who are superior to all others. In turn, this theology taught that this God-given superiority of whites made them natural masters over indigenous people and those of African descent whose situation was similarly divinely ordained as inherently inferior.[13] The late womanist ethicist Katie Cannon identified this set of racialized and racist ideas as a "theo-logic of racialized normativity." The theo-logic of racialized normativity ensured Christian colonizers, slaveholders, and other ordinary citizens that the colonization and ownership of the lands, bodies, labor, and minds of the rest of the world was their right as white people, as well as a Christian vocational responsibility.[14] This race-based and racist interpretation of Christian theology underpinned American acceptance, justification, and defense of chattel slavery and the forced labor and other abusive practices that it entailed.

Other theological ideas about work and wealth dovetailed with this theo-logic of racialized normativity. For example, the godly nature of work is a prominent theme in the theological work of Protestant reformer John Calvin. Among Calvin's most distinctive beliefs was that wealth that is generated through work signifies divine favor and blessing. Calvin understood wealth as evidence of pleasing God, and he contended that a major goal in life should be the attainment of wealth through work.[15] Calvin's view set the stage for the pursuit of wealth to be understood as both pleasing to God and as an activity of seeking God. Thus understood, work is the elemental act of the conjoined pursuits of wealth-seeking and living a life glorifying God.

In summary, the ambivalence about work and labor in US-American culture has roots in the conjunction of white supremacy and Christian theology. Belief that wealth signifies divine blessing conceals how wealth can be generated through exploitative means and in unjust ways. The theological insistence that human labor is categorically pleasing to God counters the recognition of work and labor as potential sources of oppression and harm. In essence, this theological rationality fails to account for whether the conditions under which work is performed are humanizing and ennobling to those performing it. Relatedly, it also fails to consider the level of wages that work earns for the worker. In turn, these failures produce disrecognition of exploitative labor. Similarly, disrecognition of the immorality of exploitative wealth-generating systems such as colonialism, chattel slavery, and, today, neoliberal capitalism reflects a theological rationality that interprets wealth as divine blessing and

13. Katie Geneva Cannon, "Christian Imperialism and the TransAtlantic Slave Trade," *Journal of Feminist Studies in Religion* 24, no. 1 (2008): 127–34, here 131.

14. Cannon, "Christian Imperialism and the TransAtlantic Slave Trade," 133.

15. Emilie M. Townes, "From Mammy to Welfare Queen: Images of Black Women in Public-Policy Formation," in *Beyond Slavery: Overcoming Its Religious and Sexual Legacies,* ed. Bernadette J. Brooten (New York: Palgrave Macmillan, 2010), 61–74, here 65–66.

thus sanctions the pursuit of wealth by any available means. As long as the money flows, the means through which wealth is generated are not a primary moral consideration in this theological rationality.

The ratification of the Thirteenth Amendment marked the legal end of chattel slavery in the United States. However, it is important to understand that this legal change did not dismantle, or even significantly affect, the ideological underpinnings that legitimated the practice of slavery. For one, the punishment clause of the Thirteenth Amendment stipulates that slavery and involuntary servitude remain lawful punishments to impose on people convicted of crimes. Further, key Christian theological teachings about work and wealth that undergirded the institution of chattel slavery were not challenged by this legal change. Not only do many of these theological teachings remain largely intact today; they continue to exercise considerable influence over American cultural attitudes. Taking this into account, Americans' tepid responses to forced and exploited labor in the context of neoliberal capitalism comes into focus as a manifestation of the same disrecognitions that sustained colonialism and the supporting institution of chattel slavery. For the collective preoccupation with a conception of human trafficking that turns on the melodramatic storyline of morally corrupt, sexually entitled men preying on and sexually exploiting poor, vulnerable girls directs moral attention to individual-level sexual ethics (do not buy sex). As long as the dictates of purity culture are satisfied, the collective, corporate ethics of wealth and labor disappear.

The essence of the moral quickie is to focus moral attention only on what is familiar, comfortable, and emotionally gratifying. The way that human trafficking shows up and is discussed in much public discourse, and particularly Christian moral discourse, does exactly that. The moral condemnation of commercial sex is both easier and also much more morally gratifying than squarely facing the immorality of the global economic system and our collective and individual participation in it. Essentially, pointing the finger at sexually immoral men disconnects the American public from the ways they are implicated in, and even actually *support*, the systems, dynamics, and practices that cause modern slavery.

Anthropologist Seth Holmes's investigation of the conditions of migrant farmworkers in the US agricultural system in the book *Fresh Fruit, Broken Bodies* reveals the dynamic I am describing.[16] His ethnographic account conveys the severe suffering in the lives of the Mexican farmworkers who pick

---

16. See Seth Holmes, *Fresh Fruit, Broken Bodies: Migrant Farmworkers in the United States* (Berkeley: University of California Press, 2013).

221

and process much of the produce American consumers buy in grocery stores. His study powerfully shows that the problem of modern slavery, also known as human trafficking, is not others or elsewhere. It is us and it is here, in our individual and collective participation in the global economic system.

Conclusion

Practicing slow-down ethics in relation to human trafficking permits modern slavery to be grasped in its full complexity as forced and exploited labor in the global economic system of neoliberal capitalism. Human trafficking some-times involves sexual exploitation and abuse, but this modern phenomenon is not simply an issue of sexual immorality that is easily denounced and tidily resolved by abolishing the commercial sex industry. Contextualizing mod-ern slavery in relation to the global economic system of neoliberal capitalism highlights its systemic and structural nature. Further, consideration of some of the key moral presuppositions about labor and work in US-American culture, in light of their theological underpinnings, draws attention to Christianity's ambivalent relationship with slavery. While freedom from oppression is un-doubtedly integral to the gospel of Jesus (Luke 4:18) that is the centerpiece of the New Testament, the same New Testament does not categorically condemn the practice of slavery. For example, the writer of Ephesians counsels slaves to obey their masters, and masters not to threaten them (Eph 6:5–9). Addi-tionally, the imagery of slavery is used in Romans to describe a Christian's relationship to God (Rom 16:6–20). The New Testament is ambivalent about slavery. When readers turn to the Bible looking for cues on how to respond to modern slavery, a search for one-to-one correspondences will not yield the strong antislavery stance they may hope and expect to find. Truthfully, it is easier to turn to the Bible for clear denunciations of sexual immorality (which it does multiple times in multiple ways) than it is for an unequivocal, satisfying denunciation of slavery. But again, contemporary sex trafficking is not an issue of sexual immorality, and so while these denunciations may be easier to find in the text, they do not apply to this issue.

The New Testament's ambivalence toward slavery notwithstanding, New Testament texts are still witnesses to a rich range of religiopolitical and spir-itual resistances to empire, particularly in the context of the Roman Empire in the first century of the common era. The task of responsible biblical inter-pretation invites readers to understand these practices of resistance and their contexts. Likewise, the task of responsible biblical utilization invites reflection on and production of practices of resistance to empire in the current era, especially in the context of neoliberal capitalism and the particular situation of middle-class American life.

Today as ever, the gospel of Jesus remains good news to the poor and freedom from oppression, and the primary work of the church is to witness to and participate with the work of the Holy Spirit toward that end. Therefore, responses to human trafficking and modern slavery should focus on addressing the underlying social conditions that make people vulnerable to trafficking—things like poverty, food insecurity, housing insecurity and homelessness, addiction, systemic racism, homophobia and transphobia, depressed wages, lack of worker protections, unjust immigration policies, and failures of the foster care system. None of these are fast or easy, but the reality is that the systems and structures that cause human trafficking are extraordinarily complex and will not be changed overnight. No moral quickies here. Still, building societies oriented to the flourishing of all is worth slowing down for, taking the time to sift through all the attendant complexities and shades of gray to participate in shaping a world in which no form of slavery has a place.

Discussion Questions

1. What parts of your life are made possible because of modern slavery? Why is it important to acknowledge these connections?

2. How does your sense of modern slavery's impact change when its definition expands beyond sex trafficking?

3. How does the Bible create expectations around work that implicates or encourages slavery systems? How does the Bible undermine these same expectations? What role can ambivalence play in reconciling these two interpretive uses?

Further Reading

Brennan, Denise. *Life Interrupted: Trafficking into Forced Labor in the United States.* Durham, NC: Duke University Press, 2014.

Campbell, Letitia M., and Yvonne C. Zimmerman. "Christian Ethics and Human Trafficking Activism: Progressive Christianity and Social Critique." *Journal of the Society of Christian Ethics* 34 (2014): 145–72.

Holmes, Seth M. *Fresh Fruit, Broken Bodies: Migrant Farmworkers in the United States.* Berkeley: University of California Press, 2013.

McGrow, Lauren, ed. *Religious Responses to Sex Work and Sex Trafficking: An Outrage against Any Decent People*. New York: Routledge, 2022.

Peterson-Iyer, Karen. "Sex-Trafficking, Rescue Narratives, and the Challenge of Solidarity." Pages 137–60 in *Re-envisioning Sexual Ethics: A Feminist Christian Account*. Edited by Karen Peterson-Iyer. Washington, DC: Georgetown University Press, 2022.

Glossary

abolition   Specifically referring to the movement to end (abolish) institutionalized enslavement.

athlon   (Greek) prize.

bondage   A condition of being unfree, sometimes used as a euphemism for enslavement; from the idea of binding a person to restrain them.

canon, canonical   An agreed-upon set of books, scripture, and/or writings that carry cultural, political, and/or religious authority; often used to refer to Christian and Jewish scriptures; the Bible.

carpe   (Latin) To pluck or to cut. Name of an enslaved character in Petronius's *Satyricon.*

censu   (Latin) Manumission of an enslaved person by adding their name to the Roman citizen census list.

chattel slavery   The buying, selling, and owning of enslaved persons as the property of their enslavers. Chattel are often understood as living property, including animals.

Christ-following communities   Communities consisting of early followers of Jesus's teachings, mostly made up of Jewish Christians.

colonialism   The conquering of one nation by another, whether in war or through political or economic dominance. Often followed by forced cultural, linguistic, and/or religious domination of the conquered nation.

color symbolism   The cultural relation of positive and negative meanings to certain colors, especially the relation of darker shades and skin tones to negative meanings.

cordon   To block or restrict access to.

cosmologies   Scientific studies of how the universe physically originated.

debt bondage   Condition of a person working without pay to pay off a debt.

debt slavery   See "indentured servitude."

denigration   Criticizing someone or something intensely, so as to emphasize its unimportance and lack of value.

denunciation   The public condemnation of someone or something.

deportation   The formal, and often forceful, removal of a person(s) from a country, region, or territory.

dominus   (Latin) Slave owner, enslaver.

doulos, doulē   (Greek) Slave, enslaved person, man (*doulos*), or woman (*doulē*).

ecclesia, ekklēsia   (Latin, Greek) Democratic assembly or church.

ennobling   Dignifying someone or something by giving it a title of nobility.

epistemicide   The killing of knowledge; the devaluing of knowledge or knowledge systems by unjust or systemically oppressive power systems.

ethnography   The study of people in a particular cultural or ethnic setting.

ethnopolitical   Referring to how specific ethnicities, racialized identities, or nationalities impact the politics and conflicts within political power systems.

ethnos, ethnē   (Greek) Nations; gentiles.

Eucharist   Christian religious ritual memorializing the last meal Jesus ate with his followers before his arrest and crucifixion; sometimes called Holy Communion.

eugenics Pseudoscientific practice that incorrectly theorizes that forced re-production and/or sterilization can create the perfect human being.

eunuch A person with ambiguous genitalia, whether by birth or by alter-ation. Sometimes understood as a person born male but castrated as part of their enslavement.

Eurocentric Something that elevates the importance of European culture above all others.

exonerate To relieve a person from a responsibility or obligation; to declare a person innocent.

exploitation The deliberate and unfair usage or control over someone or something.

familia (Latin) Family, specifically referring to the members of a household, including enslaved laborers.

fides (Latin) Loyalty.

forced labor Work completed by a person against their will, typically in fear of retaliation or penalty by their employer.

freedpeople Formerly enslaved persons who have been manumitted.

fungible An item that is replaceable.

genos (Greek) Term used to group together and classify people; relating to generations.

gentilis (Latin) Tribe, family, nation.

Greco-Roman The sharing of both Greek and Roman characteristics; often refers to the cultural and historical synergy between the Greek empire of Al-exander the Great and the Roman Empire.

Greek novel   Greek prose fiction; a literary genre that originated in the first century CE, often romance novels.

Hebrew Bible   Compilation of authoritative Jewish scriptures, most originally written in Hebrew; included in the Christian canon.

Hellenic   Influence of Greek culture in surrounding geographical areas; from the Greek word *Hellēn*, meaning "Greek."

hierarchy   The political organization of people into different levels of authority, rank, and perceived importance.

historiographical   The study of how scholars create historical narratives.

homogeneous   Exhibiting uniformity.

imperial period (of Rome)   Historical period from about 27 BCE to 476 CE in which the governing authority in Rome was consolidated under an emperor and territory was expanded around the Mediterranean rim.

imperialism   The expansion of a nation's power over other territories, gaining political and economic control over those territories; the process of building an empire.

indentured servitude   Form of contracted enslavement in which a person agreed to work without pay for a period of time, sometimes to account for a debt owed to their enslaver.

infallible   Assertion something has no flaws; sometimes used to assert the entire text of the Bible is trustworthy.

iniuria   (Latin) Injury.

inerrant   Without errors; sometimes used to assert the entire text of the Bible is without error.

inter amicos   (Latin) Among friends; manumission of an enslaved person by means of a community declaration.

intersectionality   The study of overlapping social and political identities; refers also to social forces of discrimination related to identities a person inhabits.

instrumentum vocale   (Latin) Literally, "vocal instrument"; term referring to enslaved persons as tools for enslavers to speak or think with.

Ioudaios   (Greek) Judean; Jewish

Jesus movement   A Jewish movement in early Christianity centered on the memory of Jesus's ministry and crucifixion.

Jewish Palestine   During the first century CE, a term describing the predominantly Jewish population of territories in and around Jerusalem, the Galilee, the Dead Sea, and the Mediterranean coast designated by the Romans as the province of Palestine.

Jim Crow laws   Laws named after the black minstrel show character "Jim Crow" that legalized racial segregation in the United States during the post–Civil War era.

kushit   (Hebrew) To be descended from Ham.

kyriarchy   Rule of the lord or master; a modern concept derived from the Greek *kyrios* for "lord" and *archos* for "ruler."

kyrios, kyria   (Greek) Enslaver; master; lord.

liberti   (Latin) Freedpeople; people formerly enslaved.

macula servitutis   (Latin) Literally, "stain of slavery"; permanent reputation of past enslavement that remains with freedpeople after manumission.

mancipia   (Latin) To be removed from the hands of an enslaver.

manumissio in ecclesia   (Latin) Manumitting an enslaved person before a church's assembly (began in fourth century CE).

manumission   The legal process of freeing an enslaved person.

Marcommanic Wars Series of wars from 167 to 180 BCE between the Roman Empire and middle Danube Germanic tribes.

matriarch A woman who is considered the head, leader, or ruler of a family or people group.

matrilineal Family descent traced through a person's mother.

mitzvah (Hebrew) Literally, "commandment"; term used to describe any law or religious duty in the Torah.

natal alienation An enslaved person's lack of connection to their birth family; a strategy used to isolate enslaved people from their heritage or ethnic community.

natio (Latin) Nation.

neoliberal capitalism Economic philosophy emphasizing the least possible amount of government control over free-market exchanges.

New Testament Compilation of Christian scriptures written by Christ followers after the lifespan of Jesus.

nomos (Greek) Law, principle, custom.

obsequium (Latin) Obligation of freedpeople to respect and remain obedient to their former enslavers after manumission.

oikonomia (Greek) Literally, the law of households; economic and social organization of a household.

oikos (Greek) House, home, household.

operae (Latin) Obligation of freedpeople to perform labor for their former enslavers as compensation for manumission.

paidiskē (Greek) Term often translated as "slave girl" that can refer to enslaved persons of any age or gender.

pagan   Term used to refer to people who engaged in religious practice other than the dominant or preferred religion, especially used in early Christianity to refer to people who attended to Greek, Roman, or indigenous gods.

parable   A fictional story that provides a religious or moral lesson about life using analogy or illustration.

paramonē **clause**   Part of some manumission agreements requiring persons to continue working for their enslaver after manumission.

paterfamilias   (Latin) The father or master of a household.

patriarch   A man who is considered the head, leader, or ruler of a family or people group.

patrilineal   Family descent traced through a person's father.

peculium   (Latin) An allowance of money or property given to enslaved persons that is controlled by their enslavers.

pedagogue   Teacher, tutor.

per epistulam   (Latin) Literally "by letter"; manumission of an enslaved person by written letter.

physiognomy   Facial characteristics or expressions, especially as they are perceived to relate to a person's ethnic, cultural, or racialized background.

polis   (Greek) City, city-state.

postexilic period   Period after 538 BCE when the Babylonian exile of Jewish persons ended.

progenitor   A direct ancestor in a family line.

proliferate   To rapidly produce or reproduce.

propriety   Socially acceptable behavior, especially applied to gender expression and sexual conduct.

proto-racism   Roots of racialization found in ancient societies; the early conceptualizing and rationalizing of racial and ethnic bias, prejudice, or bigotry.

rabbinic   Relating to Jewish rabbis post-70 CE, especially their writings on Jewish law and teachings.

racialization   The process of socially categorizing people, things, or ideas based on culture, language, ethnicity, and skin color into racial groups.

republic   A form of government in which all citizens have political power, often carried out by electing political representatives; Rome practiced this form of government until 42 BCE.

Roman comedy   Genre of ancient drama utilizing common tropes of humor, often featuring enslaved characters.

sacral manumission   A form of ancient manumission describing the sale of an enslaved person to a god, not always leading to the freedom of the enslaved person.

sacrilegious   Violating or disrespecting something considered sacred by a religious group.

servare   (Latin) To preserve, save.

servi   (Latin) Servants, slaves.

shimush hakhamim   (Hebrew) Service of sages.

slave society   A society in which enslaved labor prevails, providing a class distinction between enslaved people and their free owners.

slaving culture   A society in which practices of enslavement are interwoven within social norms and lifestyles.

slavocracy   A society in which enslavers have social, political, and economic control; used to describe pre–Civil War North American societies.

sociodemographic   Key characteristics describing a group of people, such as gender, wealth, or ethnicity.

solicitation   To request or obtain something from another person, often by coercion or through unequal use of power.

Sukkot festival   A week-long Jewish agricultural festival celebrating the fall harvest.

testamento   (Latin) Manumitting an enslaved person in a legal will put into place at an enslaver's death.

threptos   (Greek) Ancient Greek term commonly used to refer to abandoned children, sometimes also used to refer to manumitted slaves.

Torah   (Hebrew) Literally, law; first five books of the Hebrew Bible containing Jewish law.

vindicta   (Latin) Manumission of an enslaved person by the authority of a juridical official.

Contributors

Chance Everett Bonar is a postdoctoral fellow at the Center for the Humanities at Tufts University and affiliate of the Slavery, Colonialism, and Their Legacies initiative at Tufts. He holds a PhD in religion from Harvard University with a focus on New Testament and early Christianity. Previously, he held positions at Harvard Divinity School and Boston College and was a William R. Tyler Fellow in Byzantine Studies at Dumbarton Oaks Research Library and Collection. He is the author of *God, Slavery, and Early Christianity: Divine Possession and Ethics in the Shepherd of Hermas* (Cambridge University Press, forthcoming) and "Reading Slavery in the Epistle of Jude," in the *Journal of Biblical Literature* (2023). He publishes and teaches on topics including ancient Mediterranean religions, slavery, theories of authorship, gender and sexuality, race and ethnicity, and Christian anti-Judaism.

Mallory A. Challis is an MDiv student at Wake Forest University School of Divinity. She holds a BA in religious studies from Wingate University. She is a freelance journalist and regularly writes as a columnist for *Baptist News Global*. She is the author of "Martyrs of Chastity: Illuminating the Power of Peter's Disabled Daughter and Drusiana in the Apocryphal Acts," published online in the *Richard Macksey Journal* (2024). She is pursuing work in congregational ministry settings, blending her skills as a researcher, writer, and student.

Christy Cobb is associate professor of Christianity at University of Denver. She holds a PhD in New Testament and early Christianity from Drew University. Cobb is the author of *Slavery, Gender, Truth, and Power in Luke-Acts and Other Ancient Narratives* (Palgrave Macmillan, 2019) and coedited a volume entitled *Sex, Violence, and Early Christian Texts* (ed. with Eric Vanden Eykel; Lexington Books, 2022). She is also a member of the editorial board for the

Journal of Feminist Studies in Religion. Cobb's research and teaching interests include slavery, gender, sexuality, Acts, and the Apocryphal Acts.

Javal A. Coleman is a PhD candidate in classics at the University of Texas (Austin). He earned an MA in classics from the University of Texas and a BA in history at the University of North Texas along with a minor in Latin and classical studies. He has published several essays on enslavement and reception on the Society for Classical Studies Blog and has a forthcoming chapter entitled "Labor, Gender, Agency and the Status of Manumitted Slaves in Fourth-Century Athens." He also has coauthored (with Dan-El Padilla Peralta) a chapter entitled "Rhetorics" in *Writing, Enslavement, and Power in the Roman Mediterranean* (ed. Jeremiah Coogan, Joseph Howley, and Candida Moss; Oxford University Press, forthcoming). His interests include ancient slavery, Roman law, and status. He also researches Black receptions of classics.

Joseph Foltz is a PhD student at the University of Denver, focusing on the history of Christianity and the ancient Mediterranean. He holds an MA in international studies with a specialization in religion from the University of Denver. His research interests center on the intersection of violence and power in early Christianity, the Apocryphal Acts of the Apostles, and early papal politics. He has published multiple articles that focus on material culture related to apocryphal literature on the North American Society for the Study of Christian Apocryphal Literature's academic website.

F. Mira Green is assistant professor of ancient Mediterranean history in the History Department at the University of Utah. She holds a PhD in ancient history from the University of Washington. Her research focuses on questions of hierarchy and power that are intertwined with ideas about embodiment, daily routines, slavery, gender, and popular culture in the Roman world. She is the author of the forthcoming *Mastering Digestion: Embodiment, Daily Life, and Slavery in Roman Homes and Society*, as well as multiple articles about connections between slavery, gender, food, and material culture.

Midori E. Hartman is assistant professor of classical studies at Albright College. She holds a PhD in historical studies with an emphasis on Christianity in late antiquity from Drew University. Her primary research interests are Augustine of Hippo, ancient slavery, and rhetoric as it intersects with issues of gender, ethnicity, slavery, and animality. She is the author of "Sexual Violence, Martyrdom, and Enslavement in Augustine's Letter 111," in *Sex, Violence, and Early*

Christian Texts (ed. Christy Cobb and Eric Vanden Eykel; Lexington, 2022), and several other articles on the meaning of bodies in early Christianity.

Catherine Hezser is professor of Jewish studies at the School of Oriental and African Studies (SOAS), University of London. After finishing her doctoral degrees at the University of Heidelberg and the Jewish Theological Seminary in New York, she held positions at the Free University Berlin; Trinity College Dublin; and SOAS, University of London. She was a visiting professor at the Hebrew University Jerusalem and the University of Oslo. Her research focuses on the social history of Jews in Roman-Byzantine Palestine. Among her recent book publications are *Rabbinic Body Language: Non-Verbal Communication in Palestinian Rabbinic Literature of Late Antiquity* (Brill, 2017); *Bild und Kontext: Jüdische und christliche Ikonographie der Spätantike* (Mohr Siebeck, 2018); *The Use and Dissemination of Religious Knowledge in Antiquity* (ed. with Diana Edelman; Equinox, 2021); *Jews and Health: Tradition, History and Practice* (ed.; Brill, 2023); *The Routledge Handbook of Jews and Judaism in Late Antiquity* (ed.; Routledge, 2024); and *Jewish Monotheism and Slavery* (Cambridge University Press, 2024).

Marianne Bjelland Kartzow is professor of New Testament studies at the University of Oslo, Norway. In addition to several articles and book chapters, she has authored three books: *Gossip and Gender: Othering of Speech in the Pastoral Epistles* (De Gruyter, 2009); *Destabilizing the Margins: An Intersectional Approach to Early Christian Memory* (Wipf and Stock, 2012); and *The Slave Metaphor and Gendered Enslavement in Early Christian Discourse: Double Trouble Embodied* (Routledge, 2018). Kartzow has recently edited and coedited several volumes, including *The Ambiguous Figure of the Neighbor in Jewish, Christian and Islamic Texts and Receptions* (ed.; Routledge, 2022) and *Religious Responses to Pandemics and Crises: Isolation, Survival, and #Covidchaos* (ed. with Sravana Borkataky-Varma and Christian A. Eberhart; Routledge, 2024).

William Owens is emeritus professor of classics at Ohio University. His research focuses on the representation of slavery in Greek and Roman texts, especially the Greek novels. He is the author of *The Representation of Slavery in the Greek Novel* (Routledge, 2020); "Reading Apuleius's *Cupid and Psyche* from the Slave's Perspective: The Tale of Psyche *Ancilla*," in *Slavery and Sexuality in Classical Antiquity* (ed. Deborah Kamen and C. W. Marshall; Wisconsin University Press, 2021); and "Novel Evidence for Ancient Freed People: Xenophon of Ephesus' *Ephesiaca* and the *Cena Timalchionis*," in *Freed Persons in* *the Roman World: Status, Diversity, and Representation* (ed. Sinclair W. Bell, Dorian Borbonus, and Rose MacLean; Cambridge University Press, 2024).

Emerson B. Powery is the dean of the School of Arts, Culture, and Society and professor of biblical studies at Messiah University. He holds a PhD from Duke University. His recent publications include *The Good Samaritan* (Baker, 2022); *Genesis of Liberation: Biblical Interpretation in the Antebellum Narratives of the Enslaved* (with Rodney S. Sadler Jr.; Westminster John Knox, 2016); and the second edition of *True to Our Native Land: An African American New Testament Commentary* (ed. with Brian K. Blount and Gay L. Byron; Fortress, 2024). He serves as general editor of the Society of Biblical Literature's Early Christianity and Its Literature series and as (executive) general editor of the *Westminster Study Bible* (Westminster John Knox, 2024).

Ulrike Roth is reader in ancient history at the University of Edinburgh. Her chief research interest lies in the study of Roman slavery. She is the author of *Thinking Tools: Agricultural Slavery between Evidence and Models* (Institute of Classical Studies, School of Advanced Study, University of London, 2007), editor and coauthor of books on the economics of Roman slaving, freed status in Roman society, and child slavery in the Roman Empire, as well as multiple journal articles and book chapters on diverse aspects of slavery, ranging from the ancient to the early medieval world. She is also the series editor of Edinburgh University Press's Edinburgh Studies in Ancient Slavery. Beyond slavery, she has researched and published on aspects of Roman republican history, Roman historiography, and Italic and Latin epigraphy.

Katherine A. Shaner is associate professor of New Testament at Wake Forest University School of Divinity. She holds a ThD in New Testament and early Christian history from Harvard University Divinity School. She is the author of *Enslaved Leadership in Early Christianity* (Oxford University Press, 2018) as well as numerous articles on slavery in the New Testament. She is an ordained pastor in the Evangelical Lutheran Church in America (ELCA) and regularly preaches and teaches in churches around the United States.

Chris L. de Wet is professor of New Testament and early Christian studies in the Department of New Testament and Related Literature, Faculty of Theology and Religion, at the University of Pretoria. He is editor of *Journal of Early Christian History* and author of *Preaching Bondage: John Chrysostom and the Discourse of Slavery in Early Christianity* (University of California Press, 2015) and *The Unbound God: Slavery and the Formation of Early Christian Thought* (Routledge, 2018). He is also coeditor of *Revisioning John Chrysostom: New Approaches, New Perspectives* (ed. with Wendy Mayer; Brill, 2019) and *Slavery in the Late Antique World, 150–700 CE* (Cambridge University Press, 2022).

Jeremy L. Williams is assistant professor of New Testament and the inaugural director of the Center for Theology and Justice at Brite Divinity School. He holds a PhD from Harvard University. He is the author of *Criminalization in Acts of the Apostles: Race, Rhetoric, and the Prosecution of an Early Christian Movement* (Cambridge University Press, 2023).

Yvonne Zimmerman is dean of academic affairs and professor of religious studies at Clarke University. She holds a PhD in religious and theological studies from Iliff School of Theology and the University of Denver. Her primary area of research is the movement to end human trafficking, and she has published extensively on this topic, including *Other Dreams of Freedom: Religion, Sex, and Human Trafficking* (Oxford University Press, 2012).

Illustration Credits

The coeditors and contributors are grateful for the permissions granted to include the following photos and images in this book:

FIG. 0.1 The Metropolitan Museum of Art, New York (17.120.5). **FIG. 0.2** The Metropolitan Museum of Art, New York (22.24.4). **FIG. 1.1** The Getty Museum, Los Angeles (71.AA.271). **FIG. 1.2** The Metropolitan Museum of Art, New York (X.248.3). **FIG. 2.1** Wikimedia Commons; https://commons.wikimedia.org/wiki/File:Gustave_Boulanger_The_Slave_Market.jpg. **FIG. 2.2** The Metropolitan Museum of Art, New York (26.7.1417). **FIG. 3.1** © 2022 Ministero della Cultura Gallerie degli Uffizi; Le Gallerie degli Uffizi, Florence (653275). Used with permission. **FIG. 3.2** The Getty Museum, Los Angeles (77.AI.97). **FIG. 3.3** © Carole Raddato; Arbeia Roman Fort and Museum, UK (T765); Flickr; CC BY-SA 2.0; https://www.flickr.com/photos/carolemage/6782448727. **FIG. 4.1** Photograph by Marlow Green; The Soprintendenza Archeologica di Pompeii, Italy. **FIG. 4.2** Photograph by F. Mira Green; Museo Archeologico Nazionale di Napoli, Italy (145505). **FIG. 4.3** © Alberto Fernandez Fernandez; Kunsthistorisches Museum, Austria (Inv. ANSA II 9 Römisch,1. Jh. n. Chr); Wikimedia Commons; CC BY-SA 2.5; https://commons.wikimedia.org/wiki/File:Roman_mosaic_-_Love_Scene_-_Centocelle_-_Rome_-_KHM_-_Vienna.jpg. **FIG. 5.1** Itai; Hamat Tiberias, Israel; Wikimedia Commons; https://commons.wikimedia.org/wiki/File:Hamat_Tiberias_mosaic_writing.jpg. **FIG. 5.2** The Metropolitan Museum of Art, New York (25.78.63). **FIG. 5.3** © Sailko; Ostia, Italy; Wikimedia Commons; CC BY 3.0; https://commons.wikimedia.org/wiki/File:Ostia,_aula_dei_magistrati_del_grano,_mosaico_01.JPG. **FIG. 6.1** The Metropolitan Museum of Art, New York (25.78.29). **FIG. 6.2** The Getty Museum, Los Angeles (71.AA.260). **FIG. 6.3** Harvard Art Museums/Arthur M. Sackler Museum, Transfer from the Department of the Classics, Harvard University, Purchased in Rome. Photo Credit: © President and Fellows of Harvard College (1977.216.1887). Persistent Link: https://hvrd.art/o/287437. **FIG. 6.4** The Metropolitan Museum of Art, New York (18.9.2). **FIG. 6.5** © Mogadir; The British Museum, UK (1858,0819.2); Wikimedia Commons; CC BY-SA 3.0; https://commons.wikimedia.org/wiki/File:BM_GR_1858,0819.2_-_01.JPG. **FIG. 7.1** © Marco Assini; Wikimedia Commons; CC BY-SA 2.0; https://commons.wikimedia.org/wiki/File:La_Colonna_di_Marco_Aurelio_(5966172297).jpg. **FIG. 7.2** © Morgan Barrett; Flickr; https://www

.flickr.com/photos/111072739@N03/11325451546/in/photolist-ifMSKd-ifMUaY-ifNenT -ifMLiA/. **FIG. 7.3** © Sonse; Wikimedia Commons; CC BY 2.0; https://commons.wi kimedia.org/wiki/File:Arch_of_Titus_(45460435745).jpg **FIG. 7.4** Gary Todd; Flickr; Public Domain; https://www.flickr.com/photos/101561334@N08/48416942616/in/photolist -8ErJa4-21PQm-2icciey-tdjHq-2gLs5Lv-2gLsg9e-7uWdY5-8jM6JN-2gLrudG-2gLrvBd -5mToYK-ef4jYy-gthemR-5MdbRf-WrtbYP. **FIG. 7.5** The Metropolitan Museum of Art, New York (53.70). **FIG. 7.6** Photo by Danielle Kellogg; used with permission of the Amphipolis Archaeological Museum, Ministry of Culture and the Serres Ephorate of Antiquities. **FIG. 8.1** Museum Catharijneconvent; Wikimedia Commons; https:// en.wikipedia.org/wiki/File:Rembrandt,_The_Baptism_of_the_Eunuch,_1626,_Museum _Catharijneconvent,_Utrecht.jpg. **FIG. 8.2** © Dick Osseman; Wikimedia Commons; CC BY-SA 4.0; https://en.m.wikipedia.org/wiki/File:Aphrodisias_Museum_Claudius_and _Britannica_4638.jpg. **FIG. 8.3** © Carole Raddato; Flickr; CC BY-SA 2.0; https://www .flickr.com/photos/carolemage/27248284802/in/photolist-HvQzKQ-QGHkuX-QT889R -2m3akq1/. **FIG. 8.4** The Getty Museum, Los Angeles (85.AA.352). **FIG. 9.1** Photo- graph by Christy Cobb; Istanbul Archeological Museum, Turkey (1156). **FIG. 9.2** The Metropolitan Museum of Art, New York (17.194.896). **FIG. 9.3** The Cleveland Mu- seum of Art, Cleveland (2005.52). **FIG. 9.4** Gary Todd; Wikimedia Commons; https:// commons.wikimedia.org/wiki/File:Pompeii_Ruins_Brothel_Fresco_(48442300587). jpg. **FIG. 9.5** Gary Todd; Wikimedia Commons; https://commons.wikimedia.org/ wiki/File:Pompeii_Ruins_Brothel_Bed_(48442103696).jpg. **FIG. 10.1** The Metropoli- tan Museum of Art, New York (09.221.2). **FIG. 10.2** The Metropolitan Museum of Art, New York (17.190.675). **FIG. 10.3** © Carole Raddato / Ashmolean Museum, UK; Flickr; CC BY-SA 2.0; https://www.flickr.com/photos/carolemage/29462529754/ **FIG. 11.1** Ro- mainbehar; The Louvre Museum; Wikimedia Commons; Public Domain; https://com mons.wikimedia.org/wiki/File:Lyon_5e_-_Mus%C3%A9e_Lugdunum_-_Exposition _SPECTACULAIRE_-_Sc%C3%A8ne_iconique_de_la_com%C3%A9die_romaine. jpg. **FIG. 11.2** © Carole Raddato / Archaeological Museum of Cherchell, Alge- ria; Flickr; CC BY-SA 2.0; https://www.flickr.com/photos/carolemage/52466816816 /in/album-72177720303300066/ **FIG. 11.3** The Metropolitan Museum of Art, New York (36.11.1). **FIG. 12.1** Photograph by Katherine A. Shaner; Ephesus Ar- cheological Site, Turkey. **FIG. 12.2** The Metropolitan Museum of Art, New York (02.29.1). **FIG. 12.3** © Rabax63; Wikimedia Commons; CC BY-SA 4.0; https://com mons.wikimedia.org/wiki/File:ServusCollare.jpg. **FIG. 13.1** The Metropolitan Mu- seum of Art, New York (17.190.130). **FIG. 13.2** The Metropolitan Museum of Art, New York (74.51.2109). **FIG. 13.3** © Portable Antiquities Scheme; Wikimedia Com- mons; CC BY 2.0; https://commons.wikimedia.org/wiki/File:Roman_slave_shackles .jpg. **FIG. 14.1** © Friedhelm Dröge; Archaeological Park of Kato Pafos, Cyprus; Wiki- media Commons; CC BY-SA 4.0; https://commons.wikimedia.org/wiki/File:Mosaiken_Pa phos_fd_(3).JPG. **FIG. 14.2** © David Finn; The Smithsonian American Art Museum, Washington, DC (1983.95.178); Wikimedia Commons; CC BY-SA 4.0; https://commons .wikimedia.org/wiki/File:Hagar_by_Edmonia_Lewis.jpg. **FIG. 14.3** The Metropolitan Museum of Art, New York (08.242). **FIG. 15.1** The Library of Congress, Washington, DC (LOT 7479, v. 2, no. 0548 [P&P] LC-H5- 548). **FIG. 15.2** Image from the Blue Campaign; https://www.dhs.gov/blue-campaign/bli-airport-resources. **FIG. 15.3** The Metropolitan Museum of Art, New York (18.75).

Index of Subjects

FIVE RANDOM TEENS experience an unexplainable occurrence and join together to understand the messages they are given and the continued miraculous events that occur. With their ever-changing realizations about themselves and the spiritual and natural world around them, they find ways to conquer the challenges they encounter as they strive to complete a mission from God. Throw in three Angels sent to help them and a cat who changes into a black panther at will, and their lives will never be the same.

"The Crew: Named" is a fast-paced Cristian adventure filled with action, unexpected turns, and characters you can't get enough of.. Darleen Urbanek is a masterful storyteller who certainly has a hit on her hands with this well-crafted book. I can't wait for the sequel.
Linda Miller
Author of *Beyond the Crystal Ball*

The title "The Crew – Named" piqued my interest right from the start. This group of teenagers learns so many intriguing lessons and has so many exciting adventures that I could hardly put it down. Adventures of a supernatural kind seem to find them as they remember to ask God for help. So many life lessons reinforce principles of faith and remind each of us how valuable we are to God. I highly recommend it!
Sandy Casey
Pastor's Wife

I liked how each character had a different struggle so people could relate to them. The character development was really good, and I loved reading their views of religion before and after their experience with God. The storyline was very interesting and kept me entertained throughout the whole book. I think this would definitely speak to kids my age. All of the quests made me want to keep reading. It is really good!
Arianna
14-year-old

DARLEEN URBANEK'S career has been a tapestry of diverse experiences, including Disaster Recovery Planning, a role that resonates with the storyline of these teens and aids in their escapades. Her passion for creating visual worlds, as evidenced by her award-winning art, is a key element in her writing. She resides in Michigan with her husband and two dogs and has plans to pen at least four more sequels to "The Crew: Named." Keep an eye out for these future installments, where the wisdom, power, and strength of the Lord guides these young people in changing the world!

ISBN: 979-8-35097-239-9

9 798350 972399

Index of Scripture and Other Ancient Sources